British India and Victorian Literary Culture

Edinburgh Critical Studies in Victorian Culture

Series Editor: Julian Wolfreys

Volumes available in the series:

In Lady Audley's Shadow: Mary Elizabeth Braddon and Victorian Literary Genres
Saverio Tomaiuolo

Blasted Literature: Victorian Political Fiction and the Shock of Modernism
Deaglán Ó Donghaile

William Morris and the Idea of Community: Romance, History and Propaganda, 1880–1914
Anna Vaninskaya

1895: Drama, Disaster and Disgrace in Late Victorian Britain
Nicholas Freeman

Determined Spirits: Eugenics, Heredity and Racial Regeneration in Anglo-American Spiritualist Writing, 1848–1930
Christine Ferguson

Dickens's London: Perception, Subjectivity and Phenomenal Urban Multiplicity
Julian Wolfreys

Re-Imagining the 'Dark Continent' in fin de siècle *Literature*
Robbie McLaughlan

Roomscape: Women Readers in the British Museum from George Eliot to Virginia Woolf
Susan David Bernstein

Women and the Railway, 1850–1915
Anna Despotopoulou

Walter Pater: Individualism and Aesthetic Philosophy
Kate Hext

London's Underground Spaces: Representing the Victorian City, 1840–1915
Haewon Hwang

Moving Images: Nineteenth-Century Reading and Screen Practices
Helen Groth

Jane Morris: The Burden of History
Wendy Parkins

Thomas Hardy's Legal Fictions
Trish Ferguson

Exploring Victorian Travel Literature: Disease, Race and Climate
Jessica Howell

Spirit Becomes Matter: The Brontës, George Eliot, Nietzsche
Henry Staten

Rudyard Kipling's Fiction: Mapping Psychic Spaces
Lizzy Welby

The Decadent Image: The Poetry of Wilde, Symons and Dowson
Kostas Boyiopoulos

British India and Victorian Literary Culture
Máire ní Fhlathúin

Anthony Trollope's Late Style
Frederick Van Dam

Forthcoming volumes:

Her Father's Name: Gender, Theatricality and Spiritualism in Florence Marryat's Fiction
Tatiana Kontou

The Sculptural Body in Victorian Literature: Encrypted Sexualities
Patricia Pulham

Visit the Edinburgh Critical Studies in Victorian Culture web page at www.euppublishing.com/series/ecve

Also available:
Victoriographies – A Journal of Nineteenth-Century Writing, 1790–1914, edited by Julian Wolfreys
ISSN: 2044-2416
www.eupjournals.com/vic

British India and Victorian Literary Culture

Máire ní Fhlathúin

EDINBURGH
University Press

© Máire ní Fhlathúin, 2016 , 2017

Edinburgh University Press Ltd
The Tun – Holyrood Road
12(2f) Jackson's Entry
Edinburgh EH8 8PJ

First published in hardback by Edinburgh University Press 2016

www.euppublishing.com

Typeset in 10.5/13 Sabon by
Servis Filmsetting Ltd, Stockport, Cheshire,
and printed and bound in Great Britain by
CPI Group (UK) Ltd, Croydon CR0 4YY

A CIP record for this book is available from the
British Library

ISBN 978 0 7486 4068 3 (hardback)
ISBN 978 1 4744 2603 9 (paperback)
ISBN 978 0 7486 9969 8 (webready PDF)
ISBN 978 1 4744 0776 2 (epub)

The right of Máire ní Fhlathúin to be identified
as the author of this work has been asserted in
accordance with the Copyright, Designs and
Patents Act 1988, and the Copyright and Related
Rights Regulations 2003 (SI No. 2498).

Contents

Series Editor's Preface	vi
Acknowledgements	viii
A Note on Terms	ix
Introduction	1

Part I: Experiences of India

1.	The Literary Marketplace of British India: 1780–1844	9
2.	Exile	24
3.	Consuming and Being Consumed	55

Part II: Representations of India

4.	European Nationalism and British India	95
5.	Romantic Heroes and Colonial Bandits	104
6.	Imagining India through *Annals and Antiquities of Rajast'han*	127
7.	Transformations of India after the Indian Mutiny	154

Afterword: Reading India	185
Bibliography	190
Index	206

Series Editor's Preface

'Victorian' is a term, at once indicative of a strongly determined concept and an often notoriously vague notion, emptied of all meaningful content by the many journalistic misconceptions that persist about the inhabitants and cultures of the British Isles and Victoria's Empire in the nineteenth century. As such, it has become a by-word for the assumption of various, often contradictory habits of thought, belief, behaviour and perceptions. Victorian studies and studies in nineteenth-century literature and culture have, from their institutional inception, questioned narrowness of presumption, pushed at the limits of the nominal definition, and have sought to question the very grounds on which the unreflective perception of the so-called Victorian has been built; and so they continue to do. Victorian and nineteenth-century studies of literature and culture maintain a breadth and diversity of interest, of focus and inquiry, in an interrogative and intellectually open-minded and challenging manner, which are equal to the exploration and inquisitiveness of its subjects. Many of the questions asked by scholars and researchers of the innumerable productions of nineteenth-century society actively put into suspension the clichés and stereotypes of 'Victorianism', whether the approach has been sustained by historical, scientific, philosophical, empirical, ideological or theoretical concerns; indeed, it would be incorrect to assume that each of these approaches to the idea of the Victorian has been, or has remained, in the main exclusive, sealed off from the interests and engagements of other approaches. A vital interdisciplinarity has been pursued and embraced, for the most part, even as there has been contest and debate amongst Victorianists, pursued with as much fervour as the affirmative exploration between different disciplines and differing epistemologies put to work in the service of reading the nineteenth century.

Edinburgh Critical Studies in Victorian Culture aims to take up both the debates and the inventive approaches and departures from convention that studies in the nineteenth century have witnessed for the last half century at least. Aiming to maintain a 'Victorian' (in the most positive sense of that motif) spirit of inquiry, the series' purpose is to continue and augment the cross-fertilisation of interdisciplinary approaches, and to offer, in addition, a number of timely and untimely revisions of Victorian literature, culture, history and identity. At the same time, the series will ask questions concerning what has been missed or improperly received, misread, or not read at all, in order to present a multi-faceted and heterogeneous kaleidoscope of representations. Drawing on the most provocative, thoughtful and original research, the series will seek to prod at the notion of the 'Victorian', and in so doing, principally through theoretically and epistemologically sophisticated close readings of the historicity of literature and culture in the nineteenth century, to offer the reader provocative insights into a world that is at once overly familiar, and irreducibly different, other and strange. Working from original sources, primary documents and recent interdisciplinary theoretical models, Edinburgh Critical Studies in Victorian Culture seeks not simply to push at the boundaries of research in the nineteenth century, but also to inaugurate the persistent erasure and provisional, strategic redrawing of those borders.

Julian Wolfreys

Acknowledgements

Some material in Chapters 4 and 5 has previously appeared as part of 'Transformations of Byron in the Literature of British India', *Victorian Literature and Culture* 42.3 (2014): 573–93, and is published by permission of Cambridge University Press.

I am grateful to Patrick Brantlinger and another (anonymous) reader who both made helpful suggestions in response to my initial proposal for this book; to Nicola Royan, for her generosity with Latin translations; and to Julian Wolfreys and the editors at Edinburgh University Press for their support throughout.

A Note on Terms

'British India' is used in this book to indicate all the territory under the formal or informal control of the East India Company and later the British government, including the princely states.

I have used the term 'Indian Mutiny' (rather than an alternative such as 'Indian Rebellion' or 'Anglo-Indian War', which would better indicate the extent of the conflict of 1857–8), because it accurately reflects the view of events held by those writers whose work is discussed. The term 'Anglo-Indian' also reflects nineteenth-century usage, referring to the British community in India.

Place names in English are given in their nineteenth-century forms where these were standard and widely used (Calcutta, not Kolkata). Words transliterated from the indigenous languages of India appear in the form used by the writer in question, with current spellings supplied in parentheses if required. Where place names or personal names appear in several variants (as in the stories of Alauddin's invasion of Chitor in pursuit of Padmini) I use current spellings outside of direct quotations.

Introduction

This study explores the crystallising of a colonial literary culture in early nineteenth-century British India, and its development over the course of the Victorian period. It focuses on a wide range of texts, including works of historiography, travel writing, correspondence, fiction, and poetry, produced by amateur writers as well as writers who were better known and more professionalised. Its aim is to delineate the parameters and operations of a literary culture that is both local, in that it responds to the material conditions and experiences specific to colonial British India, and transnational, in that it evolves from and in reaction to the metropolitan culture of Britain. The writers I discuss were British, and lived and worked in British India (anglophone writing by Indians falls outside the parameters of this study). They often published their work for limited circulation within the colonial marketplace, but also with an eye to the more extensive readership of 'home'. While individual authors' works may be inconsequential or ephemeral, and sometimes apparently derivative of metropolitan texts and genres, the corpus in total constitutes a significant body of literature with its own concerns, themes and formats.

My work in this area is informed by previous work in the field of colonial literature and history, and by more recent scholarship on the literature of British India in particular. A great deal of this scholarship is underpinned by the concepts and methods of colonial discourse theory, and its formulation of the connections between literary discourse and the colonial relationship between Britain and India at all levels, from policy-making and rule to the experiences of individual colonisers. Readers will recognise behind much of my analysis in this book the foundational ideas of Edward Said and Homi Bhabha, particularly concerning the polar opposites of colonial difference and racial and cultural hybridity, and the tension between them in the history and literature of colonialism, as well as the insights of Gayatri Chakravorty Spivak into the ways in which race and gender hierarchies intersect to the detriment of those most excluded from power.[1] In my own work, however, these theories underlie the analysis of specific texts and contexts.

Scholarship on this literature over the past thirty years has tended to focus on a narrow set of individual authors, primarily Rudyard Kipling, whose work has cast a long shadow backwards over earlier Victorian India. Critics including Edward Said and Bart Moore-Gilbert have explored the colonial relationship depicted in Kipling's Indian fiction, making connections between this relationship and the larger topic of British perceptions of and responses to India more generally in the late nineteenth century; this work has been more recently continued by others such as Peter Havholm.[2]

More recent analysis, much of it carried out in the course of the last ten years, has also paid more attention to the authors of an earlier period: the essay collection edited by Bart Moore-Gilbert, for instance, sets Kipling's work alongside other texts, including novels and poems produced by Philip Meadows Taylor in the mid-nineteenth century and women writers of the late Victorian period.[3] Other scholarship in this area has focused on several different aspects of what Moore-Gilbert identifies as a local and colonial, as opposed to metropolitan, discursive constitution of India in literature.[4] These include travel writing, where Nigel Leask, Indira Ghose and Pramod Nayar are among those retrieving and analysing the forms and themes of British travellers' engagement with India.[5] Significant work has been carried out on discrete issues or flashpoints within the colonial relationship between Britain and India, most notably the representation of *sati* and the Indian Mutiny of 1857. On the former, and on the wider issue of the representation of colonised women, my thinking has been guided by works produced by Lata Mani and Andrea Major, among others.[6] On the latter, major works by Gautam Chakravarty and Christopher Herbert have explored the impact of the Mutiny on literature both in Britain and in India.[7] In the last few years, scholarship in this area has also focused on describing and extending the body of literature produced in nineteenth-century British India.[8] Daniel White and Mary Ellis Gibson both in different ways explore the connections and transitions between Britain and India, and take up in particular the theme previously identified by Rosinka Chaudhuri of the interaction of British writers and anglophone Indian writers in the cosmopolitan literary culture of Bengal.[9]

This book examines a wide range of material, looking especially to the relatively neglected and ephemeral texts published in small print runs and/or in newspapers and periodicals, starting from the early nineteenth century and then spanning the length of the Victorian period. This enables me to offer a broadly-based analysis of this literature, and pay attention to a range of colonising voices, not confined to canonical or elite actors on the literary stage.

The time frame of this study also allows me to situate the discussion of topics such as the literature of the Indian Mutiny within the larger context of the literary culture of British India more generally. In this way, the characteristic tropes of the early nineteenth-century bandit narrative, for example, can be seen to have an impact on literary and political representations of India throughout the Victorian period. At the other end of the nineteenth century, post-Mutiny literary representations of British relationships with India are shaped not just by the events of 1857, but also by rhetorical tropes and narratives developed through engagement with Indian mythology and history. The view that emerges is of a long, complex literary tradition, marked by traumatising events and controversial practices, but not determined solely by them.

This literary tradition is also formed in negotiation with the metropolitan culture of the Victorian period, and several aspects of that culture have a strong impact on the literature of British India. One of these is the strongly gendered nature of Victorian thought and social organisation, with its particular emphasis on female identities founded on principles of self-fulfilment through sacrifice and service to others – a theme which finds an echo in some of the indigenous traditions of India, and is apparent throughout the development of a colonial literature during this period. Other shaping aspects of metropolitan literary culture include the look to history for explanatory and justificatory accounts of British interventions in the colonial world, as well as a complementary concern with ideas of imperial decay and degeneration. These find expression across the breadth of the literature of British India.

I further argue that this literary tradition, in both its metropolitan and colonial aspects, plays a key role in creating the 'imagined community' of British India. In doing this I draw on Benedict Anderson's now much-critiqued concept, arguing that it has literary and cultural (if not political) resonance in this area. The specificity of the language and cultural tropes of British India (concerning, for example, issues of the material experience of the émigré community such as distance from 'home') contributed to the formation of a shared communal identity. Through deploying the language and knowledge associated with the colonial project, the writers were also able to challenge or subvert the relationship of dominance and derivation normally present between the metropolitan centre of 'home' and the colonial periphery of British India. The study draws in this respect on current analyses of local negotiations and interactions between coloniser and colonised, as distinct from earlier theoretical preoccupations with overarching theories of colonial relationships.

The book is arranged in two parts: Experiences of India, and Representations of India (the brief introduction you are currently reading is supplemented by introductory chapters beginning each section). The introductory chapter for Part I, 'The Literary Marketplace of British India, 1780–1844', discusses the material conditions for the emergence of a publishing and print culture in early British India and throughout the first half of the nineteenth century; it also considers the salient demographic and economic factors which affected the development of the publishing industry. The two chapters following each include a consideration of some prose and poetry appearing in the periodical press, while also broadening the focus to take into account other forms and genres (travel writing and memoirs).

Chapter 2, 'Exile', examines the ways in which the émigré community conceived of their absence from 'home' as a kind of exile, an experience that often evoked powerful emotions of fear, alienation, homesickness, and (post-Mutiny) disaffection and anger. (Although I recognise Said's uneasiness about the term 'exile' being used for those expatriates who have not undergone banishment or forced relocation, my analysis reflects the self-ascription of the word by the writers in question, and also takes account of the social or familial pressure to travel to India they often felt.[10]) While apparently artless, the trope of 'home' was not simple. The nostalgic or picturesque representation (privileging aesthetics over experience or memory) of the homeland served to reinforce affective connections between the exile and those left behind; in addition, sentimentalised images of the homeland were projected onto the Indian landscape, again effacing or limiting the value of the authentic experience of exile. Ambivalence was also at the heart of how 'home' was understood: it was seen, for instance, as a place of loss, death and alienation – a place to which the exile could never return – as well as a place of innocence and lost childhood. The experience of India expressed in these varied ways of understanding 'home' is often a suppressed or negated experience, recuperated only in the later century, in the works of Kipling, for example, as disaffection with Britain post-Mutiny led to the establishment of a sense of community, and indeed a kind of 'home', in British India itself.

The exiles' fears, traumas and losses in British India also found expression in the discourse of consumption and predation given impetus by the high-profile trial of Warren Hastings towards the end of the eighteenth century and evolving further throughout the Victorian period. The East India Company's transformation from a commercial concern into a government was accompanied by intense public debate over its role in India, focusing on economic relationships of exploitation, and moral relationships of corruption. The 'nabobs' of the Company were represented as exploiting India and its residents for their own material gain, and simultaneously as being themselves corrupted by contact with India. Their return to Britain gave rise to a sense that their moral and financial corruption was being imported into the British body politic. While this political moment quickly passed, the debate established the terms and metaphors – greed, excess, predation and contamination – in which British people imagined their role in India, and India's effect on them, throughout the Victorian period. This is the topic of the next chapter, 'Consuming and Being Consumed'.

The second part of the book is concerned with representations of India itself – as opposed to the representations of the experience of being in and relating to India that form the subject of the first half. A brief introductory chapter, 'European Nationalism and British India', sketches the moment of preoccupation with emerging nationalism in India as well as in Europe at the beginning of the nineteenth century, when an incipient discourse of Indian nationalism appears in British writing, albeit in limited and evanescent form. The three chapters following examine some of the reverberations of this British sense of a potential Indian agency and self-determination expressed in opposition to the British colonial project, as they are manifested in several different forms of literature throughout the Victorian period.

Chapter 5, 'Romantic Heroes and Colonial Bandits', explores how British literary representations of Indian practices (such as banditry) criminalised by the colonial state had the effect of transforming the eighteenth-century stereotype of the 'mild Hindoo' into a predatory Indian masculinity formed in opposition to a weak and victimised femininity. In a series of representations of India developed through the appropriation of British metropolitan forms and texts (notably the writings of Scott and Byron), the potential for threat to the British colonial state implicit in depictions of Indian agency is disabled or negated by the distancing or alienation of Indian figures from British readers. The following chapter, 'Imagining India through *Annals and Antiquities of Rajast'han*', focuses to a greater degree on representations of Indian agency derived from British scholarship on Indian history and mythology. It also discusses the story of the sacrificial death of the Rajput princess Kishen Kower, which becomes an exemplary vehicle for tracing the changing representation of female agency in the literature of British India, and exploring its interactions with British ideas of gender norms and femininity.

The final chapter, 'Transformations of India after the Indian Mutiny', explores British responses to the events of the Indian Mutiny and the rise of Bengal nationalism towards the end of the Victorian period. This period is characterised in some ways by a British turning away from both 'home' and indigenous India and towards an insular colonial mindset. An examination of some representative texts from this period shows that at the same time, the literature of the colony engages in a set of transformative narratives of India and the British role in India, forming a literary tradition more complex than is first apparent. The tropes and themes of depictions of India in the earlier pre-Mutiny period are now co-opted and turned to the depiction of British heroism and British sacrifice, in a process which also involves the incorporation of aspects of a stereotypically Indian character into an evolving ideal figure of British colonial rule, whose femininity makes it paradoxically impossible for her to be accorded a place in the male-dominated society of the colony.

A brief afterword, 'Reading India', returns to the issues of perception and expression arising throughout this book, and places them in the context of British descriptions of *sati*, one of the most complex and emotive tropes developed throughout this literature. A further analysis of three accounts of the *sati* rite explores the multifaceted interaction of lived experience and narrativisation in British responses to India, suggesting that representations of the colony are also, inescapably, discoveries of the colonial self.

Notes

1. Said, *Orientalism*; Bhabha, *Location*; Spivak, *Critique*.
2. Said, *Culture and Imperialism*; Moore-Gilbert, *Kipling and 'Orientalism'*; Havholm, *Politics and Awe*.
3. Moore-Gilbert, *Writing India*.
4. Moore-Gilbert, 'Introduction', *Writing India*, pp. 21–5.
5. Leask, *Curiosity*; Ghose, *Women Travellers* and *Travels, Explorations*; Nayar, *English Writing*.
6. Mani, *Contentious Traditions*; Major, *Pious Flames*.
7. Chakravarty, *Indian Mutiny*; Herbert, *War of No Pity*.
8. Gibson, *Anglophone Poetry* and my collection *Poetry of British India* take different approaches to this task, mine concentrating on colonial authors; see also Gibson, *Indian Angles*.
9. White, *From Little London*; Gibson, *Indian Angles*; Chaudhuri, *Gentlemen Poets*.
10. Said, 'Reflections', p. 181.

Part I
Experiences of India

Chapter 1

The Literary Marketplace of British India: 1780–1844

From small beginnings in the late eighteenth century, the periodical press became the powerhouse of literature in British India during the first half of the nineteenth century. Newspapers and literary titles were set up, in many cases, to serve as a conduit for the distribution of the news and culture of 'home' across India, casting the colonial readers of these texts in a peripheral relation to the political and cultural centre of the British metropolis. The periodicals also provided a forum in which the British community in India could write for (and often about) itself, thus enabling the development of a sense of local and colonial identity, related to but also set apart from the identity of the British at 'home'.

One of the most important aspects of the periodical press is its role in the formation of the 'imagined community' of Anglo-India, in the process described by Benedict Anderson whereby texts create and maintain the connections between individuals that overlay individual consciousness with collective identities.[1] Bart Moore-Gilbert argues for the recognition of British India as a community with a sense of its own cultural identity distinct from that of Britain, a difference marked by the evolution during the nineteenth century of a distinctively Anglo-Indian dialect and literary tradition.[2] Simply in terms of the amount of material involved, the periodicals constitute a significant part of that literary tradition. In the period covered by this chapter, texts published in periodicals assume a particular importance in comparison with the handful of notable volumes of poetry and novels directly or indirectly produced from British India. There is an argument to be made for travel writing as the most important and representative form of 'national literature' for Anglo-India, certainly in the first half of the nineteenth century, but travel writing is by its nature usually published from outside, looking back, while periodical contributions are typically produced by writers still living and working in India, as part of the community created by their texts and shared by their readers. B. S. Cohn describes the society of British officials in India as 'a fossil culture, cut off from close contact with home, recruited from several groups in English middle- and upper-class society, and with diverse educations'.³ One of the things they did have in common was the experience of being in India. Periodical writing chronicled and sustained that experience, allowing writers to articulate responses to the country, the colonial state and their own encounters with exile and alienation.

The Periodical Press of British India

The periodicals of the late eighteenth century were small and short-lived, published on one or two days a week and containing an eclectic mix of contents, of which literary material sometimes formed a small component. The first to be established, James Hicky's combative and sensational *Bengal Gazette; or, Calcutta General Advertiser* (1780–2) included some satires in verse form among other material, and this set the pattern for many of the titles that succeeded it.⁴ A critic of the 1820s, looking back forty years, described the press of the time as 'conducted in the most slovenly manner possible', and continued:

> The printer of a journal generally acted also in the character of editor, and filled his pages with a few ill-written paragraphs of domestic intelligence, some extracts from the English prints, ... and occasionally ... some wretched stanzas of rhyme, or a trite string of mawkish, stupid trusims, under the imposing title of An Essay ...⁵

This description, though unkind, is reasonably accurate: news from Britain, generally in the form of extracts from British periodicals, was a priority for newspapers (and was to remain so throughout the period), while other types of publications served small audiences for short periods of time until their demise. The *Oriental Magazine; or, Calcutta Amusement* (1785) described itself as 'a universal repository of knowledge, instruction, and entertainment', and displayed a particular interest in satiric commentary, often in verse, on the politics surrounding the East India Company's conduct and the impeachment of Warren Hastings. The *Calcutta Monthly Register* (1790–1) and the *Calcutta Magazine and Oriental Museum* (1791–2) focused mainly on current affairs; despite the latter's claim to contain the 'philosophy, literature, science, history, politics, arts, manners and amusements of the age', such literary material as it contained was normally poetry extracted from British titles. The *Asiatick Miscellany* (1785–6) was an eclectic combination of 'original productions, fugitive pieces, translations, imitations and extracts from various publications'; while the later *Oriental Miscellany* (1798) was targeted at students of oriental languages at the Fort William college, containing facing-page translations. The most consistently 'literary' in focus was Hugh Boyd's *Indian Observer* (1795), a one-man enterprise on the model of Johnson's *Rambler*, consisting of a series of weekly essays on a range of subjects, some of which were on subjects to do with India (Hindu doctrine, the work of William Jones, etc.). While these titles were short-lived, this period also saw the establishment of three newspapers: the *Bengal Hurkaru* (1795–1866), the *Calcutta Gazette / Government Gazette* (1784–1947), and the *India Gazette* (1780–1834).[6]

During the early years of the nineteenth century, in India as in the UK market, the economic climate generally, and the relatively high price of materials such as paper necessary for literary production, militated against periodical publication. While the daily newspapers listed above continued to be distributed, the smaller titles of the early years did not, and were not replaced.[7] Towards the end of this period, however, the *Calcutta Journal* (1818–23) became an important radical voice, until its editor, James Silk Buckingham, was expelled from India over his criticism of the East India Company's administration. Alongside polemic articles and other newspaper material, the *Calcutta Journal* also included some literary works. The same economic conditions that stacked the odds against periodicals fostered the domination of the British literary marketplace by poetry, particularly the works of Scott and Byron, which ultimately had an effect on the India marketplace as well.[8] David Kopf identifies the 1820 publication in Calcutta of Byron's *Don Juan* as the springboard for the appearance of several works of anti-establishment satire in the Calcutta periodicals of the early 1820s.[9] These were easily accommodated within the *Calcutta Journal*, where poems such as 'Rinaldo, or the Incipient Judge' targeted the East India Company's structures of law and government, the orientalist emphasis on proficiency in the languages of India among its elite members, and the eagerness of British society at 'home' to send its unwary youths to India.[10] Texts such as this, identifying and locating a British Indian constituency in oppositional relationship to both 'home' and their colonial surroundings, are among the early examples of what would become a long tradition of exile literature.

From the early 1820s onwards technological innovations – stereotyping, the Foudrinier paper-making machine, the power press – began to make publishing cheaper, and tilted the balance away from poetry and towards other forms of literary expression.[11] By 1834, a reviewer for the *Calcutta Literary Gazette* was of the opinion that India was 'as bad a market for poetry as can well be conceived. . . . The only way to circulate poetry here, is to print it in the periodicals.'[12] At the same time, numbers of British residents in India were rising (and continued to do so throughout this period), increasing the pool of potential readers. The Bengal periodical press underwent a period of expansion, as existing newspapers printed more and larger issues, and new titles, some with a more distinctly literary focus, were instituted.

Among the first of these was the weekly *Trifler* (1823–4), which advertised itself as 'a channel of pure literary discussion', but which appeared to be less than confident about its own prospects of success. 'Calcutta is singularly barren in literature', it claimed, and authors' reward for their labours was to have their work 'wither unnoticed and unlamented'.[13] The *Trifler* itself proved a less than welcoming haven for these authors, as the editor rejected any 'localities' offered by its contributors – the desirability, or not, of local material was to prove a vexed point throughout this period. The occasional item of 'original poetry', thus, was not generally on any India-related subject, though some translations from the Persian were included. Several letters to the editor lamented the difficulties of editing a periodical in India, foremost among which were the absence of contributors, and the absence of readers. These obstacles notwithstanding, the *Trifler* lasted fourteen issues, expiring with a prospectus for another publication, the *Spy* (which never appeared), and the publisher's complaint that 'our charge to Subscribers hardly pays us more than the actual expenses incurred for publication'.[14]

Other publications lasted longer: the monthly *Oriental Magazine and Calcutta Review* (1823–4; thereafter the *Quarterly Oriental Magazine, Review and Register*, 1824–7) aimed to publish on 'subjects connected with the History, Religion, Laws, Manners and Customs' of India, although in the event much of its output concerned other countries. Its main literary interest lies in its book reviews, on topics including both British-published and locally-published volumes of poetry; and some 'original poetry' by local authors (most of this is not on Indian subjects). Also published at the same time was the quarterly *Asiatic Observer: or, Religious, Literary, and Philosophical Miscellany* (1823–4), with a similar mix of general-interest works – many of a religious nature – reviews and poetry.[15]

The group of titles published by Samuel Smith dominated the Calcutta periodical scene for much of the 1820s and 1830s. Edited by David Lester Richardson – whose army career rapidly took second place to his literary and pedagogical interests – and publicised by cross-publication of material in the widely read daily *Bengal Hurkaru*, they included weekly, monthly and quarterly titles, all containing substantial local and

India-related material. The *Bengal Weekly Messenger* (1824–5), and its successor the *Calcutta Literary Gazette* (1826–35) – conceived of along the lines of Jerdan's London *Literary Gazette* – published work by local authors alongside literary extracts from British publications.[16] By 1834, when Richardson took over as proprietor as well as editor, the balance of contents had shifted almost entirely over towards original material: literary articles, serial prose and poetry. The paper was absorbed by the *Bengal Herald* (a weekly abridged edition of the *Bengal Hurkaru*, started in 1833, and also edited by Richardson) in 1836.[17] The monthly *Calcutta Magazine* (1830–2) contained local essays and poems as well as extracts from British periodicals; it was replaced by the *Calcutta Quarterly Magazine and Review* in April 1833, but the new title apparently did not last beyond the end of that year.[18] The flagship periodical of the group in terms of literary material was the *Bengal Annual* (1830–6), an imitation of the expensive literary annuals of the metropolis such as *Fisher's Drawing Room Scrap Book* which, for at least the first few issues, included engravings as well as print matter. If the metropolitan annuals functioned, as Hofkosh argues, as 'recognized signs of education, taste, and luxury', the colonial equivalent carried also the implicit claim to a status for its readers equivalent to that of their metropolitan counterparts.[19] This title is further discussed in the next chapter.

The *Oriental Observer* (1827–41), printed from the *John Bull / Englishman* presses, was both newspaper and literary journal, with the emphasis shifting between the two at various points during its existence. Under the editorship of Emma Roberts (1830–1), and later as the *Oriental Observer and Literary Chronicle* (1837 onwards), it included material by local authors alongside extracts from UK periodicals, particularly the work of Laetitia Landon and Maria Jane Jewsbury, Roberts's associates in London. The *Kaleidoscope* (1829–30) drew entirely on local contributors.[20] The *Orient Pearl* (1833–5) was a literary annual published by Thacker & Co., on the model of the *Bengal Annual*, and similarly comprising contributions from local writers, some of which were on India-related topics. The *East India United Service Journal* (1833–9), edited by J. H. Stocqueler of the *Englishman* and published from the *Englishman* press, included some literary prose and poetry, though its main concern was matters relevant to the army.[21]

With the demise of the *Calcutta Literary Gazette* and the *Bengal Annual*, there were few high-profile outlets for literary work in the Calcutta marketplace between the mid-1830s and the establishment of the *Calcutta Review* in 1844. The monthly *Eastern Miscellany* (1838) drew on many of the same contributors as the *Bengal Annual*, and produced the same kind of material, but it lasted for only six issues. David

Drummond's *Weekly Examiner; and, Literary Register* (1840–1) was primarily a newspaper with some literary content, including some original works by local contributors, and reviews of volumes by Richardson and others. The *Oriental Observer* was absorbed by the *Bengal Herald* in 1842; and the *Bengal Herald* itself closed at the end of 1843.[22]

Outside of Calcutta, periodicals were becoming more established, with a similar pattern of literary or para-literary periodicals printed from newspaper presses. Of the general newspaper titles printed in north India from the early 1830s onwards, only the *Agra Ukhbar* (1832–46) appears to have contained any substantial literary material.[23] The *Delhi Gazette* (1832–59) included a 'literary sheet' for the first two years of its existence, but was apparently impelled to stop doing so because of competition from the *Calcutta Literary Gazette*.[24] The *Meerut Universal Magazine* (1835–7) specialised in ephemeral parody and satire alongside current affairs. John Lang's *Mofussilite* (1845–76), published from Umballa from 1847, fulfilled by and large its promise in the first issue that the 'Literary Columns' would be 'supplied with original articles written in India'; these included serial fiction, often written by Lang himself, and occasional poetry.[25] The Madras *Government Gazette* (1801–32) and its successor the *Madras Male Asylum Herald* (1833–6) included a section devoted to poetry during the 1830s, though most of its material appears to be selections from British publications. The short-lived *Madras Literary Gazette* (1834–5) carried some material by local authors, virtually none of it India-related. The annual *Madras Comic Almanac* (1843–7) contained topical and local satiric material by local authors. In Bombay, the *United Service Gazette and Literary Chronicle* was briefly edited by Roberts until her death in 1840, and lasted another two years thereafter.

The evanescence of most of these periodicals – with the exception of the main newspapers – and the relatively small space occupied by local contributors, compared to that devoted to selections from British and other imported material, suggests that writing of any kind on the subject of India, apart from local news and gazette-type announcements, was of limited interest to a community still looking to 'home' for cultural leadership. Within the marginal space allocated to it, however, a developing body of British writers' representations of India, and their own relationship to India, can be seen to take shape. The nature and extent of this response to India is determined in part by the material circumstances surrounding its writers and readers.

Writing in the Literary Marketplace

The main difference between the literary marketplace of British India and that of the metropolis was one of size. While there are no very reliable figures available for British residents of India in the first half of the nineteenth century, P. J. Marshall offers a tentative estimate, derived from the *Parliamentary Papers,* of between 40,000 and 50,000 in c. 1830 (compare a London population of over a million in the same period), with soldiers making up by far the greatest number of these.[26] The pool of potential readers for literary periodicals was therefore limited, to an extent that the market was unable to sustain any fully professional enterprise (that is, one where both editors and contributors were paid for their work). The literary periodicals were generally printed from newspaper presses, and circulated through their distribution networks. While London editors, and their regular contributors, could expect to live what Lee Erickson terms 'a fairly comfortable life' on the proceeds of their literary work, their equivalents in British India worked on a more amateur basis.[27] The editors of the main newspapers were salaried – John Lang is reported to have been offered the sum of Rs.1,200 a month 'and a house rent free' – but those in charge of smaller papers and literary periodicals were usually well established in other and more lucrative professions.[28] Contributors were unpaid, creating a sometimes problematic situation, as Richardson complained: 'It is not to be expected that gentlemen who contribute to a periodical from motives of friendship to the Editor, or for their own amusement, or even for the benefit of the public at large, should sacrifice their own convenience by a very rigid adherence to punctuality.'[29] Motives of friendship often proved insufficient to sustain a periodical. The *Madras Literary Gazette* cited lack of support from its subscribers as the reason for its failure after thirty-six issues, but the fact that it had only eleven regular contributors must also have been a factor.[30]

The literary marketplace of British India also suffered from its orientation towards, and dependence on, its metropolitan counterpart. The *Calcutta Review* considered India a location particularly unconducive to literary pursuits: the climate made people indisposed to exertion; the administration overworked its employees; and, above all, the audience preferred 'the imported to the indigenous article'.[31] This last point is the most important one: the India market was peripheral to that of the metropolitan centre in three respects: first in dependence on publications from 'home'; then in interest above all in material from or about British subjects; and lastly in reliance on metropolitan responses for critical validation as well as practical support.

One of the greatest obstacles to locally produced literature in British India was the availability of 'home' material. While technological advances empowered the growth of locally produced literature in Calcutta, improvements in the journey time from Britain to India meant that British imports were increasingly competitive. Even before the introduction of a steam-powered route via the Red Sea cut journey times for mail from six months to two months in 1835, literature from Britain was readily available in India. H. H. Spry, a doctor, and therefore representative of the military and civilian professional classes who produced most of the literature of British India, writes in 1833 of having 'a decent supply of books of my own', and also had access through the Book Club in Saugor, where he was stationed, to 'all the periodical publications of the day as well as all the new works as they are published'.[32] New books from Britain might be 'unattainably expensive' on their first arrival, but only a few months later, 'when the gloss of novelty is over', would be sold at a fraction of their original price in the bazaars, together with cheap American editions of British titles, and translations from French and German works.[33] Calcutta printers were also able to produce pirate editions of British titles.

The circulation of periodicals published in India was small compared to their metropolitan equivalents. In Bengal, literary periodicals in the 1830s generally printed between 200 and 350 copies per issue.[34] In London during the same period, a weekly or monthly circulation of 2,000–3,000 was respectable for a literary periodical; and the *Literary Gazette* was selling 4,000 weekly in the 1820s.[35] The contrast with London circulation figures has to take account of relative population sizes, however; Marshall's comparison of the British population of Calcutta pre-1858 to that of 'a large village or small town' suggests that the achievement of the Calcutta literary press in sustaining their publication figures is, relatively speaking, impressive.[36]

The India titles were also expensive compared to their British counterparts. Prices of periodical publications were falling in Calcutta as well as in London during the 1820s and 1830s, but the general tendency was for Calcutta publications to cost at least as much as their London equivalents.[37] Even when the Calcutta booksellers were charging more than a 25 per cent markup on their stock, citing the costs of shipping,[38] the London titles were still competitive economically with their local alternatives, as well as carrying the sought-after 'home' material.

As a result of these economic constraints, relatively few 'local' periodicals were published, and those that were depended heavily on material from 'home'. For contemporary readers, the main task of the Anglo-Indian press, in news or in literature, was to provide a conduit through which the culture of the metropolitan centre of Britain could be channelled to India, maintaining the essential link between 'home' and colony. The works of Felicia Hemans, Laetitia Landon and other mainstays of the London literary periodicals all feature in the Calcutta press. These 'literary selections' were not imported uncritically; rather, they often became the occasion for critical or political debate in editorials and readers' letters, as in the correspondence across several titles concerning the merits, or otherwise, of Landon's poetry; or the responses to 'Cinnamon and Pearls', Harriet Martineau's work on Ceylon, across several titles.[39] British material always remained the prime interest, however, in literature as in news: the *Calcutta Courier* ran an editorial anticipating the approaching death of 'poor Nelly' in *The Old Curiosity Shop*, and another four weeks later mourning her demise.[40]

In this literary climate, editors' desire for distinctively 'local' works, dealing with the India context, were likely to run counter to readers' wish for material from 'home'. Several publications specifically asked for material of 'a local or Oriental description'; or 'notices of the various tribes, the natural history, the climate and the soil of different parts of India' as the one kind of local writing that might compete with British selections.[41] While encouraging the submission of items for publications was a commercial strategy for editors seeking to maximise an audience's sense of connection with the publication, it was one that might backfire in the special circumstances of the India marketplace. Sales of the *Oriental Observer* improved, according to a contemporary account of the Calcutta press, once Roberts's policy of encouraging local material had been abandoned after her return to London.[42] Readers' objections to the preponderance of local material in the *Calcutta Literary Gazette* were met by Richardson's claim that its sales were up, and still increasing, since the change was made; however, the title ceased to exist as an independent publication a few months afterwards.[43]

While the day-to-day survival of literary periodicals depended on their ability to satisfy their local subscribers, titles such as the *Bengal Annual* and the *Orient Pearl* were produced with an eye to the London market as well. Both were designed on the model of, and in competition with, the literary annuals that dominated the British literary market from the mid-1820s to the early 1840s, and that already were strongly established in the colonial markets.[44] In many respects, the competition was unequal: Richardson justified the Rs.16 per issue price of his *Bengal Annual*, against a London annual's Calcutta price of Rs.12, with reference to the economies of scale available to a London title such as the *Souvenir*, with a circulation of over 6,000, and the 'nearly doubled' cost of printing and paper in Calcutta.[45] The professionally produced engravings that were the most important selling feature of the London annuals were also out of reach for their Calcutta competitors: Richardson's attempt to replace them with 'the friendly contributions of Amateurs' was unsuccessful, as they were deemed not up to standard.[46] The India annuals' only distinctive attribute, their access to 'local' material – poetry and prose representations of India and the British exiles' experience of it – was as likely to alienate as to attract an audience whose primary interest was 'home'. Richardson addressed this problem by positioning his *Bengal Annual* as a title marketed, albeit indirectly, at British readers and critics. It was a reasonably successful marketing strategy, as the *Bengal Annual* made an impact on sales of British annuals in India.[47] And, while most of the titles of British India remained peripheral to the larger colonial marketplace, the literary annuals, with their concentration of literary texts, and especially poetry, had, as Gibson argues, a 'lasting impact in the formation of a poetic canon' – more so, she suggests, than in the metropolis.[48]

If economic circumstances were thus less than favourable for the development of a literature of British India, other aspects of the literary marketplace were more so. This was not immediately apparent to Richardson, whose pessimistic account of 'The Literati of British India' points to the make-up of British Indian society as one of the forces running counter to the establishment of a viable literary scene. There were no 'men of letters' who lived by writing, in his view, because of the lack of 'unproductive labourers in our community', who turned to authorship for want of a better profession.[49] Those who did write in their spare time were predominantly members of the civil service, or – in locations such as Agra or Meerut – army officers; in other words, the professional middle classes which provided in Britain the vast majority of contributors to and editors of periodicals.[50] As McLaren points out, the effective written 'communication of information, explanation and opinion' was an increasingly important and valued aspect of civil servants' professional role.[51] Other aspects of the exile community's experience also fostered the impulse to write: the only form of contact with families in Britain was by letter, and since many of these letters might be expected to be lost on the voyage, they had to be written diligently and often. In these respects, conditions in the literate, narrative-aware society of British India, where writing was common currency and of central importance in both professional and personal lives, were ideally suited to the production of literature.

This was also a predominantly male society, and one surprisingly unaffected by any contact with the people of India among whom they lived. Women of any class were few in number – a fact that had an impact particularly on the literary end of the periodical marketplace.[52]

While the London literary annuals were in large part written by women, and marketed to an overwhelmingly female readership, the contributor lists of their Bengal equivalents is dominated by men.[53] Despite the cosmopolitan quality of Calcutta in the 1820s and 1830s, the periodical press was also almost entirely white British: the understandable focus on outstanding figures such as the 'East Indian' H. L. V. Derozio (and later the Dutt family) in the work of Chaudhuri and Gibson, while casting welcome light on the productive cross-cultural relationships of the age, entails the risk of overstating the extent of indigenous participation in the nineteenth-century literary scene.[54] Derozio was indeed active in the literary community of Calcutta; his poetry was extensively published in literary periodicals, and both his considerable personal following among Bengali students, and his early death, contributed to his literary reputation.[55] Kasiprasad Ghosh, a graduate of the Hindu College, was widely published in literary periodicals of the 1830s, and Michael Madhusudan Dutt also published in English periodicals in the early 1840s.[56] While those writers might have been accorded, as Chaudhuri argues, a 'social status regardless of race', and their work certainly appeared alongside those of British writers in the periodicals, they were atypical of their contemporaries.[57] Another 'East Indian' was less well received than Derozio, with some of the hostile reaction apparently directed at the poet's ethnic identity as well as the quality of the writing. Reviewing J. F. Delanougerede's *Wuzeerally and Other Poems*, with its self-conscious placing of the author as a Bengal nationalist – 'My wretched country, while I write, I mourn! / By insatiate England of her freedom reft' – the *Englishman* commented: 'We wish Mr Delanougerede would let us know to what country he lays claim and what degree of freedom we unhappy English have robbed her of?' The review ends with a stern injunction to the poet: '*Va te coucher*, Delanougerede, and don't let your friends allow you to write poetry.'[58] Even while including Derozio's work in his *Selections from the British Poets*, Richardson gave it a strictly demarcated space: a section of British Indian poetry is followed by a separate section of 'Poems by an East Indian' (Derozio), and a solitary 'Poem by a Hindu' (Kasiprasad Ghosh).[59] Along the same lines, but from the other side, it is notable that the *Kaleidoscope* appears to draw on a pool of contributors distinct from those of the other periodicals, with the exception of Derozio himself.[60] British responses to the work of Kasiprasad Ghosh and his compatriots were frequently patronising, giving the impression that the work was being printed for curiosity value more than anything else, as with the remarks accompanying the 'Introductory Lines' from G. C. Dutt's *School Hours*; or the Madras *Government Gazette*'s 'delight at witnessing so great a progress in polite literature among the Natives of the East'.[61] While the periodical press was willing to open, on occasion, its columns to those outside the community of British India, it remained for the most part mono-vocal in its representation of that community.

The literary marketplace of British India changed in several ways during and after the 1840s. Poetry (and fiction) continued to appear in the pages of newspapers such as the *Bombay Times / Times of India*, the Lahore *Civil and Military Gazette* and the Allahabad *Pioneer* – the latter two notable as vehicles for the early work of Rudyard Kipling. At the same time, the weight of literary output moved towards volume publication of fiction, and towards London as the main location of publication. From the 1840s onwards, metropolitan publishers started to produce cheap editions of British texts for the colonial market, which in India saw fiction in particular become more widely available throughout the Victorian period.[62] A focus on local literary culture was maintained, however, by the quarterly *Calcutta Review*, founded in 1844 by John Kaye, which offered a regular and authoritative commentary throughout the second half of the nineteenth century. When its first issue noted the transformation of communications brought about by steam travel, which meant that 'letters and papers' posted in Bombay could be 'delivered in London five weeks after they are despatched; and in little more than two months an answer to a letter sent from Bombay may be received at that place', it marked a change also in relations between the émigré communities and the homeland, constituting 'an extreme provocative to frequent correspondence, not only between parties engaged in business, but between private individuals'.[63] The network of relationships between writers and readers, in Britain and abroad, was taking on new forms. In many ways, however, their concerns – with the fact of exile, with the relationship between 'home' and colony, with the everyday interactions between coloniser and colonised – remained unchanged, given enduring form by the literary tradition developed from the late eighteenth century onward. These aspects of the experience of life in India, as represented through the poetry, fiction and travel writing of the Victorian period, form the subject matter of the next two chapters.

Notes

1. Anderson, *Imagined Communities*; Alex Tickell describes the readers of the Anglo-Indian press as envisaging themselves as a 'sub-national community' (*Terrorism*, p. 82).
2. Moore-Gilbert, *Writing India*, pp. 20–2.

3. Cohn, 'Recruitment', p. 545.
4. See, for example, Nair, pp. 36, 169–70, 187–8.
5. Bannatyne, 'Indian press', pp. 134–5.
6. While these and other newspapers are generally outside the scope of this study, it should be noted that they included some literary material – normally poetry and book reviews – from the late 1820s onwards, though this was usually copied over from other titles, both local and metropolitan. The *Bengal Hurkaru* often included material from the *Calcutta Literary Gazette* (printed at the same press, and at one time owned by the same publisher); while the *Calcutta Courier* (1832–9), a spin-off from the *Calcutta Gazette / Government Gazette*, carried regular items of poetry and literary debate. The *India Gazette* and the *John Bull* (1822–33) / *Englishman* (1833–1934) also carried some literary material.
7. Chanda also attributes this lack of new titles to the 'deadening influence' of the Press Regulations of 1799, which required papers to be approved prior to their publication (*English Press*, p. 417).
8. Erickson, 'Market', pp. 350–1.
9. Kopf, *British Orientalism*, pp. 222–3; see also Leask, 'Anglo-Indian poetry', pp. 73–5.
10. 'Rinaldo', *Calcutta Journal* 22 January, 1 February, 16 February 1822; see also *Ruin: A Familiar Tale of the East* (1820).
11. Erickson, 'Market', p. 345.
12. *Calcutta Literary Gazette*, vol. 10 (1834), pp. 127–8.
13. *Trifler*, 1.1 (1823): 1–2.
14. *Trifler*, 1.14 (1824): back matter.
15. Chanda, *English Press*, pp. 77–9.
16. The *Calcutta Literary Gazette* took its title and its weekly format from Jerdan's *Literary Gazette*, but was substantially different in content: Jerdan's paper relied heavily on advertising, and each issue included mainly book reviews, with one or two items of 'original poetry'; while the Calcutta version had more poetry and some fiction, with few advertisements. While the newspapers generally depended heavily on advertising revenue (Chanda, *English Press*, p. 399), the weekly literary periodicals, with their smaller subscription base, were less attractive vehicles for advertisers.
17. The *Calcutta Literary Gazette* was revived as an independent title for a few years in the 1850s.
18. Chanda, *English Press*, p. 159.
19. Hofkosh, *Sexual Politics*, pp. 86–7.
20. This periodical was possibly edited by H. L. V. Derozio; see Chaudhuri, *Derozio*, p. 289.
21. Chanda, *English Press*, pp. 160–4; see also Peers, 'Colonial Knowledge'.
22. Chanda, *English Press*, pp. 106, 117.
23. Chaudhuri, 'India', p. 186.
24. *Calcutta Literary Gazette*, 2 April 1834.
25. *Mofussilite*, 2 August 1845.
26. Marshall, 'British immigration', pp. 182–4. An alternative figure of c. 30,000 is suggested by Finkelstein and Peers, 'A great system', p. 11.
27. Erickson, *Economy*, p. 83.
28. 'Starting a paper', p. 94. The *Calcutta Courier* announced its incoming

editor as 'Mr Osbourne, the Barrister' (9 December 1837); his salary was Rs.800 a month, and that of his successor Rs.500 (Chanda, *English Press*, p. 148) – Lang may have exaggerated his own salary. Robert Adair Macnaghten, an officer in the Bengal Army, was for a time the editor of the *John Bull*, and later of its successor the *Englishman*. David Lester Richardson, the most successful of the 'literary' editors, was an army officer during the first years of his literary career, and thereafter Professor of English Literature at the Hindu College; he apparently also had 'considerable' independent means (Laurie, *Sketches*, p. 318). David Drummond, the editor and proprietor of the *Weekly Examiner; and, Literary Register*, was also a schoolteacher and writer. The East India Company's 1826 prohibition on its employees being associated with the press excluded literary and scientific titles.

29. *Bengal Annual* 1833, n.p.
30. *Madras Literary Gazette* vol. 2, p. 273.
31. 'Literary labours of D. L. Richardson', *Calcutta Review* vol. 10 (1848), pp. 26–7.
32. Spry-Leverton, 'Spry Letters', p. 338.
33. 'Reflections of a returned exile', *Asiatic Journal* (January–April 1837), pp. 353–4.
34. In 1833, circulations for the *Calcutta Quarterly Magazine and Review* and the *Oriental Observer* were estimated at 200–230, with the *Calcutta Literary Gazette* and the *Bengal Annual* achieving figures in the mid 300s (*Bengal Hurkaru*, 5 October 1833).
35. Marchand, *Athenaeum*, pp. 43–4; Sullivan, *Romantic Age*, p 243.
36. Marshall, 'White town', p. 309.
37. In 1834, Calcutta booksellers were advertising Ackermann's *Forget-me-not* and the *Literary Souvenir* at Rs.10 each, compared to Rs.12 for the *Bengal Annual* (*Calcutta Literary Gazette*, 15 February 1834). The *Edinburgh Review* and the *Quarterly Review* both appear to have sold for Rs.4 per issue (*Calcutta Literary Gazette*, 18 January 1834), the same price as the *Calcutta Quarterly Magazine and Review*. A similar trend may be observed across other sets of comparable publications.
38. Advertisement, *Weekly Examiner: and, Literary Register*, 14 March 1840, p. 26.
39. On Landon's work, see the *Calcutta Magazine* (i–ii, 1830, pp. 517–47), and the *Oriental Observer*, 27 June 1830. The *Bengal Hurkaru* reprinted correspondence on 'Cinnamon and Pearls' from the *Ceylon Gazette* and the *Government Gazette* (Colombo), as well as its own contributions: see issues of 13, 15, 20, 21, 22, 28, 29 March 1834.
40. *Calcutta Courier*, 11 March, 6 April 1841.
41. *Oriental Observer*, 29 June 1828; 'Prospectus for the *Calcutta Quarterly Magazine and Review*', *Bengal Annual* 1833.
42. *Bengal Hurkaru*, 8 October 1833.
43. *Calcutta Literary Gazette*, 27 September 1834.
44. As Alison Adburgham points out, the long lead times of the London annuals enabled them to be shipped overseas in time for Christmas ('Women in print', pp. 261–2).
45. *Bengal Annual* 1831, n.p.

46. *Bengal Annual*, 1830, v.
47. Bose, 'Verse', p. 51.
48. Gibson, *Indian Angles*, p. 108.
49. *Bengal Annual* 1830, p. 4. Richardson's 'men of letters' excludes women, a group whose middle- and upper-class members, at least, had, in the words of Roberts, 'many temptations to idleness and few incitements to industry' (*Scenes and Characteristics*, vol. 2, p. 50).
50. Parker, *Literary Magazines*, p. 34. The occasional contributors to the *Bengal Annual* from outside these groups, such as J. M. Harris, identified as 'Serjeant, 3rd Troop 2nd Brigade Horse Artillery' (1836), are few and far between.
51. McLaren, *British India*, p. 3.
52. Marshall, 'British immigration', pp. 182–4.
53. See Cronin, 'Romantic Victorians', p. 97. The *Bengal Annual* for 1833 had a female to male contributor ratio of 1:7, and is typical in this respect.
54. See Chaudhuri, *Gentleman Poets*, pp. 30–2; Gibson, *Indian Angles*, pp. 65–71; the same argument might be made with respect to the recent interest in the work of Roberts, whose career as a female professional writer and editor was unique in British India.
55. See, for example, the extract from a *Literary Gazette* article on Derozio as a young boy reprinted in the *Bengal Hurkaru*, 12 November 1833.
56. Ghosh's poems appeared in the *Calcutta Literary Gazette*, the *Bengal Annual*, the *Government Gazette* (Madras) and the *Orient Pearl* (and in the London *Fisher's Drawing Room Scrap Book* for 1835); his name is spelled in several variant forms. See Gibson, *Indian Angles*, pp. 140–154. On Dutt, see Saha, *Indian Renaissance*, p. 16; Gibson, *Indian Angles*, pp. 154–68.
57. Chaudhuri, *Gentlemen Poets*, p. 32.
58. *Englishman* (14 March 1836); see also the *Calcutta Courier* (15 March 1836), and the *Bengal Hurkaru* (28 March 1836). The normally combative relationship between the *Englishman* and the *Hurkaru* makes their joint condemnation of the unfortunate poet the more remarkable.
59. Richardson, *Selections*, pp. 1519–20.
60. The *Kaleidoscope* items are generally identified by initials or pseudonyms; some are directed specifically at mixed-race readers, such as the essay 'East Indians in the Mofussil' (vol. 1, pp. 5–16).
61. *Calcutta Courier*, 25 March 1839; *Government Gazette* (Madras), 17 February 1831. On the other hand, David Drummond's reluctantly condescending acceptance of a 'Sonnet to the author of the Literary Leaves, by a Native' (*Weekly Examiner*, 16 May 1840) is characteristic of his attitude to contributors in general, regardless of their race.
62. See Joshi, *In Another Country*, Chapter 3; the focus in this work is on Indian readers of anglophone fiction, but the first part, 'Consuming Fiction', also sheds light on the availability and consumption of metropolitan material in India more generally.
63. 'English in India', p. 3.

Chapter 2

Exile

The writers and readers of the British community in India occupied a complex set of relationships to 'home': they were set apart from familiar locations and individuals by physical distance, differences of experience and perception, and the time elapsed and yet to elapse before a possible return might be contemplated; and united by their experience of exile. Their literary works, and the envisaged and actual readerships of these works, reflect these relationship in a dual focus, looking outwards at India – in a gaze shaped often by the fact of being enacted at least partly for the benefit of distant private and public readerships – and also back to the homeland, in a nostalgic recreation of distant scenes and relationships which serves the dual purpose of reminding the exile of the lost 'home', and reminding those at 'home' of their importance to their distant loved ones. The first of these literary representations, the depiction of India, has been, for obvious reasons, the main concern of scholars working on the literature of British India. The nostalgic vision of 'home' is, however, often of equal interest. Writers who produced picturesque visions of India wrote of their homeland in the same picturesque mode, developing an image of 'home' as shaped by the colonial encounter. Writers who produced comic or dystopian accounts of India did so sometimes in counterpoint to a nostalgically idealised 'home', but sometimes also brought the lens of satire to bear on the homeland. The image of 'home' developed in these writings is many-faceted, often contradictory: 'home' is a space of domestic comfort and remembered bliss, land of childhood and innocence; and also a land of cold, loss, senescence, and the anticipation of death.

The importance of 'home' to exiles over the entire period of the British presence in India is a point that has been noted throughout scholarship in this area. Elizabeth Buettner argues that the fact of absence, even though it distanced expatriates from Britain, also functioned to maintain their connection to the homeland, and to others in the expatriate community, producing 'nostalgic sentiments that kept them mentally anchored within Britain even while living far away'.[1] Even the act of encountering a new land can become an opportunity for re-inscribing the connection with 'home', as when Anne Elwood looks at a ruined fort in Kerah, only to be reminded of Pevensey Castle in East Sussex; or sees a gathering of fighting men in Cutch which 'reminds one of similar scenes in the Highlands, as described by Sir Walter Scott'.[2] The circulation of narratives and illustrations between 'home' and the colony, both in published works (notably the literary periodicals, which frequently carried poems and essays on this theme) and in private correspondence, sustained and renewed these connections.

A similar purpose was served also by the practice of transporting valued objects (with their inevitable associations and memories) from Britain to India, creating what John Plotz terms 'mobile containers of Britishness' which 'strengthened settlers' bond to their alma mater, even as they reminded them of their distance from home'.[3] Indeed, some of these objects, such as the views of the Great Exhibition of 1851 described by G. O. Trevelyan, have the effect of reminding their distant owners that 'home', as well as the colony, is a location of empire. 'Everywhere', Trevelyan writes, 'you see views of the interior and exterior of the building, crowded with Turks and Albanians, Highlanders and Esquimaux, with here and there an individual in the hat and coat of modern civilization directing the attention of a female on his arm by pointing his stick at some interesting object in mid-air.'[4] Here, the lines between homeland and otherland are less than clear, as the Highlanders (of Scotland) are to be found outside the category of those associated with 'modern civilization'. The scene reminds us that the 'home' so fervently and expensively remembered, and carried in effigy and symbol to India, is itself changed by the experience of participation in the empire. It also reminds us that the remembering of 'home' is a process, one which involves the economic relationships of the marketplace as well as the affective relationships of individuals. Both these aspects of the exile / 'home' dynamic are apparent in the literature produced in British India, as writers locate themselves, and their readers, in relation to both 'home' and colony.

While periodicals and newspapers marketed the news and the culture of 'home' to their colonial readership through reprinting selected material from the metropolitan press, their representation of that readership's local surroundings often constitutes also a version of 'home'. It is visible, not just in poems straightforwardly expressing emotions of loss and homesickness, but also in works apparently concerned only with representations of India, as D. L. Richardson seems to suggest in his 'Introductory Stanzas' to the opening issue of his *Bengal Annual*.

> We would twine a wreath of Eastern flowers,
> But we think of those which blow
> Far off in our own native bowers,
> And our task moves sad and slow;
> We have blushing fields of roses here,
> Where glittering song birds roam;
> And Indian lilies sparkle clear, –
> But they're not the flowers of Home.
> Home! – Home! – how many in vain
> Shall sigh for thy blessings once again.

Richardson proceeds to set up a series of similar oppositions between 'Home' and 'here' – a deictic which is identified with the indeterminate East, signified by 'Eastern flowers', etc., as well as the exiles' gazing 'upon the west' to think of home. The elements of 'home' are of apparently low status, but carry emotional significance deriving from their personal associations with the speaker. In the speaker's mind, the 'shells that sleep / By his own sweet native stream' are valued above the 'pearls of Serindeip', the 'Ava ruby', or 'Golconda's gems'. Amidst the dismal reality of life in India – 'the jackall's dreary yell' – the exiles find a 'fever'd sleep' interspersed with 'happy dreams' of home. These staple tropes of the literature of nostalgia figure largely in the poetry and prose written by Richardson and his compatriots. The relationship of homeland and otherland is complicated, however, by two further aspects of the work. First, the representation of India is simultaneously an implicit representation of home, which appears to arise spontaneously during the act of writing:

> We would strike the lyre with bolder hand,
> But when we woo its tone
> To tell some tale of this far land,
> It murmurs of our own.

Secondly, the representation of India is inflected by the writer's imagined and implied reader – gendered and idealised as 'Beauty' – whose response is what makes the material worthwhile:

> Perchance bright eyes may scan these tales,
> Where the honeysuckle weaves
> Cool bowers – while violet-scented gales
> Play o'er our Indian leaves.
> Then – where our flowers less sweetly bloom,
> Our gems less brightly shine,
> Think – Beauty – think – 'tis Exile's gloom
> Lies dark upon the line.
> Home! Home! there – there alone
> The minstrel's harp gives all its tone.[5]

In the context of the *Bengal Annual*, the personification of the predominantly female readership of the literary annuals as the flattering 'Beauty' may be regarded as a transparent marketing ploy. That female readership was much more likely to be found in Britain than in India, where even in the elite classes women were far outnumbered by men.[6] The need to appeal to this demographic underlies the final lines of the poem, where the exile writer, it is implied, is capable of only a partial and inadequate performance if read by a migrant audience. The full 'tone' of the work is apprehended only when it is read at 'Home'.

Though this appeal to a 'home' audience has its roots in a strategic awareness of the gender and class dynamics of literary readerships, it also suggests a broader theme of concern with 'home' as the source of critical recognition as well as commercial success. Further issues of the *Bengal Annual* reflect this preoccupation, as introductory lines in each case re-cast the relationship between exile writers and exile and metropolitan readers. The 'Introductory Stanzas' of the 1831 issue describe the *Annual* as 'a British garland', wrought by 'British hands' – 'Western blossoms reared in Orient bowers'. Addressing its India-based readers as 'Fraternal Exiles', the poem requires their 'gracious favour' for these works:

> And if some living blooms less bright appear
> Than glorious genius sheds o'er Britain's soil,
> Scorn not their fainter glow; as doubly dear
> Regard these products of the wanderer's toil;
> Their hues are eloquent of home-sick hearts
> Whose fancy's vernal freshness soon departs.[7]

As the writings of those 'wanderers' are inferior in quality to those of 'home'-based authors, so the writers themselves are transformed by their exile, having lost the 'vernal freshness' originally theirs. In 1834, another set of 'Introductory Lines' used a similar image of the poetic 'flowers' of exile, but this time placed the responsibility for their care at least partly with their 'home' readers:

> Our country's rose,
> Parch'd in its bud, but palely blows;
> Yet cherish'd by the fostering hand
> Of friends from its own native land,
> 'Twill blossom into life . . .[8]

The 'Introductory Sonnet' of the 1835 issue similarly invokes the 'fraternal Exiles' oppressed by 'sultry skies', war and disease; and addresses them alongside 'ye that tread our distant father-land – / Dear, unforgotten friends'.[9] Richardson persists in the use of flower imagery to characterise the writings of his authors: in 'Summer and Winter', the *Bengal Annual* itself is described as 'an English winter floweret, reared by English hands, and blossoming beneath a foreign sky'. As the writings of exiles are conceived of as transplanted products of 'home', so the look back at 'home' in these works negates the process of exile: 'On the remotest foreign strand, we do but turn a pensive eye towards our native shore, and the mist of many years and the vast waste of waters that roll between us are as if they had never been.'[10]

That gaze towards the native shore is not straightforward. As both Richardson and Emma Roberts recognised, the interests of the exile community did not coincide with those of the British at 'home'. For those at 'home', the value of material from India was in its difference: the first-hand accounts offered by British writers of a land and experiences unfamiliar to most of those who read their work. Roberts's second edition of *Oriental Scenes*, published in London, omits two-thirds of the original material, keeping only those poems on Indian subjects, and supplementing them with others of the same kind. The dedication to Lady William Bentinck, wife of the Governor-General, in the 1830 edition is replaced in 1832 by an address to Roberts's friend Laetitia Landon, a prominent figure on the London literary scene. The preface of this work offers an accurate formulation of the place occupied by exile material more generally, as Roberts excuses her publication of a 'work of inferior pretensions' with reference to the 'irresistible' temptation to 'illustrate scenes and incidents, which, during my travels in India, struck me as being particularly interesting and picturesque'.[11] Roberts's disingenuous disavowal of her poetic abilities serves the dual purpose of reassuring metropolitan readers of their own superior position, while highlighting the value of the exotic associated with exile writing. Demonstrating a similar sense of what British readerships valued, Richardson prefaced the *Bengal Annual* for 1833 with a response to those 'London critics' who had expressed the wish that 'the Eastern character had entered a little more into its contents'. Those critics were assured by Richardson that the volume was 'more decidedly Oriental than any of its predecessors'; and that the writers had 'this year paid more than usual attention to eastern subjects'. He also suggests that 'the contents of this volume will probably be esteemed in England, in proportion to the foreign cast of its contents', and implies that this 'might render it less welcome to readers in Bengal'.[12]

The problem of holding the attention of this dual audience is addressed by the satirical 'Oriental Tale' by Henry Meredith Parker that stands first in this issue of the *Bengal Annual*, and targets every aspect of the process of packaging India for the West. Imagining himself at work in a room scattered with 'little mountains of roses', the writer incorporates in series several of the clichés of Anglo-Indian writing: from the heat strong enough to crack 'a tyger's tooth' to a *sati* scene where the heroine, 'eyes down-cast in terror and modesty', is exposed 'unveiled before many men' to the reader's gaze.[13] In the process, however, Parker sets one stereotype against another, the 'chilly and chilblained English reader' against an Anglo-Indian teller of tall tales, a 'medical officer of undoubted veracity' (2). The homeland's supposed ignorance of India lies behind Parker's traps for the British reader, like the appearance of a brahmin who calls the Muslim faithful to prayers (5), and the translation of 'hookahburdar' as 'commander of a thousand' (8). The deeply insulting 'Soor [swine] and son of a soor' is glossed as a term of endearment, 'so soft and expressive in the tongues of the East, so untranslateable into the languages of Europe' (8). As Daniel White argues in a perceptive analysis of this work, Parker's approach produced 'a tale so Oriental that practically no one who hadn't lived in India could possibly have understood the vocabulary or grasped just how ludicrous, not to mention how full of historical, religious, and cultural solecisms' it was. The tale thus functions to assert exile readers' and writers' mastery of what White terms 'that most metropolitan of tropes, the depiction of extreme alterity', as well as their membership of a 'cosmopolitan literary sphere' beyond the reach of a 'home' audience.[14] At the same time, the exile reader is not permitted uncomplicated enjoyment of these linguistic jokes: both audiences, the metropolitan and the local, are in turn satirised.[15] Playing off the conventional depiction of British men at rites of *sati* as onlookers and potential rescuers,[16] Parker's *sati* scene features a 'British hero' sharing the role of victim. The traditional account of the heroine's appearance and demeanour is replaced by a minutely particular description of his 'white shorts and silks, ... red coat and brass buttons, with a pair of tasty fringe epaulettes hanging well in front, a narrow tight white neckcloth, hair elaborately curled and powdered, a gold laced three-cornered cocked hat, and a pig tail' (14) – that last detail raising an echo from the 'soor' of several pages back, so that the Anglo-Indian reader's privileged recognition of both European (outmoded) fashion terminology and Indian terms of abuse may be brought to bear on a ludicrously feminised protagonist. The act of colonial mockery of metropolitan preconceptions produces, not a figure of the triumphant coloniser, but something akin to Homi Bhabha's hybrid figure that 'breaks down the symmetry and duality of self/other, inside/ outside': a version of the coloniser whose impotent clownishness is most apparent to those who are versed in the language of colonialism.[17]

As a writer, Parker was certainly not immune from an exile's nostalgia for the land of his birth. 'Stanzas written on the River', for example, offers a picturesque account of an Indian landscape constructed in dialogue with memories of a distant English home. This home is barely described – 'a mild breeze, like that of England's June' is the nearest thing to an account of it – but the exile's loss, and the alienness of the exile landscape, is apparent throughout, from the metaphor of the 'bud that loves the shade' and fades in the 'glare and splendour' of an Indian sun, to the final lines which make explicit the irreplaceable nature of the lost homeland:

> So though around me golden fountains sprung
> Of riches and of pleasure – if for me
> Honour and power their proud trumpets rung,
> And all life's splendours sparkled georgeously, [sic]
> What lustre in a foreign land can come
> To dim the halo round our sacred HOME?[18]

While Parker as a chronicler of his own experience can thus give free rein to nostalgia, Parker as commentator on the literary marketplace is aware of the complex position of the exile writer, and the ways in which writing from exile necessarily involves awareness that 'home' is a constraining and shaping force on the exile's voice, as well as being the subject of exile fantasies of safe return. This awareness of 'home' in the literature of the colony, and the exiles' representation of the homeland, forms the subject of the remainder of this chapter.

Literary Constructions of 'home'

The oscillating journeys of travellers and their correspondence set up a dialogue that constructs 'home' through a process of recollection and negotiation, as the exiles' response to news of change is developed alongside their own reiteration of those abiding memories of the homeland to be recalled for those who shared them at their inception. The representation of 'home' in this literature is neither transparent nor simple, despite the apparent artlessness of many examples of exile writing. The processes of negotiation, and the ways in which 'home' is shaped by those metropolitan genres and forms that constitute part of the exiles' baggage on their journeys, are apparent even in private correspondence written by those whose main audience was the inner circle of friends and family, and whose primary aim was the sustaining of their relationships with those absent interlocutors.

Samuel Sneade Brown, who carried on an active correspondence with his mother and sisters in the course of fourteen years' service as a local administrator in India (1827–41), was not writing directly for publication, though the carefully worked poems included in some of the letters suggest that he might have had publication at the back of his mind. (A selection of his letters was eventually edited for private circulation after his death, and forms the basis of the analysis of his work in this chapter.) The movement apparent in his work, from straightforward nostalgia to an exploration of mixed feelings of loss and alienation, all the while sustaining an anticipation of eventual return, indicates the complex and multifaceted nature of the exile relationship. These are letters about England, to England, so carrying the burden of his relationship with family and friends as well as being a record of his own memories. They also constitute a narrative into which he fits these memories, a narrative of both loss and uncertainty about what 'home' might prove to be, or to have become, when he experiences it again.

Brown constructs his life in India as a negative image of English normality, writing to his mother from the isolated station of Sahuswan: 'You who live in happy England, and meet white faces wherever you go, cannot well imagine an existence like mine, unbroken by the voice of cheerfulness, or murmur of sympathy.'[19] The letters he receives serve for consolation in this lonely existence, as he learns of the daily lives of family and friends. His own letters back are equally important: these recreate the 'home' of his memory and imagination. The recapitulation of events and experiences in this correspondence serves to reinforce memories of 'home', but also to falsify these memories – a process of which Brown shows himself strikingly aware, as in this passage written to his sister Ellen:

> I think frequently, with tears in my eyes, on our quiet summer evening walks . . . with the trees and mounds and ferns, and the bright shining sea, and, forgetting my own captious temper, wonder that I viewed such objects with such indifference, and that I did not enjoy to the utmost such tranquil pleasures. This memory sheds a peaceful light over past scenes, brightening the dark shades, and tempering the bright parts of the picture.[20]

This composite vision of 'home' – the memory of home itself overlaid with the qualities retrospectively associated with it over time and distance – is a recurring trope among the exile writers. Richardson, for example, refers to his 'native strand, / Where shadows of departed dreams still float o'er hill and grove'.[21] These 'departed dreams' perhaps form the true matter of exile recollections, as when Brown declares that 'whatever length of time I may remain in India, I shall always remain the same, unchanging and unchanged as to my longing for England'.[22]

While these memories of 'home' are specific to each individual traveller, they are framed and coloured through the prism of existing literary forms. Brown's occasional poems sent to his family offer several examples of this process, as he adapts and responds to canonical published works in order to develop his own representations of the homeland he remembered. 'England', for instance, takes as its model Byron's celebrated opening lines from 'The Bride of Abydos' and transforms its representation of an idyllic Eastern location into a version of England 'where the fountain is springing', a pastoral landscape of songbirds, where 'peace sits in smiles at the cottager's door', and the 'spirit is borne of the free and the brave'. Crucially, however, this is not the 'real' England, but the 'isle of the west,' a space as unreal (geographically speaking) as it is idealised: 'Far – cradled afar on the blue ocean's breast – Where the hearts of its exiles in dreams ever roam, / 'Tis the clime of my fathers – 'tis England – 'tis home.'[23] The creation of 'home' as an occidental fantasy, based on and rivalling the oriental idyll of the original, demonstrates the extent to which the homeland is valorised in exile literature, but also the extent to which it is a construction of the literary imagination.

Brown was not a professional or a very practised writer of poetry, something evident from the ways in which his work tends to the banal or the simplistic when compared to its source-texts. 'I shall never be a poet', he wrote to his mother, while exhorting her to 'pass over the faults' of his poems 'for the sake of the feelings expressed in them'. The lines to which he refers are 'meant as a continuation' of the work Brown calls 'a beautiful little poem': Felicia Hemans's 'The Spells of Home'.[24] Hemans's original develops the theme of the 'spell' cast upon the heart of the wanderer by the experience of childhood:

> By the soft green light in the woody glade,
> On the banks of moss where thy childhood play'd;
> By the household tree thro' which thine eye
> First look'd in love to the summer-sky,
> By the dewy gleam, by the very breath
> Of the primrose tufts in the grass beneath,
> Upon thy heart there is laid a spell,
> Holy and precious – oh! guard it well![25]

In this poem, the spell is inspirational and character-forming, its 'gentle might' leading 'the freeman forth to stand / In the mountain battles of his land', and summoning the 'weeping prodigal' to return 'to the gates of his father's hall'. Brown retains the nostalgic element of Hemans's work, but does not venture beyond that: whereas Hemans's spell is constituted by and gains its power from memory, Brown's version of the 'holy spell' is simply another term for memory itself, the 'heart's best treasure' of the wanderer. The poem resolves the didactic tension of the original into a simple contrast between a picturesque image of India and a yet more attractive image of 'home':

> For a vision of home on his spirit beams, –
> He hears the voice of its thousand streams,
> He sees the pearl-drops of its summer showers
> Flinging a bloom o'er the woodland bowers,
> And the wavy gleam of the feathery grass,
> And the spring birds twittering as they pass,
> And the primrose bank, more dear to his eye
> Then the citron blossoms of Araby,
> Whilst Memory pours from her fairy shell
> The oft-heard tones of that holy spell.[26]

In this case, the language of the picturesque and the pastoral used by Hemans is the crucial element of Brown's representation of 'home', evidence of the influence of metropolitan modes and genres on the version of 'home' evolving in the colony.

The Picturesque Vision of 'home'

These visions of home are inspired by images as well as words, as is apparent in Brown's response to a volume he dwells long upon: *A Picturesque Tour to the English Lakes*, published by Ackermann in 1821. The close attention paid by Brown to this work translates into his own recollections of time spent in that location:

> It almost appears as if the artist had accompanied us step by step in our tour . . . They have set me a-dreaming the whole day. One would have been sufficient for that purpose, but the whole form a kind of magic mirror, not merely of the scenes themselves, but of the recollections connected with them.[27]

Those recollections tend, again, toward the banal – 'here is the identical mountain stream on the bank of which I lunched in my pedestrian excursion from Wast Water to Buttermere the day previous to the episode of the jug; and here is the spot where we had a squabbling match' – but the feelings of 'melancholy' and awareness of the passage of time inspired by the images speak effectively of their impact on the writer: 'Twelve long, long years [to be spent in India] . . . in an utter dearth, at least, of the heart's best affections.'[28] Brown himself appears to be consciously aware only of the subject-matter of the images, but their form, and in particular their framing in the mode of the picturesque, is also important.

Recent scholarship has emphasised the prevalence of this mode in framing literary responses to India, and Sara Suleri has argued that the 'proper colonial function' of the picturesque is to make 'memorabilia out of a culture still alive but one that it must nevertheless take pains to embalm'.[29] This tendency is also apparent in the construction of accounts of 'home' seen from India. The imagery of these accounts is drawn from the natural world, and the prevailing note is that of melancholy – as in Brown's rueful response to a letter from his mother 'redolent of spring – the beautiful spring of old England, with its flowers, and buds, and blossoms', which leads him to question: 'Shall I ever see again one of those hedgerows you speak of, or an autumn sunset, or a spring violet?'[30] This pastoral and elegiac voice is an echo of that found in several of Brown's contemporaries in India; the effect across this literature is to delineate an image of 'home' as distinctive, and as much set apart from the mundane pursuits of its ordinary inhabitants, as the orientalist image of India.

The 'home' of this representation is predominantly rural, despite the fact that the background of the writers concerned was urban. Richardson and Roberts, for instance, both moved to and fro between London and India (though Richardson also was familiar with the countryside of Devon).[31] Their work, however, focuses almost exclusively on the countryside; and also offers a vision of that countryside peopled by the rural poor. Richardson's poem 'England and Bengal', for example, describes England as a pastoral idyll: a green hill where the speaker stands and sees a 'meandering rill' of a stream and sheep on the hillside 'like little breakers bright, / Sprinkled o'er a smiling sea, / Seem[ing] to float at liberty'. The picturesque disorganisation and random freedom of movement associated with the animals is transferred onto the buildings 'scattered' around: 'White cots on the meadows green, / Open to the sky and breeze, / Or peeping through the sheltering trees'. The human inhabitants are children swinging on a gate. This is a land of play, of purposeless activity, where the principle of organisation is aesthetic.

The second part of the same poem offers a variant on the same scene; here the landscape of England is more populated, but populated with a select category and kind of people.

> How proud a sight to English eyes
> Are England's village families!
> The patriarch, with his silver hair,
> The matron grave, the maiden fair,
> The rose-cheeked child, the sturdy lad,

On Sabbath day all neatly clad; –
Me thinks I see them wend their way
On some refulgent morn of May,
By hedgerows trim, of fragrance rare,
Towards the hallowed House of Prayer?

This is a landscape peopled with a stereotypical and idealised family. The individuals are either old – the silver-haired patriarch, the grave matron – or young: the maiden, the child, the 'sturdy lad'. No work takes place: this is Sunday. The first half of the stanza is a static set piece; the movement of the second is a gentle 'wend their way'.[32] The main quality of the stanza is a dainty and well-ordered stillness.

The limited lexicon and range of reference in this vision of 'home' is apparent in the recurring use of familiar tropes and images. They reappear, for instance, in Richardson's 'The Return from Exile', where a landscape of white cottages and sheep is peopled with youth – a 'rural group of ruddy boys, that gaily loitered nigh' – as unproductive as the empty landscapes celebrated in the picturesque image of India.[33] 'An English Landscape' offers a countryside 'sun-lit', 'brightly beautiful', traversed by little streams, with 'sweet children' playing on their 'daisied' banks. This is a land of 'luxurious leisure'; the pastime of the 'village maids' is to 'blend their artless songs with laughter gay', while the only man visible is the 'herdsman old' who 'in yonder shade reposes'.[34] 'Sonnet to England' invokes 'nest-like cottages and silver streams'.[35] In these works, 'home' is a composite picture in a range of muted and sentimental hues, a fiction whose impact depends on its familiarity for both writer and reader.

The extent to which this image of 'home' is stereotypical, rather than simply the result of individual taste or memory, becomes apparent when recollections of the English homeland are contrasted with those of other countries. G. A. Vetch's poem on Scotland, for example, delineates a pastoral landscape similar to that of the nostalgically remembered England, but also marked as Scottish: the streams and rills of the English countryside are replaced by the 'crags and dells' and 'fern and heather' of Scotland. The image of youth is given a Scottish flavour by reference to the 'lads and lasses' dancing a 'strathspey' reel; and the sound of the bagpipes recalls to the speaker the 'plaided clans' of Scotland's martial history, 'to the combat dashing'.[36] In the same vein, the speaker of 'Kathleen's Lament', looking back to an Irish 'home', invokes the 'sparkling Bann' and 'proud Lough Neagh', but also offers an image of the sentimentally supernatural, with 'fairy-guarded' hills, the 'Benshee's [sic] sable thorn' and 'the shamrock's triple leaves'.[37] In both these cases, as in the representations of England more generally discussed in this section, 'home' is constituted by a set of emblematic images and associations, becoming a performance of rural Englishness, Scottishness or Irishness, and drawn in such a way as to exclude the urban or the modern.

The fact that this mode of writing is so prevalent in the periodicals of this period, and that it is also adopted by unpublished writers such as Brown, suggests that its 'sameness' may have been one of its virtues for both writers and readers. Certainly, editors were happy to print nostalgic poems, and readers (who could, and did, comment on the quality of the work they were offered) did not object to the repetition many times over of their sentiments and motifs. One reason for this tolerance may lie in the tendency of this invocation of an absent 'home' to reinforce the shared experience of the British in India, uniting a community of exiles around the reiteration of their feelings of loss.[38]

As well as constituting a force for cohesion within the Anglo-Indian community, the poetry of nostalgia also prompts several observations about the nature of that community, and its relationship to India, as well as to Britain. The implicit or explicit comparison of the exotic with the domestic is a staple of these texts. Brown, for instance, slots the Ganges immediately into such a relationship: 'The broad Ganges is, I confess, an exhilarating object . . . My thoughts, notwithstanding, are constantly reverting to our English May, and, with my recollection of that month, the banks of the Wye are inseparably united.'[39] Such parallels are frequently indicative of more complex relationships between 'home' and India, however.

Roberts's 'Stanzas Written in a Pavilion of the Rambaugh' offers many of these predictable oppositions of the exile's lament: a 'lonely exile' gazes at the 'winding river, turret, spire, and dome' of the Indian landscape, exclaiming 'It is not home! alas, it is not home!', and thinking of the 'gurgling brook, the narrow-winding dell' of a British countryside.[40] Despite these conventional features of the text, 'Stanzas Written in a Pavilion' also exemplifies a complexity and sometimes contradiction in Roberts's view of exile that leads Gibson to describe her work as 'devolv[ing] into a kind of incoherence'. Gibson's analysis traces the back-and-forth movement between 'home' and India carried out in the course of the poem, as the exile subject 'longs for the painted scenes of India because "his own earth" does not possess such scenes; this same exile longs for the humble villages of "his native land"'.[41] This displacement is finally stabilised (here my reading diverges from Gibson's), when the final passage locates the exile in India, and constructs 'home' as a fantasy, as the 'pensive gazer would rejoice to see', but by implication cannot see, its familiar characteristics:

> The soft green sward with daisies spangled o'er,
> The brawling stream by rustic arches spanned,
> The jasmine trailing round the cottage door,
> The humblest village of his native land.[42]

'The Ganges,' similarly, starts and ends with a self-reflective look back at home. The speaker declares in the opening stanza: 'farewell, thou regal stream! / Henceforth thy pomp will be to me nought save a gorgeous dream'. This future is deferred for most of the succeeding fifteen stanzas, as the speaker is preoccupied with an address to the eponymous river, and a recapitulation through it of many of the standard exotic associations and trappings of India as imagined through a lived experience heightened by literary acquaintance with stereotype. These include tigers and alligators on the riverbanks, the 'lofty towers' of cities, 'blood-cemented battlements' of forts, and the 'countless Hindoo host, / By wild fanatic zeal impelled, in adoration lost'. It is not until the penultimate stanza that the speaker returns to that opening thought, anticipating a future occasion to 'stand / Beside some rippling brooklet's bank in my loved native land', when 'Not all the wealth thy waters bear could tempt me to remain, / Or cross the seas to gaze upon thy stately realms again.'[43] As in 'Stanzas Written in a Pavilion', the complex movement of those final lines, where the speaker in India imagines being in the homeland and imagining India, has the effect of positioning both locations as equally unreal and unreachable, the 'rippling brooklet' of 'home' as stereotypical as the tigers and alligators of India. Here as in other exile texts, the reality of a distant homeland is replaced by the elusive fantasy of an unattainable 'home'.

'Home' as Location of Change and Death

Part of what makes the reality, as opposed to the stereotype, of this distant 'home' unimaginable is the exiles' pervasive anxiety about the changes that might have worked upon the homeland in their absence. In its simplest form, this involves the possibility that those loved residents of 'home' may not survive the period of the exile's absence, as J. Tytler's poem 'Exile' suggests:

> Where are the Friends whose loss I mourn?
> Beneath the silent tomb they sleep:
> O'er ocean why must I return
> On their cold monuments to weep?[44]

Samuel Brown expresses as his 'most earnest wish that when I find the hour of my departure draw nigh, I may see myself in my native land'; but the recurring theme in his letters is his fear and anticipation of his mother's death, rather than his own.[45] 'I dreamt a few nights ago', he writes, 'that your silver cord had been loosed, and your pitcher broken at the fountain, and I awoke in a flood of tears' (133). On observing in her handwriting a 'slight . . . tremulousness . . . which tells of increasing years', he imagines his heart to be 'like a sealed fountain in the wilderness', which will be unsealed 'only by your death, and then the waters will flow forth freely' (148). His untitled lines of verse written on (and to) his mother, panegyric in tone, end with a vision of her death:

> Till when beneath the verdant sod
> Thou tread'st the path that all have trod
> To meet thy Father and thy God,
> My mother. (99)

History does not record Mrs Brown's response to these thoughts. Death, however, is not the greatest fear in these texts. 'Time will blunt even the keen edge of a mother's affection' (56), observes Brown; and a similar apprehension that 'home' will have changed, or that those at home will have changed, or that the exile has been changed by the years of absence, is visible in the work of many others. Richardson's essay 'On Going Home' describes a 'mistrustful mood' in which the exile imagines 'a thousand melancholy images' of abandonment: relatives dead, home empty, the 'hearth of his infancy' cold. The greater fear expressed here is the fear of alienation: 'if the halls and lands of his fathers are not lonely and neglected, they are perhaps in the possession of the stranger, and his own birth-place is like a scene in a foreign land'. Most tellingly, the pastoral landscape of the exile's imagined 'home', here a 'sweet flower-garden', has become 'a dreary wilderness'.[46] Elsewhere, he describes a lived rather than an imagined alienation, comparing the ideal England he, 'a mere boy', had left – 'the glory of the earth and the favourite of heaven' – with the land of 'cold and cautious strangers' he found on his return sixteen-odd years later. 'It was the observer, however, that had changed', he writes, 'and not the people. They were neither worse nor better; but my own head had grown clearer and my heart colder.'[47]

These fears of transformation of the self, or alienation of the self from the distant 'home', are evident in much of this literature, reflecting Edward Said's observation that for exiles, 'homes are always provisional'.[48] W. Stacy's poem 'The Wanderer's Return' describes how the process of leaving home changes home itself:

> My poor deserted home!
> I gaze upon thy mouldering walls,
> And see each vacant chair,
> While memory bitterly recalls
> The forms that should be there.

This is not simply a matter of the passage of time: the absent dead 'never loved me – not a smile / Of love was given', though the speaker even while affirming this, 'cannot think of them ... Without a deep regret'. The poem concludes with the recognition of alienation and estrangement as constitutive of identity – 'I'm but a stranger now / In mine own land of birth' – as the speaker leaves for 'some foreign shore' to 'forget in strangers' love / How cold these hearts have been'.[49] A lost 'home' is doubly lost, as having never had in the first place the 'homely' associations of love or belonging; and the quest for 'strangers' love' by one who now describes himself as a 'stranger' marks a decisive separation from that place of origin. A similar dynamic is apparent in the work of other writers, as in Patrick Scott's 'The Exile's Return', when the exile's 'home he loved when young' proves so disappointing that he leaves again, '"Mid alien tribes to roam, / And scarce could find another spot / So foreign as his home!"[50] In the case of Calder Campbell's 'Sonnet', the impact of alienation is destructive of the speaker's poetic as well as personal identity: 'home' is 'altered – *altered?* is it so, / Or is the change in me?' He finds 'my home, / Which is no more my home, and with it fled / The minstrel-spark within me – *that* is dead!'[51]

This idea of 'home' as foreign or alien to the exile also finds expression in a re-casting of the returned traveller's own relationship to the homeland. The England of R. A. Macnaghten's poem 'A Sort of Lay Jocund, on my return to India' is a tourist destination, and his sojourn there disappointing in that it has failed to meet his expectations of its promised attractions: 'The King and I have never met,' he observes, and 'I know not one bas bleu'. The 'native land' of the poem's ironic address is further defamiliarised as the speaker composes a farewell that runs in counterpoint to the conventional exile's lament:

> So my native land, good night! – or if,
> You would rather, I'll say good morning!
> I am happy to tell you the breeze is stiff,
> And the pilot has given us warning.
> I go! – with a heart too light to swell,
> I sail! – with a tearless eye! –
> Land of Umbrellas, Fare thee well;
> Land of caught colds, good bye![52]

This sense of 'home' having become unfamiliar is also apparent in Emily Eden's anxious comparison of the 'starving districts' of Cawnpore, where drought led to famine during the 1830s, with an imagined England of the future:

> Perhaps two thousand years hence, when the art of steam has been forgotten, and nobody can exactly make out the meaning of the old English word 'mail-coach,' some black Governor-General of England will be marching through its southern provinces, and will go and look at some ruins, and doubt whether London ever was a large town, and will feed some white-looking skeletons, and say what distress the poor creatures must be in; they will really eat rice and curry; and his sister will write to her Mary D. at New Delhi, and complain of the cold, and explain to her with great care what snow is, and how the natives wear bonnets, and then, of course, mention that she wants to go home. (66–7)

Deirdre David's influential account suggests that this passage demonstrates Eden's ability, unusual in her time and among her class, to 'admit the root meaning of imperialism', recognising it as 'power not as duty', and so 'unsettles powerful early nineteenth-century ideas about racial difference and superiority'.[53] A different reading might suggest that Eden is also concerned with the otherness of 'home' – though the transformation suggested is safely distanced to 'two thousand years hence' – and the experience of alienation from it. The passage above continues: 'Do you like writing to me? I hate writing in general, but these long letters to you are the comfort of my existence.'[54] Home is imagined as there, and yet not there, familiar and yet alien; the writing by which the relationship to 'home' is maintained is both hated and comforting.

This sense of alienation from 'home' finds expression also in a recurring theme of this literature: the temperate climate of Britain, with its cold winters, contrasted to the heat and sunshine of India. Richardson's dogged insistence on the superiority of England seems rather forced at times, as when he claims that the 'wholesome frigidity of England' and its 'external gloom and bleakness enhance our in-door comforts, and we do not miss sunny skies when greeted with sunny looks. If we see no blooming gardens, we see blooming faces'.[55]

The vocabulary of this passage, with its stress on the absence of sunshine and fertility, rather belies Richardson's positive comparison; and the association of 'home' with gloom, bleakness and frigidity finds an echo in other works, such as Vincent Tregear's poem 'The Wanderer', where (to turn around the intended message) the fact of its being 'home' is the only redeeming aspect of the 'rude built hut' and the 'hills so drear' that characterise his native land, and appear so far inferior to the 'land of sun and flowers' that is India.[56]

These examples also demonstrate how the language descriptive of climate and personality takes on a metaphoric character that goes beyond the literal. 'Home' is a location without warmth or sunshine, devoid of sensual pleasure, characterised as not only frigid, but wholesomely frigid. This becomes particularly apparent in looking at a poem that addresses a potentially sexualised relationship directly. 'Stanzas', by 'S. T.', combines longing for a woman with nostalgia for home, and contrasts both with the lush and sensuous landscape of India. Against India's almond trees, orange flowers, and mango groves, its fruits and flowers with their 'gay perfumes', the woman is held up as icily chaste, her 'pure unspotted brow' the only physical feature to draw comment. As the woman's unattainable, distant status is signalled and emphasised by the surroundings of her 'northern home', the fantasy of 'home' is revealed as driven by Thanatos rather than Eros – if feminised India is a land of life and growth, 'home' is a land of chilly lifelessness. Brown's correspondence offers a comic version of this trope, as he energetically rejects his mother's discussion of a possible future for him as husband and schoolteacher: 'Why, this is an airy vision, indeed; a vision of romance and happiness, of seclusion and elegance, of refinement and enjoyment! Oh, murder!'[57]

Other writers also associated 'home' with death. W. F. Muston describes the 'fairy picture' of the Dorset countryside left behind by the exile – 'Thy down, thy flock, and meads unbounded charms' – but ends by acknowledging that this 'Summer's past', and looking forward to an increasingly conditional future: 'yet Autumn may be ours; / Adieu! Adieu! e'en Winter has its flowers'.[58] This theme is treated in more depth by Parker in 'The Return from India', which initially describes the familiar emotions of the exile – loneliness, alienation, appreciation for the 'well-remembered scenes' of home. These feelings, however, are not associated with the exile phase, but with the experience of the speaker on his return to what was once 'home'. 'Still I have reached my home at last; / But other hands now cull its flowers'; the hearth is 'lonely'; the speaker laments: 'I am a stranger in my hall, / The hearts which made it glad are cold'. Though the pastoral vision of 'home' appears in its familiar form, with 'hazel copse' and 'gushing rill', the speaker asks 'But where are all the feelings, where! / Which made it still more dear than bright?' As the day becomes night, and the summer moves towards winter – both signalled by the 'harvest moon' rising – the speaker looks towards his last 'home':

> The bells of many a harvest wain
> Come soft and sweet; but sweeter yet

Yon spire on which the moonshine glows,
That tells me where I shall forget
Life's toils and hopes in death's repose.[59]

'Home' as Land of Childhood

The uneasy anticipation of old age and death is replaced, in some cases, by the exiles' imagination of 'home' as a location of memory, the home of their childhood. In 'Return from Exile', Richardson pictures the return 'home' as also a chronological turning back: on seeing the 'bright cliffs' of England, 'I paced the swift bark's bounding deck, light-hearted as a child; / And when among my native fields I wandered in the sun, / I felt as if my morn of life had only just begun.'[60] For him and many others in the exile community, Britain is the location of their own childhood, and the memories of 'home' are also memories of being a child. Eden makes the connection explicit when she describes the aftermath of a storm in Simla:

> Such nice clear air, and altogether it feels English and exhilarating; and I think of you [her sister], and Eden Farm, and the Temple Walk, and Crouch Oak Lane, and the blue butterflies, and then the gravel-pit, and your reading 'Corinne' to me; and then the later days of Eastcombe and our parties there, with G. V. in his wonderful spirits, with all his wit, and all the charm about him; and all this because the air is English. I should like to go back to childhood and youth again – there was great enjoyment in them.[61]

Vetch similarly invokes an association with youth as a central aspect of the nostalgically-conceived 'native land': 'childhood's blissful day, / Ere yet one pang from sorrow griev'd us', before 'Love betray'd – or friends deceiv'd us'.[62]

One of the central tenets of British Indian society was the idea that 'home' is a fit place for children, both morally and materially better suited to their development than the alien climate and culture of India. As Buettner's study of Victorian and early twentieth-century sources demonstrates, medical and other advice literature advocated that the health of younger children, and the sexual and moral development of adolescents, required them to be returned to what a contemporary author describes as the 'more bracing and healthy ... atmosphere' of Europe, and more specifically, England – 'The child must be sent to England, or it will deteriorate physically and morally.'[63] Britain is thought of as the natural location of childhood, as 'J. P.' indicates in *The Care of Infants in India*: 'few sights are more pleasing than to see these puny, pallid, skinny, fretful little ones converted, by British food and British meteorology, into fat and happy English children'.[64] This is not an uncomplicated notion, of course, as Roberts indicates when she remarks on how 'gratifying' exiles such as herself found 'groups of healthy-looking, tidily dressed English children' of British soldiers, who were able 'to preserve their strength and vigour in a climate considered to be exceedingly detrimental to the juvenile classes of Europeans'.[65] But whether Roberts was implicitly excluding her working-class compatriots from the category of 'exile', or distancing herself from contemporary ideas about the harmfulness of the Indian climate to children in general, her association of 'home' and childhood is a theme recurring throughout this literature.

Less obviously, the return 'home' also serves to prevent children and parents becoming alienated from one another, in the ways suggested by Roberts when she describes the effect on children of being looked after primarily by Indian servants, and learning their language rather than English: 'In numerous instances, they cannot make themselves intelligible to their parents, it being no uncommon case to find the latter almost totally ignorant of the native dialect, while their children cannot converse in any other.'[66] Paradoxically, the forced separation between child and parents involved in the child's return 'home' is designed to bring them linguistically and in other ways closer together. In returning to Britain, the child re-enacts the parents' own experience of childhood at 'home', while acquiring the linguistic, cultural and class attributes of their parents.

Poems such as Richardson's 'Consolations of Exile: or, An Exile's Address to his Distant Children' explore this process of bringing together in imagination the parent and child separated by distance: 'Fair children! still, like phantoms of delight, / Ye haunt my soul on this strange distant shore'. By the final passages, absence has been succeeded by an imagined reunion, as he first looks at his children's painted images, and then invokes the fantasised location of 'home' as the space where he can see them directly:

Oh! then how sweet,
Dear Boys! upon remembered bliss to dwell,
And here your pictured lineaments to greet;
Till Fancy, bright Enchantress, shifts the scene
To British ground, and musical as rills,
Ye laugh and loiter in the meadows green,
Or climb with joyous shouts the sunny hills![67]

This unproblematic imaginative union of the sundered family on the ground of 'home' is not, however, the only take on the association of childhood with 'home' in these texts. Others suggest a more complex and darker set of memories and associations carried by exiles, or perhaps a process whereby the memory of the homeland becomes darker and more complex over the years spent away from it.

Robert Cotton Money makes it clear in his letters to his parents and sister that nostalgia, memories of 'home' and family, and fond thoughts of England took up a considerable amount of his mind during his absence. In the correspondence published as *Journal of a Tour in Persia*, his main focus is, naturally, on the sights and experiences of the journey; but these are interspersed with episodes of longing for 'home':

> The many, many a summer day like that which I had spent in England came to my recollection. The sweet faces of those who shared these pleasures flitted across me. I fixed my eyes on one little cloud, which, as Milton beautifully says, 'turned forth its silver lining on the sky,' and tried to people it with those whom I love so much. I tried to make it my home. . . . Sweet, sweet hours! but sweeter will they be when we meet again. How sweet after such a separation![68]

The combination of pastoral – the summer day, the cloud – the invocation of absent loved ones, the anticipation of a later reunion, even the quotation of Milton may all be said to represent attempts to recreate a version of 'home' in exile, and to maintain by the correspondence in which this experience is described a connection and a relationship between the writers and the absent recipient of the letter. Money's sense of what 'home' might be also extends beyond the personal. In the course of his observations on Persia, he pauses several times to draw unflattering comparisons with 'our dear native land', as when describing an attractive pastoral landscape blighted by 'innumerable musquitoes', which oblige him to 'pitch my tent in a yard attached to a miserable and dirty hovel'.[69] Here as elsewhere, the landscape, customs and inhabitants of Persia are implicitly compared to an English ideal. In the poem 'Stanzas written at the Rain Ghat', the irreplaceable aspects of England are explicitly listed: they include a vision of the pastoral in 'summer beds of green', the 'jewel month of May', and 'peasant cottages'; but also a 'lion-maned strength', and a history that includes the 'shout of Freedom's jubilees / For full a thousand years'.[70]

When Money addresses the topic of a personal memory of England directly, as in the poem 'Thoughts of Home in India', a different vision becomes apparent. Even as the structure of the following stanza, for instance, sets the homeland – 'ours' – above all those the poet has seen on his travels, the overwhelming impression for the reader is the richness and colour of these other lands:

> O'er golden river'd lands I've run,
> Lap-full of fruits and flowers,
> Like scenes before the Fall, but none –
> None half so sweet as ours.

At 'home', by contrast, the river has become a 'distant wintry waterfall / Half icicled and dumb'; and the robin 'piping for a crumb' is an image of want and neediness as well as a cliché of the English countryside. Although the poem locates 'childhood's happy dream' in England, the specific elements of these memories of childhood are edgy and at least ambiguous – such as the 'ghostly story' told 'to scare the little flock'.[71]

The same or a similar memory of a ghost story appears in a poem written by Robert's brother David Money at around the same time. 'Domum, Domum, Dulce Domum' – or 'home, home, joyous home' – expands on Robert's brief mention of storytelling with a catalogue of horrors that belies the poem's title:

> How some poor donkey or a post
> Was taken for a fearful ghost –
> How 'neath some tree was always heard
> The sound of that mysterious bird,
> Whose cry at midnight rises shrill,
> And clear, and loud, foreboding ill,
> And how the ominous sound had scared
> All . . .
>
> We heard of sudden-sinking floors,
> Of frightful noises, and trap-doors,
> Of heavy nightmares, and of screams
> In restless after-supper dreams;
> How highwaymen were seen about
> Drear Shooter's Hill, and such like places –
> How murders always were found out,
> Though time had swept away the traces!
> The forest lodge – the bloody bed –
> And underneath a shaggy head
> Just peeping out; – the lonely inn –
> The landlord with a murderous grin –
> The sleeping draught . . .[72]

This is clearly an evocation of childhood excitement and the thrill of sensation, and also an account of the shared experience of heightened emotion and the individual's role in a larger audience – all aspects of the lost 'home' that might be considered particularly appealing to a writer now distanced from that community. The line 'murders always were found out' gestures towards the crime narrative's role of reinstating

46 Experiences of India

order and security. At the same time, the overall effect of the lines is to highlight the unreliability of the familiar and domestic: the donkey taken for a ghost, the 'ominous sound' of a bird, the floor no longer solid but sinking at a footstep. Places of apparent safety – the forest lodge, the bed, the inn – become locations of fear and death. While the poem insists that 'happy too were summer days', the writer chooses to dwell instead on an anecdote of winter, where a carefree childhood memory of skating is underlaid with the 'Crack! crack! crack!' of ice, again an evocative image of 'home' as a space of danger unrealised by the child whose memories are being shared.[73]

'Home' as Beyond Reach

While the exile concept of 'home' is clearly problematic in the ways discussed above, it is also unattainable, retreating even as the exile affirms its significance. Against the graveyards of India, Roberts positions home, 'beyond the western wave', as an unreachable resting-place – idyllic compared to these 'gloomy cemet'ries', but vainly hoped for by the 'weary spirit' who imagines it:

> Oh! since beyond the western wave
> I may not hope to find a grave,
> Nor yield my weary spirit up,
> Where springs the glittering butter cup,
> And daisies lend their silvery shrouds,
> And violets mourn in purple clouds,
> Where the green moss is over spread,
> In spring time with the primrose pale,
> And the red wall flower lifts its head,
> And sheds its sweets on autumn's gale.[74]

Similarly, the grammatical structure of Tregear's 'Lines – Home' creates a parallel movement of unfulfilled yearning, positioning his native land behind a series of conditional negatives, each of which emphasises the attractions of 'home' while simultaneously distancing the exile from it:

> Land of my birth! although my feet no more
> May pace thy fields, or wander on thy shore;
> Though ne'er again my brow may feel thy gale;
> My lips no more thy fragrant breeze inhale

That series of conditional clauses is concluded in the final lines with a declarative:

> Be thou the idol still, on memory's shrine
> The kibleh of my heart, where'er I roam,
> Heav'n bless thee still, my lost for ever home!⁷⁵

Here the 'Land of my birth' with which the sentence began is finally picked up and referred to as 'kibleh of my heart' – an unglossed use of the Arabic قبلة, or 'qibla', the direction to be faced when praying. Positing 'home' as Mecca, and as the 'idol ... on memory's shrine', the poem enacts the process by which home has become 'lost for ever', through the poet's own movement away from it, both literally and in terms of experience. Made problematic through its cross-cultural identification as both 'idol' and subject of blessing, 'home' is paradoxically a stable point in the exile's mental landscape, while simultaneously 'lost for ever'.

This is the dilemma underlying the insistence on 'home' as a constant which appears in the work of exiles such as Julia Maitland. 'Home always means England', she writes; 'nobody calls India home – not even those who have been here thirty years or more, and are never likely to return to Europe; even they still always speak of England as home.'⁷⁶ In the case of some of these exiles, however, while their sense of England (or Scotland or Ireland) as 'home' remains constant, the imagined nature of that 'home' changes in the course of their experience of India. Eden, at the very end of her tour of the Upper Provinces in 1840, returns to the house she shared with her brother and sister in Calcutta, thinking of her father's anecdote of the Duke of Marlborough, who went from the house of a poverty-stricken friend to his own residence of Blenheim Palace and remarked: 'Well! home is home, be it never so homely.' Eden echoes this:

> So say I, on coming back to this grand palace, from those wretched tents, and so shall I repeat with still greater unction when we arrive at our dear little villa at Kensington Gore. If it should please God that we ever do so, mind that you and your girls are on the lawn to greet us.⁷⁷

The word 'home' is charged with increasing levels of significance here: the initial location of 'home' in Calcutta cannot be permitted to stand, but is replaced immediately in a domestic space with sentimental associations, a 'dear little villa' in London. By the final sentence, the declarative 'when we arrive' has become the conditional and implorative 'If it should please God that we ever do so': home is a refuge, but that refuge is receding, becoming more unattainable, even as the final letter home raises up the image of the welcoming family waiting to greet the exiles on their return.

'Home' Relocated to India

Rudyard Kipling's work offers several examples of this ambivalence towards 'home', deepening in complexity as he moved away from India. Some of his later works represent a British 'home' as seen from India, or experienced as a contrast to an India lately left, but are in fact written at many years' remove, and at a far distance. The early 'letter in rhyme' to his aunt Edith Macdonald draws on the conventional trope of the exile's misery, locating the author, self-described as 'your parboiled nephew', in an infernal India of heat, noise and 'pitiless sunlight', where he can only imagine an absent 'home': 'If I shut my eyes and the parrots were hushed in the palms outside, / I might fancy myself for a time by some wholesome English tide'.[78] 'The Moon of Other Days', similarly, offers a conventional scene of England being recalled while the speaker is in exile, sitting at evening-time in the 'deep veranda's shade', and watching the moon rise. The memory of his walks with 'little Kitty Smith' – 'When arm in arm we wandered long / Through Putney's evening haze' – sets up an opposition between the sentimental memory of 'Home', reduced to a romantic vision of 'golden gorse', and the unpleasantly material reality of India:

> But Wandle's stream is Sutlej now,
> And Putney's evening haze
> The dust that half a hundred kine
> Before my window raise.
> Unkempt, unclean, athwart the mist
> The seething city looms, –
> In place of Putney's golden gorse
> The sickly *babul* blooms.[79]

The prevailing tone of the poem is ironic: Kitty Smith's description as 'Sweet Saint of Kensington', and the unlikely image of Putney and Hammersmith as pastoral retreats, suggest that this is a version of the exile's lament which at least gestures toward satire of the mode, or of the speaker. The relish with which it dwells on the dust, drains, smells and fevers of the Indian city, together with the pseudonym of 'Dyspeptic' under which it was first published, further suggests a sardonic playing with the genre.[80] The lived experience of exile and the performance of the exile's role have become intertwined.

The biographical context within which this response to exile was developed became apparent as Kipling went on to publish several accounts based on his own return with his sister Trix to England in 1870, when they were sent as young children to board with the Holloway family in Southsea. Their house, Lorne Lodge, was referred to by Kipling as the 'House of Desolation', and became the space of his oppression by Mrs Holloway and her son in his autobiography, *Something of Myself*, and in the short story 'Baa Baa Black Sheep'.[81] These works have been exhaustively analysed by critics and biographers of Kipling, and the extent to which they are (literally or substantially) accurate portrayals of his childhood experience much debated.[82] The salient point for the current discussion is the way in which a childhood sensation of 'belonging' in India is, in these texts, contrasted to a 'home' in England which is perceived as alien.

This is particularly clear in *Something of Myself*, which opens on the author's recollection of his earliest memories. None of these concerns a building which is the physical location of 'home': they feature instead public spaces, as the child remembers 'early morning walks to the Bombay fruit market', visits to 'little Hindu temples', and 'evening walks ... by the sea in the shadow of palm-groves'. No mention is made of his parents, but Indians appear as reassuring and caring figures, from the ayah to 'Meeta, my Hindu bearer' to the 'dimly-seen, friendly Gods' of the Hindu temples which are, like the rest of the landscape, freely accessible to him. The exile's concern with the dangers of India is invoked with reference to the 'menacing darkness of tropical eventides', but this is immediately subsumed into the overriding narrative of comfort: 'I have [always] loved the voices of night-winds through palm or banana leaves, and the song of the tree-frogs' (3). 'Home' is in this passage not associated with a dwelling place or with parents (though both make an appearance in the following pages); rather, the entirety of India is represented as a familiar and welcoming environment.

By contrast with the 'daybreak, light and colour and golden and purple fruits' of India', the England of the child's first encounter is repellent:

> There was next a dark land, and a darker room full of cold, in one wall of which a white woman made naked fire, and I cried aloud with dread, for I had never before seen a grate. Then came a new small house smelling of aridity and emptiness, and a parting in the dawn with Father and Mother ... (5)

Here the fireplace – traditionally the domestic heart of the home – becomes an object of fear, the familiar made strange, in the same way as the 'white woman' is perceived not as another self but as the 'other' distinguished by her race. Like the house itself, they constitute aspects of a supposed 'home' which is wholly unhomelike, a representation further substantiated by the details of the child's mistreatment, culminating in the episode where his mother, having come to visit her children, goes into her son's room to 'kiss me goodnight', and finds the half-asleep boy putting up a hand to 'guard off the cuff that I had been trained to expect' (40).

In contrast, the equally fictional, but idealised and romanticised, version of a child's life in the opening chapters of *Kim* takes some of its idyllic quality from the protagonist's ability to find acceptance wherever he goes, and enter into child-parent relationships with adults from across the races and societies of India. The abundance of parental figures he acquires in the course of his *Bildungsroman* – the lama, Mahbub Ali, Father Victor, Colonel Creighton, and Lurgan all take on aspects of the father's caring and protective role; while the Sahiba and the Woman of Shamlegh both function partially as mother figures – makes India again the protective and endlessly enabling 'home' of Kipling's early childhood, notwithstanding the manufactured dangers of the spy story which supplies the motivation for the novel's plot.[83]

The first chapter of *Something of Myself* concludes the tale of misery at Southsea with a redemption of sorts, when the returning mother rescues the two children from the 'House of Desolation' and brings them to happiness in London. The abiding memory of that time is their happy possession of season tickets for the 'old South Kensington museum' where they 'owned that place' and 'roved at will' through its treasures (40). In fiction, however, Kipling transferred that experience to India, where Kim brings the lama to the 'Wonder House' that is the Lahore museum. As he 'click[s] around the self-registering turnstiles' into the space where he, like the child Kipling in Bombay, has free entry, and listens to the curator (in real life, Lockwood Kipling, Rudyard's father) expound to the lama the knowledge of the East gained by the 'labours of European scholars', he becomes the personification of Kipling's fantasy of colonial knowledge, the British coloniser for whom India is the authentic 'home'.[84]

Those who did not seek to imagine India as 'home' could, on occasion, find a similar refuge in the shared experience of exile itself. 'The Emigrant's Song', by Patrick Scott, begins with the exile's conventional emotion of homesickness: 'With heavy hearts we stray, / For our thoughts are in our father-land / While we are far away!' Solace is found, for these exiles, not in thoughts of return, but in the migrant community: 'We'll turn to those who share our fate, / Our exile and its pain.' The final stanza resolves the conundrum of exile by ascribing to the emigrant community an emotional value that encompasses and surpasses the 'home' that has been lost:

We'll drown in scenes of present bliss
The thoughts of past delight.
And as with brightened looks we gaze
On each accustomed face,
The home we knew in other days
We'll find in their embrace![85]

Notes

1. Buettner, *Empire Families*, p. 189.
2. Elwood, *Narrative*, vol. 2, pp. 184, 205.
3. Plotz, 'First strawberries', p. 659. See also Agnew's discussion of the attempts by British women in India to 'recreate an anglicised home' through the deployment of imported material goods ('Relocating domesticity', pp. 100–1).
4. Trevelyan, *Competition Wallah*, pp. 36–7.
5. Richardson, 'Introductory Stanzas', Bengal Annual (1830), pp. 1–3.
6. Marshall, 'British immigration', pp. 182–4.
7. Richardson, 'Introductory Stanzas', *Bengal Annual* (1831), p. vii.
8. R. H. Rattray, 'Introductory Lines', *Bengal Annual* (1834), p. xi.
9. Richardson, 'Introductory Sonnet', *Bengal Annual* (1835), n.p.
10. Richardson, 'Summer and Winter', *Bengal Annual* (1834), p. 269. The conceit of a poetic 'anthology' or gathering of literal and metaphorical flowers continues to inform his work: a later collection is entitled *Flowers and Flower-Gardens*, and includes 'an appendix of practical instructions . . . respecting the Anglo-Indian Flower-Garden'.
11. Roberts, *Oriental Scenes* (1832), p. vii.
12. Richardson, 'Preface', *Bengal Annual* (1833), p. v. One reviewer made a point of advising 'our friends in Bengal . . . that if they look to home for the popularity of their . . . works, they will find it very much to the advantage of their lucubrations to stamp on them a thoroughly Indian character' (*Monthly Review* [August 1832], p. 570).
13. Parker, 'Oriental Tale', *Bengal Annual* (1833), pp. 1–16. Here, and in other instances where a text is subject to sustained analysis, further page references are given in parentheses.
14. White, *From Little London*, pp. 142, 148–9.
15. White's proposed third audience, the reading public of returned Anglo-Indians in Britain, is beyond the scope of my discussion: see *From Little London*, p. 148.
16. See Mani, *Contentious Traditions*, pp. 161–4.
17. Bhabha, *Location of Culture*, p. 165.
18. Parker, 'Stanzas Written on the River', *Bengal Annual* (1831), p. 50. See also a similar work by Parker, 'Songs of Spring', which contrasts a homeland in the 'temperate zones of earth' with the deictic 'here' where spring comes 'on the wings of the fiery blast', and 'scorching whirlwinds sweep the plain' (*Bengal Annual* [1832], pp. 150–1).
19. Brown, *Home Letters*, p. 103.

20. Brown, *Home Letters*, p. 13.
21. Richardson, 'Home Visions', *Literary Leaves* vol. 1, p. 60.
22. Brown, *Home Letters*, p. 18.
23. Brown, *Home Letters*, p. 119; cf. Byron, *Selected Poems*, p. 209. Byron's work, and this poem in particular, often served as a model for the poets of British India: see my article 'Transformations', pp. 580–1. The vision of England as a literary construct is found in the work of other poets as well: H. M. Parker's 'Sonnets on Shakespeare', for example, uses the first sonnet, 'As You Like It', to raise the vision of an England which is itself inspired by Shakespeare's Forest of Arden (*Bengal Annual* [1833], p. 101).
24. Brown, *Home Letters*, pp. 71–2.
25. Hemans, *Records*, p. 286.
26. Brown, *Home Letters*, p. 71. See also another poem (pp. 51–2), which Brown describes as a poetic response to 'Call of the Wanderer', by Mrs Hemans – Hemans did not, to my knowledge, publish a poem by that title, but the trope of the wanderer appears frequently in her work.
27. Brown, *Home Letters*, p. 137.
28. Brown, *Home Letters*, p. 138.
29. Suleri, *Rhetoric*, p. 103; see also Leask's discussion of the picturesque mode in travel writing (*Curiosity*, pp. 166–78); and Nayar on the 'missionary picturesque' (*English Writing*, pp. 94–131).
30. Brown, *Home Letters*, p. 157.
31. See Priyali Ghosh, 'David Lester Richardson', pp. 25–6. Mary Ellis Gibson argues that this focus on the rural is a necessary part of imagining 'home' as 'a longed-for destination', because 'the urban is too close to the twin economic realities of empire and industry' (*Indian Angles*, p. 132).
32. Richardson, 'England and Bengal', *Literary Recreations*, pp. 18–27. An earlier and shorter version, dated 1839, appears in *Literary Leaves*, vol. 1, pp. 151–4; Ghosh suggests that these 'flat and unconvincing figures are remnants from Richardson's earlier poetry' ('David Lester Richardson', p. 315) . The association of a pastoral 'home' with the rural working classes reaches beyond the poetic form. Roberts, for instance, writes of how those of the elite classes in India are moved to emotional response by 'meetings with country people of an inferior class in the jungles of India', when 'the homely provincial accents of some untaught soldier come in music on the ear' (*Scenes and Characteristics*, vol. 2, p. 125).
33. Richardson, *Literary Recreations*, pp. 140–1.
34. Richardson, *Literary Recreations*, p. 451. Compare, for example, Roberts's description of the Indian picturesque river scene and its idle boatman in 'The North-Wester' (*Oriental Scenes* (1832), pp. 42–5).
35. Richardson, *Literary Leaves*, vol. 1, p. 224.
36. G. A. Vetch, 'Lines: On hearing the Bagpipes of the Cameronians at Chinsura', *Bengal Annual* (1831), p. 401; on the strathspey dance / music, see Lamb, 'Reeling in the Strathspey'. The look back at Scotland was a recurring motif in Vetch's work; as well as several poems in the *Bengal Annual*, see 'My Highland Hame' and related correspondence, *Calcutta Courier*, 2 June 1834.
37. S. V. V., 'Kathleen's Lament', *Bengal Annual* [1831], pp. 323–4.
38. Nigel Leask comments on an earlier exchange of poetry between Malcolm

and Leyden that 'sentimental memories of home' have the 'patriotic function' of 'cementing the homosocial bonds of Anglo-Indian identity' ('Anglo-Indian Poetry', p. 60).
39. Brown, *Home Letters*, p. 91.
40. Roberts, *Oriental Scenes* (1832), p. 110.
41. Gibson, *Indian Angles*, pp. 89, 90.
42. Roberts, *Oriental Scenes* (1832), pp. 110–11, 112.
43. Roberts, *Oriental Scenes* (1832), pp. 163–4.
44. Tytler, 'Exile', *Bengal Annual* (1832), p. 214.
45. Brown, *Home Letters*, p. 21.
46. Richardson, *Literary Leaves* vol. 1, p. 63.
47. Richardson, 'When I Left England', *Literary Leaves* vol. 2, p. 13.
48. Said, 'Reflections', p. 185.
49. Stacy, 'The Wanderer's Return', *Bengal Annual* (1833), pp. 104–5.
50. Scott, *Oriental Musings*, pp. 67, 68.
51. Campbell, 'Sonnet – Lament for the Muse', *Bengal Annual* (1834), p. 360.
52. Macnaghten, 'A Sort of Lay Jocund', *Calcutta Magazine* (1830), pp. 250, 252. It should be noted that Macnaghten also produced other and more conventional poems of exile: see 'The Daisy' and 'Return Song of the Exile', in Richardson, *Selections*, pp. 1496–8.
53. David, *Rule Britannia*, p. 39. See also Mukherjee's discussion of this passage and the Edens' representation of India more generally (*Natural Disasters*, pp. 63–6).
54. Eden, *Up the Country*, p. 67.
55. Richardson, 'Summer and Winter', *Literary Leaves* vol. 2, p. 6.
56. Tregear, 'The Wanderer', *Bengal Annual* (1835), p. 184.
57. Brown, *Home Letters*, pp. 46–7.
58. Muston, 'Lines from India, addressed to his Friends at Home in 1801', *Bengal Annual* (1833), p. 210.
59. Parker, *Bole Ponjis*, vol. 2, pp. 94–6.
60. *Bengal Annual* (1831), p. 194.
61. Eden, *Up the Country*, p. 161.
62. Vetch, 'Lines on a Sweet Briar in India', *Bengal Annual* (1831), p. 317.
63. Sir Joseph Fayrer, *European Child-Life in Bengal* (London, 1873), pp. 29–30, quoted in Buettner, *Empire Families*, p. 29; see also Buettner's wider analysis pp. 29–36.
64. Quoted in Buettner, *Empire Families*, p. 52.
65. Roberts, *Scenes and Characteristics*, vol. 2, pp. 126–7.
66. Roberts, *Scenes and Characteristics*, vol. 2, p. 333.
67. *Bengal Annual* (1835), pp. 289, 291.
68. R. C. Money, *Journal of a Tour in Persia*, pp. 13–14.
69. R. C. Money, *Journal of a Tour in Persia*, p. 29.
70. R. C. Money, 'Stanzas written at the Rain Ghat, near Belgaum, in 1834', *Bengal Annual* (1835), pp. 344–6.
71. R. C. Money, 'Thoughts of Home in India', *Bengal Annual* (1834), pp. 266–8.
72. D. I. Money, 'Domum, Domum, Dulce Domum', *Orient Pearl* (1835), pp. 21, 22. The poem takes its title from a school song, 'Dulce Domum', most often associated with Winchester; Money himself was a pupil at

another English public school, Charterhouse (Venn and Venn, *Alumni Cantabrigienses*, vol. 2, part 4, p. 439).
73. D. I. Money, 'Domum, Domum', *Orient Pearl* (1835), pp. 23, 20–1.
74. Roberts, 'Indian Graves', *Oriental Scenes* (1832), pp. 117–18.
75. Tregear, 'Lines – Home', *Bengal Annual* (1836), p. 398.
76. Maitland, *Letters from Madras*, p. 66.
77. Eden, *Up the Country*, p. 396.
78. Kipling, *Letters*, vol. 1, pp. 36–8. A letter in rhyme to Edith Macdonald, 12–13 June 1883.
79. Kipling, *Complete Verse*, pp. 51–2. The poem was first collected in *Departmental Ditties* (1886).
80. See McGivering, 'Notes to "The Moon of Other Days"', 21 February 2011, <http://www.kiplingsociety.co.uk/rg_moon_other1_p.htm> (last accessed 31 August 2014).
81. Kipling, *Something of Myself*, p. 7; and 'Baa Baa, Black Sheep', in *Something of Myself*, pp. 137–70. See also the opening chapter of *The Light that Failed*, where Dick and Maisie take the place of Kipling and his sister.
82. The details of Rudyard and Trix Kipling's years in Lorne Lodge have been discussed and evaluated in several biographies; see Birkenhead, Carrington, Gilmour, Seymour-Smith; also Buettner, *Empire Families*, pp. 122–5. Trix's story based on the Southsea years, 'Through Judy's Eyes', is included in Fleming, *Trix: Kipling's Forgotten Sister*, pp. 345–66.
83. See my Introduction to *Kim*, pp. 14–16 for a more detailed discussion of these aspects of the novel.
84. Kipling, *Kim*, pp. 8, 12.
85. Scott, *Oriental Musings*, pp. 73–6.

Chapter 3

Consuming and Being Consumed

Elizabeth Inchbald's farce *The Mogul Tale: or, The Descent of the Balloon* (1788) offered late eighteenth-century audiences the spectacle of three English travellers making a balloon journey. Blown off course, they find themselves in the land of the 'Great Mogul'. On their arrival, they are overcome with panic – Fanny is afraid of being left alone 'amongst tygers, land monsters, and sea monsters' – although none of these entities makes an appearance, and the travellers are eventually permitted to depart unharmed. The notable point is that the travellers themselves are regarded with an equivalent fear by the inhabitants of India. The second lady of the seraglio, on seeing the balloon, exclaims that 'I am afraid it is a great ravenous bird, coming to devour us.'[1]

The literature of British India frequently represents British people as driven by the need to incorporate the material substance of India and/or Indians into themselves, while a contrapuntal narrative chronicles a fear of bodily disintegration or re-incorporation into the 'other', often depicted in fantasies of being consumed by the Indian landscape or its human or animal inhabitants. The dual portrayal of the British in India seen here in Inchbald's work (where the travellers are simultaneously potential consumers / predators and consumed / victims) has its origins in the political landscape of the second half of the eighteenth century. At this time, the question of Britain's role in India, with its accompanying stereotypes of India as simultaneously oppressed by British colonisers and a threat to them, was developed in the course of successive political debates, culminating in the impeachment of Warren Hastings on a variety of charges including those of personal and political corruption. The trial lasted from 1788 to 1795. Hastings was eventually acquitted of all charges, but the process focused public attention on the activities of the East India Company and its dealings with India, and aroused a rancorous debate carried out through the means of pamphlets and articles. The language of the debate about Hastings itself was steeped in tropes of predation, excess, and consumption, and, as I shall discuss below, its divided discourse of consumption spread throughout a wide range of literary forms in Victorian British India.

The Turn Against the 'nabobs'

The word 'nabob' originates from the Urdu term 'nawab', a ruler of a province or territory whose formal role was that of a representative, or deputy, of the Mughal emperor. While retaining this sense in Anglo-Indian usage, it was also applied to a British person who made a fortune in India, and carried it home to fund a luxurious lifestyle and the purchase of political influence. Several contemporary texts offered polemic accounts of their activities, directed against both this exploitation of India, and the disruption to the social and political hierarchies of England caused by wealth being acquired by individuals of relatively lower social class.[2]

From the 1760s onwards, the activities of these Company employees, the 'nabobs', became the focus of public concern. Their extravagance, and their use of their new-found wealth to acquire political influence, became the target of satiric portraits in a variety of media.[3] The nabobs were associated in this literature with both destruction and consumption. In *The Nabob: A Moral Tale*, for example, the Nabob, his wife Mrs Rapine (a former servingwoman) and daughters return to England and buy an estate, on which they live in a state of estrangement from their neighbours, who detest them for their haughtiness and meanness. The Misses Rapine's encounter with a poor but respectable widow, the owner of an apricot tree, demonstrates the qualities of acquisitiveness and destructiveness characteristic of this portrait: having 'surveyed the fine ripe apricots with an eye of desire', they damage the tree in the attempt to gather them, and eventually destroy it altogether in order to obtain revenge upon its owner.[4] Much of this literature focuses on the British context for the nabobs, with authors like Samuel Foote and the pseudonymous 'Timothy Touchstone' charging them with disruption of the social and political order of the time.[5] There is evidence also, however, of contemporary anxiety about the impact of East India Company employees' conduct within India itself. The works of William Bolts and Harry Verelst, both of whom decried abuses by Company servants (while accusing one another of complicity in these practices), had the effect of publicising and drawing attention to the deleterious effects of British greed on the economy of Bengal, as well as individual Indians who suffered by it.[6]

A metaphorical thread runs through much contemporary writing on the nabobs, associating them with a physical hunger for and material consumption of Indian territories, goods and bodies. This way of thinking was not unique to writing on the nabobs, however: it was so deep-rooted in the mindset of the British in India at this time that it is to be found in the rhetoric of conquest used by servants of the Company themselves. Governor-General Richard Wellesley writes to Henry Dundas, the President of the Board of Control, after the fall of Tipu Sultan's stronghold of Seringapatam, when the Company was extending and establishing its control of southern India:

> I hope ... the treaties of partition and subsidy have satisfied your anxiety respecting the settlement of Mysore ... if you will have a little patience, the death of the nizam will probably enable me to gratify your *voracious appetite for lands and fortresses*. Seringapatam ought, I think, to stay your stomach a while; not to mention Tanjore and the Polygar countries. Perhaps I may be able to give you a supper of Oudh and the Carnatic, if you should still be hungry.[7] [Emphasis in the original.]

As the conventionally metaphorical 'voracious appetite' ascribed to Dundas becomes the more disquieting hunger for Indian states, the trope of eating is established as a shared approach to India.

This metaphorical association of Indian conquest with consumption, and the rhetorical trope of literalising the metaphor, is also visible in the work of those who criticise or condemn the East India Company's actions. The German writer Friedrich Wendeborn's evaluation of those 'who might be called English East-India nabobs' as being 'still worse' than those 'Asiatic despots' who oppress their own people is, in James Raven's analysis, 'an attitude shared by dozens of diarists, letter-writers, and other witnesses' of the time.[8] It is Wendeborn's imagery, however, that stands out in this context: 'Many of them arrive very hungry and in an emaciated condition in India; they suck as eagerly as leeches, to fill themselves the quicker, that they may return the sooner to their own country.'[9] In similar vein, Bowen describes some of the popular feeling against nabobs in the late eighteenth and early nineteenth centuries, including Horace Walpole's reference to the Company and its employees as a 'crew of monsters', and William Cobbett's observation that they 'have long been cooking and devouring the wretched people of both England and India'.[10] Thus a rhetoric of predation was already in circulation in texts about 'nabobs', as well as in official documents of the East India Company. It was in the course of the impeachment of Warren Hastings, Governor-General of India from 1773 to 1785, that this discourse became particularly virulent, and its use widespread.

Warren Hastings

Against the background of anxiety and revulsion over the actions of British colonisers in India, a compelling, albeit contested, narrative of Britain's exploitation of India emerged from the public debate surrounding the Hastings impeachment. Hastings's conduct in office came under attack in Britain and in India during the final years of his administration. He had several opponents, chief among whom was Sir Philip Francis, on the governing council in Calcutta: Francis and others accused Hastings of incompetence or criminal intent in his management of the Company's dealings with Indian rulers, and of being personally corrupt in financial matters, accepting large bribes and selling offices. One of his accusers, the Bengali politician Nandakumar, was tried on a dubious charge of forgery, and executed in 1775; the judges in the case were allies of Hastings. Other accusations concerned the supposed mistreatment of elite Indian women. In Britain, the main opponent of Hastings was the Whig politician Edmund Burke, a longstanding critic of the Company. He worked for several years to prepare a case against Hastings, and in 1786 laid a set of charges before the House of Commons. The Commons voted to impeach Hastings in 1787, and his trial before the House of Lords began in 1788. He was acquitted of all charges in 1795.

There is a considerable body of scholarship on the substance of the charges against Hastings, as well as the changes in the role of the Company at this point, as it began the movement from trading company to governing state.[11] There is also critical discussion of the philosophical implications of Burke's engagement with the role of the East India Company and British imperial responsibility in the course of his long career, extending far beyond the question of Hastings's direct involvement. (Luke Gibbons, for instance, makes the important argument with regard to Burke that his lifelong engagement with the question of the 'cultural' as well as corporal suffering caused by the Company – such as his observations on the social exclusion of Indian women – constitutes a 'radical extension of Enlightenment thinking'.)[12] In the specific context of the representation of British actions in India, it is Burke's imagery of physical despoliation and mutilation of the body – deployed both verbally by him and others and visually in the caricatures and images that surrounded the trial – that proved highly influential in contemporaneous debate, and that makes its way into the later texts, rather than his political and philosophical arguments. My aim in this section is therefore to discuss the language of this debate, and in particular the language of predation and consumption used to such effect by Burke.

As the Hastings trial began, Burke had previous form for associating the Company with excessive and material consumption. Five years earlier, speaking on Charles James Fox's India Bill of 1783 (which aimed to transfer the government of British India away from the East India Company to a board of commissioners), he cast the 'young men' who 'govern' in India as rapacious and without empathy:

> Animated with all the avarice of age, and all the impetuosity of youth, they roll in one after another; wave after wave; and there is nothing before the eyes of the natives but an endless, hopeless prospect of new flights of birds of prey and passage, with appetites continually renewing for a food that is continually wasting.[13]

Two years later, in 1785, Burke charges the Company's administrators that

> they felt nothing for a land desolated by fire, sword, and famine; their sympathies took another direction; they were touched with pity for bribery, so long tormented with a fruitless itching of its palms; ... they felt for peculation which had been for so many years raking in the dust of an empty treasury; they were melted into compassion for rapine and oppression, licking their dry, parched, unbloody jaws.[14]

The impact of such rhetoric was to implicate the Company as a corporate body in the corrupt and oppressive practices described by Burke and his associates. Whelan argues that in many cases Hastings's 'questionable policies' were attributable to pressure on the Company's finances; he instances the land settlement in Bengal to increase revenue; the acceptance of 'presents' that went into the Company treasury; the actions taken to gain possession of the wealth of the Begums of Oudh, etc.[15] These examples do not so much suggest Hastings's personal greed as imply that the foreign policy and practice of the Company required such extortionate behaviour, a point which is relevant to the contemporary and later unease about British 'consumption' in India more generally: it was not just one individual who was implicated, but Britain in India. During the seven years of the impeachment and trial, the arguments and evidence put forward by both prosecution and defence, and the circulation of this material in contemporary newspapers and journals, brought to the fore the issue of India and the conduct of the Company and its employees.

The high drama of the trial, however, focused attention on Hastings's personal conduct, and the sensationalism of the accusations against him set in motion the dissemination of the imagery of consumption with which he was repeatedly associated. Leading the case against Hastings, Burke depicted him as corrupt, predatory and motivated by personal gain, and used the idiom of sentimentality to evoke his audience's sympathy with the Indians who were supposedly victims of his cruelty. The trial left Hastings's supporters and his detractors both unmoved – indeed, there is still no consensus among scholars over his behaviour and its consequences.[16] This is partly a function of the way in which the charges were put together: Whelan argues that Burke's 'primary intention' in the impeachment was the arousal of 'public opinion in Great Britain against abuses in the Indian empire', rather than the conviction of Hastings himself. To this end, Burke stressed the larger context of his charges against Hastings – the future conduct of British government in India, and the welfare of Indians living under that government – and deployed tactics designed to further this aim, educating the public with detailed narratives of events in the 'Articles of Charge', making the most of 'sensational episodes' that would engage the public interest, and emphasising the spectacular possibilities of the trial as a public event.[17]

Among the articles of impeachment, Article 7 makes reference to the 'dreadful Famine and Mortality [in Bengal and Bihar], by which at least One-third of the Inhabitants generally, and in many Places near One-half of the Inhabitants, perished', and charges that Hastings, despite his knowledge of 'the calamitous and distressful State of the Country, from the Famine and Mortality aforesaid', refused to mitigate revenue demands on the population.[18] In the context of these accusations, and the reports of famine to which they alluded, Burke's deployment of the imagery of predation and consumption added a hard edge of reality to its rhetorical flourishes. While space does not allow me to provide a systematic account of the language used, even a brief examination of a text such as the contemporaneous *History of the Trial of Warren Hastings* reveals the trial's emphasis on the language of predation and consumption. The editors wrote, for instance, that:

> He [Hastings] gorged his *ravenous maw* with an allowance of 200£. a day. ... He never *dines without creating a famine*. He feeds on the *indigent*, the *decaying*, and the *ruined* ... like the *ravenous vulture*, who feeds on the *dead*, and the *enfeebled*; who destroys and incapacitates *nature* in the destruction of *its object*, while devouring the carcases of the dead. ... Mr Hastings feasts in the dark alone; *like a wild beast he groans in a corner over the dead and dying* ... He comes a *heavy calamity* to the nation, as we say a country is visited by *famine* and *pestilence*.[19] [Emphasis in the original.]

Burke's colleague and fellow orator, Richard Brinsley Sheridan, also focused on the image of Hastings as predator and offered sentimental and sensational vignettes of his Indian victims, such as the Begums of Oudh, imagined as gathered 'together in fluttering trepidation, like a flock of resistless birds in the air, on seeing the felon kite'.[20] These characterisations of Hastings, received with rapt attention and horror by the audience in Westminster Hall (packed for the opening speeches, though later emptying as the trial dragged on), contributed to a set of associations of him, and of the Company more generally, with the exploitation and oppression of India.

The question of the impact of British actions upon India was developed not only in the speeches made by Burke and Sheridan, which reached a wide audience, but in the paratexts of the narrative they developed – pamphlets, newspaper articles, and caricatures. These were produced by both Hastings's opponents and his supporters, since the contest was carried on in the media of the day as well as in Westminster Hall.[21] Several contemporary caricatures illustrate the extent to which the tropes of consumption permeate this body of work. For instance, William Dent's 'The Raree Show' satirises proceedings by depicting audiences fighting for access to the Raree Show booth within which the trial is played out as a farcical performance.[22] Burke and Sheridan feature as clowns, together with Charles James Fox. The figure of Hastings appears at top left, with an inscription identifying him as the 'prodigious monster arrived from the East': he is consuming the body of an Indian woman, while the bodies of others are trampled under his feet.[23]

Such visual and verbal images of predation and consumption were so prevalent that they eventually made their way into the writings of Hastings himself. In a sardonic verse account of his own portrait as represented in the course of the impeachment, Hastings draws on the language of the gaping mouth thirsting for blood:

> A mouth extended fierce from ear to ear,
> With fangs like those which wolves and tigers wear;
> Eyes whose dark orbs announce a sullen mood,
> A lust of rapine and a thirst of blood –
> Such Hastings was, as by the Commons painted
> (Men shuddered as they look'd, and women fainted)[24]

In the event, Hastings was acquitted of all charges, and a change in the culture of the East India Company, and its more rigorous oversight by the British government, contributed to changes in attitude and policy during the nineteenth century, while the political and social rhetoric of progress and civilisation functioned to legitimise the increasingly powerful British regime's expansion across the subcontinent. Nevertheless, the tropes of rapaciousness, greed, and predation continued to circulate, in texts concerned not only with Hastings, but with the impact of the Company presence and British policy more generally.

Famine

The inclusion of Article 7 (on famine) in the charge sheet against Hastings points towards one of the factors troubling British perceptions of India, that is, their own role in and responsibility for Indian suffering. The Bengal famine of 1770, which caused devastation in Bengal and attracted public attention in Britain, was but one episode in a succession of famines and epidemics from the mid-eighteenth century to the end of the nineteenth century, and beyond.[25] In a letter to the Court of Directors sent by Hastings in his role as Governor-General in 1772, he comments on the negative publicity the famine engendered for the Company, as 'laboured descriptions' of its impact 'have been accumulated to raise Compassion and to excite Indignation against your Servants, whose unhappy lot it was to be the witnesses and spectators of the suffering of their fellow-creatures'. Hastings also deplores the impact on the surviving population as the Company continued to maintain (and in fact increase) its revenues by the custom of levying a tax on 'the wretched Survivors' in order to 'make up for the Loss sustained in the Rents of their neighbours who are either dead or have fled the Country'.[26] This communication highlights the essential problem: the commercial imperatives of the Company's operations often ran counter to the best interests of the majority of India's people, while it is clear from many of the encounters with famine in India recorded by British people that the writers themselves were troubled by their own participation, witnessing, or even complicity in the events they described.

Famine and scarcity were not directly caused by British action, but in many cases were exacerbated by the social and economic impact of British rule. The 1770 Bengal famine, for instance, was precipitated by drought, but the Company's enforcement of high levels of taxation intensified its impact (the levels were unchanged from those of the previous administration, but enforcement was strengthened), as did the activities of individual employees who were also commodity traders on their own account.[27] As periodic famines continued to afflict the Indian inhabitants of territory controlled by the colonial state throughout the nineteenth century, the state developed clearer policies aimed at ameliorating their effects (though these policies were also governed by the intention to avoid the development of any dependency on government assistance on the part of the Indian people).[28] At the same time, the transition from indigenous to colonial government continued to have unintended consequences: Bayly's analysis of the 'crisis in the political economy' of north India in the 1830s, for instance, shows that it was attributable to climactic and ecological factors as well as British actions, but he also notes the impact of 'a conquistador imperialism using Mughal methods to push for a degree of centralisation which the Mughals had never achieved'.[29] To similar effect, Sharma argues that the colonial state, by 'limiting its role in the market and the rural credit network ... eroded some traditional checks on vulnerabilities without providing dependable alternatives'.[30] These East India Company policies meant that cash crops replaced food crops; revenues were expected to remain constant even during times of scarcity; and revenue-gathering was enforced with an unaccustomed and onerous efficiency.

It is not possible, of course, to draw a straight line from these Company policies which brought about and/or exacerbated the conditions for famine in British India, to the individuals who wrote of their own emotional responses to what they saw. But the contrast between the British observers' situation and that of the famine victims, if nothing else, is clear in these texts, such as this anonymous response to famine in 1845:

> Alas how little do we think
> (From famine's fangs secure,)
> Of those now standing on the brink
> Of Death – the many Poor.
> On dainties brought from distant lands
> We revel – and we thrive,
> While millions wring their shrunken hands!
> Stern flood of Forty Five![31]

Where that direct contrast is absent, there is still visible the impact of scenes of famine on the writers. John Shore's recollection 'nearly forty years afterwards' of the Bengal famine of 1770 jumbles together the dying and their predators, emphasising the impact on the observer and his inability to represent what he saw adequately:

> Still fresh in Memory's eye the scene I view,
> The shrivell'd limbs, sunk eyes, and lifeless hue;
> Still hear the mother's shrieks and infant's moans,
> Cries of despair, and agonizing groans.
> In wild confusion, dead and dying lie; –
> Hark to the jackall's yell, and vulture's cry,
> The dog's fell howl, as, midst the glare of day,
> They riot, unmolested, on their prey!
> Dire scenes of horror! which no pen can trace,
> Nor rolling years from Memory's page efface.[32]

In other instances, that emotional impact is accompanied by allusion to or discussion of the observer's own role, or that of the British more generally, in the alleviation of famine. An account of the famine in

Tulligong in 1805–6, when 80,000 perished, repeated at second hand by Maria Graham, accentuates the details of Indian suffering with an example of British intervention, even while the narrative expresses its own doubt as to the efficacy of that intervention:

> [The] bones strewed the fields around. The inhabitants of many towns and villages emigrated, hoping to find elsewhere that sustenance which failed at home; thousands perished on the road side, and many, at the very moment when they stretched forth their hands to receive the means of life which the charity of the British afforded, sunk to death ere the long wished-for morsel reached their lips.[33]

Here, as in other cases, the causes of famine are unexamined. John Dunbar's 'Sonnet – Famine' (1832) casts famine as an event divorced from human and/or social causes: 'sheer down upon every plain, / [the sun] darts his searching fire, and every green / And tender herb doth fade'. The human response is passive: 'Men's hearts are faint, and mournful mothers weep, / While weak with want, their starving infants sleep'.[34]

Emily Eden's account of her travels with her sister, as they accompanied their brother George Eden, Lord Auckland, on his progress as Governor-General through north India in 1838, expresses both the wish to ameliorate famine, and implicitly the apprehension of culpability as regards its causes. In the vicinity of Cawnpore, Eden records her experience of what she terms 'the starving districts', where a famine of long standing had left the countryside in 'perfectly dreadful' distress: 'You cannot conceive the horrible sights we see, particularly children; perfect skeletons in many cases, their bones through their skin, without a rag of clothing, and utterly unlike human creatures.' In apparent response to the implicit contrast between this and the activities she had just described, when their little dog Chance was fed cake, and the Governor-General invited 'five and twenty people to dinner', Eden writes 'Our camp luckily does more good than harm. We get all our supplies from Oude, and we can give away more than any other travellers.' The party distribute what food they have available, but Eden's text suggests the hopelessness of the endeavour: 'We can do no more than give what we do, and the sight is much too shocking. The women look as if they had been buried, their *skulls* look so dreadful.' She retreats, with some relief, to the thought that 'dear Shakspeare knew all about it', and the quotation of Romeo's lines to the Apothecary on the subject of poverty: 'Famine is in thy cheeks, / Need and oppression startle in thine eyes, / The world is not thy friend'.[35]

W. H. Sleeman's characteristically pragmatic and strategic account of famine in Bundelkhand in 1833, with its insistence that famine relief should not equate 'what may be considered a *full rate* of subsistence to able-bodied persons, as it tends to keep concentrated [at certain points] vast numbers who would otherwise be scattered over the surface of the country', is unable to maintain its detachment in the face of 'exceedingly distressing' scenes where 'in spite of the best dispositions and greatest efforts on the part of government and its officers, and the European and native communities, thousands commonly die of starvation'. His insistence that 'here all who suffer attribute the disaster to its real cause, the want of rain in due season; and indulge in no feelings of hatred against their rulers, superiors, or more fortunate equals in society, who happen to live beyond the influence of such calamities' is not entirely convincing.[36] As an example of wishful thinking, it demonstrates the difficulty he, and others in his position, had in reconciling the suffering they recognised around them with the impact of their own actions, however well intentioned.

A similar stress and tension is evident in the work of T. S. Burt, who also wrote about famine in Bundelkhand, this time in 1838, drawing on anecdotes gleaned from British residents of the area, as well as his own experience. His host in Cawnpore tells him of having seen 'in one small field ... upwards of 100 dead bodies in different degrees of putrefaction from that of a fresh body to that of a skeleton with numerous vultures ... close at hand'. Burt is naturally disturbed by these accounts, and by the news that while the destitute are employed on famine relief works, 'the helpless or those who cannot work get nothing at all'. He finds himself unwilling to believe that this might be the case, but maintains that it was 'the account I received, I forget from what source, and I do not venture to assert its correctness. It is unnecessary further to notice these distressing subjects as the Newspapers give daily accounts of them with painful truth.'[37] The verse narrative of these events in 'The Exile's Return', similarly, peters out after eleven stanzas, perhaps in response to this inability or unwillingness of its writer to further confront the subject matter. In those eleven stanzas, however, Burt's laboured verses tally many of the familiar images of famine: 'wretched half starved creatures' with 'faces pale and wan'; 'skeletons that glared upon my route, / From staring skulls that told the horrid fate / Of those whose flesh was ate by the wild brute'; and those still alive when 'greedily attack'd' by vultures. The unease over the colonial state's response to famine (see above) is reflected here in the paratextual insistence that 'Nine thousand persons were *daily* fed, under my supervision, at Delhi, by order of the Government of India, and thousands elsewhere', while Indian farmers 'never spared a grasping hand / to rob them of their food'. Unease is further reflected in the meandering text's apparently random return to England, meditating on the whiteness of the bones of famine victims, left clean by wild beasts:

> But what the deuce should render them so fair?
> Was it the effect of sunshine, which alone's
> The finest linen-bleacher? – as at home
> In England, you will find, if much about you roam.

'You' implicates the reader, while the sunshine which brightens the bones is the same sunshine which bleaches linens in England. While this is not sophisticated or crafted verse, it expresses the writer's uneasy, contradictory desire to contrast the people of India – victims and exploiters – with the people of Britain, while also metaphorically relocating the horror of what he sees to a domestic context.[38]

These issues never wholly faded from British India. The colonial administrator G. H. Trevor, whose obituary noted the 'practical and effective' measures taken under his control to provide relief to victims during a series of famines in the latter half of the nineteenth century, celebrated the use of the rail network to import grain in his poem 'Famine in Rajputana' (1892).[39] The 'dried-up wells / And barren fields' of famine are located in 'former days', whereas in the contemporary present, the 'Iron Horse has saved the land and scared / The spectre Famine, like some carrion bird / Disturbed at its foul feast'.[40] Even in Trevor's pedestrian verse, the past and the present combine: 'like chime / Of bells o'er hills the railway's scream is heard' – a distress cry that reflects the suffering that continued for much of the 1890s, and that was only partially alleviated by relief efforts. In some other cases, indeed, the response by government seems to have had a negative impact on the sufferers.[41]

In this context of British awareness of Indian suffering, and the complex reactions of distress, denial and anxiety manifested in contemporary writing, it is not surprising that concern over the impact of famine, and the politics and realities of consumption, should stretch beyond a focus on the colonised to imagine that British policies and actions in India might have unintended consequences for the colonisers themselves. The pseudonymously published poem *The Grand Master*, for example, has two recurring and counterpointed themes: the rapaciousness of the British in India, and the haplessness of the British protagonist, 'Qui Hi'. At the outset of his journey to India Qui Hi sees himself as a successful predator, a theme the poem delineates with the familiar overlap between imagery of metaphorical and literal consumption: 'Filling his knapsack with rupees, / Or fruit from the pagoda trees'.⁴² There is also already present a corresponding anxiety about this predatory approach, visible in comments such as the reference to the people of Ascension Island: 'And tho we don't enslave or beat them / Like Africans, we're known to eat them!' (22). On Qui Hi's arrival in Bengal, this vision becomes transformed, as the human body becomes that which is consumed, rather than consuming:

> While mosques and old pagodas rise,
> In solemn grandeur, to the skies.
> Hundreds of human bodies lay,
> A horrid feast for birds of prey;
> While fun'ral piles, on either side,
> Some savage sacrifice imply'd (29)

From this point on Qui Hi is subject to a steady decline in his circumstances and his ability to exert agency over his surroundings. Fleeced by a 'rascal' who offers himself as his servant, and then further victimised by the inadequate pay which leads him to borrow money at ruinous interest, he finds himself in difficulty.⁴³ His inability to shape his own destiny is evident in the hunt where he falls asleep through drunkenness, and is carried along with no control over his journey: 'For all the time he was asleep, / The horse (quite sober) knew the way, / Without direction, to Bombay' (231). His marriage with the Indian beauty Goulaub further reinforces this theme: his desire for her is clearly regarded as misguided by the narrator (who describes her as 'black as soot – / Blacker, aye blacker than your boot!') – and it leads him into a further loss of control, as she takes over while he sleeps. 'She unconcern'dly got astride / On Qui Hi's horse, and took the lead, / Keeping of all the rest the head; / And guided Qui Hi down the steep' (166): this suggests both a loss of agency on his part, and a reversal of the gender and racial hierarchies that underpinned British society in India. His failure in this respect is complete by the end of the poem, when imprisonment leads to his illness and eventual death.

Underlying this narrative of colonial ineptness, however, is another narrative of colonial exploitation and domination, summarised in an Indian's lament of how the English arrived, were well treated and given a house, built many more, and then 'Declar'd our people all were slaves' and 'Trod down the temples of our god' (40–1). The imagery of eating reappears in connection with this theme, as the text of the poem is supplemented with paratextual notes glossing the vocabulary of Anglo-India in terms that highlight the gluttonous nature of the protagonists. 'Tiffin', for example, is described in a footnote as a meal where 'both ladies and gentlemen literally *stuff* themselves to such excess, that they are obliged to go to bed for three or four hours', after which dinner is then 'another stuffing match' (45). Qui Hi's company of soldiers 'march to barracks, where with joy, / Their masticators they employ, / On curry, rice, and beef, and goat, / Voriously [*sic*] they cram each throat' (66). The footnote in this case expands on 'voriously', as the narrator avers that no other term can 'convey to the reader the indelicate method both ladies and gentlemen eat'. He has himself 'absolutely been disgusted at seeing one of the *prettiest girls* in Calcutta eat about two pounds of mutton-chops at one sitting!' (67). Leaving aside for the moment the gender implications of representing overeating as particularly unfeminine, we may see that the text clearly offers a direct link between this excessive consumption of food and the predatory ways of the British in India:

> And now the natives often think
> Our worship, is to eat and drink;
> And take by force their homes and land,
> In every place where we command;
> Their lands, their money, or their wives,
> Nay, we may even take their lives. (68)

This theme is further developed in the 'Fable', supposedly part of Hindu mythology, which appears in Canto VI. This recounts how Brahma created both Hindus and the '*vicious* tribes' of the '*west'rn* country's' [*sic*] who 'live by rapine, war, and plunder' (124). One of these tribes 'went, / To visit ev'ry continent' (126), and Brahma, 'angry with us here', brings them to India. Having celebrated the '*good*' done to India by these invaders (and identified this as an example of irony in a footnote), the poem goes on to detail their actions:

> Some of their chiefs, 'tis true, act wrong,
> (To them authority belong;)
> We to their individual crimes,
> Impute the present iron times;
> Bad men cannot be calculated
> To be with sov'reign pow'r *inflated*;
> Under the hand of noxious power,
> Locusts each day our crops devour;
> Famine and pestilence attend,
> The footsteps of each *foreign friend* (127–8)

The Rowlandson illustration accompanying these lines in *The Grand Master* shows the horsemen of the apocalypse, including the then Governor-General, Lord Moira, a skeletal figure on a horse which emanates 'pestilence' and 'desolation'.[44]

These twin strands of invasion and food come together when Qui Hi is transformed by a Brahmin into a flying fish, which is then caught by British sailors. He is killed immediately after telling his story, thereby completing the cycle by which the protagonist in India is victimised both by India and by the larger community of Britain which has dispatched him there. This also brings us full circle back to the figure of the nabob, whose excesses formed the subject of criticism in the eighteenth-century satirical tradition: as Christina Smylitopoulos suggests, *The Grand Master* may also have been written as a means of countering such attempts to distance the metropolitan 'home' from the excesses of the colonists.[45] With Qui Hi's metamorphosis into a creature predated by humans, the discourse of consumption has another element added to it: that of the food chain, and with it, threats to the integrity of the individual and state body through involuntary incorporation or contamination from within.

Troubling the Food Chain

The imagery of predation and consumption in the texts described above reveals a prevailing anxiety about the impact of British consumption of India (literal and metaphorical) not just on India but on the consumers themselves. Burke's description of Hastings as feeding on the dead was, of course, entirely rhetorical; and the imagery of predation and consumption in *The Grand Master* and similar texts is largely metaphorical in nature. In other texts, a theme of the literal consumption of Indian substances becomes indistinct. This reflects in part the movement from metropolitan representations of the nabobs to accounts of Anglo-Indian life written from India: in the latter, eating indigenous food and/or food produced in India is part of the everyday reality of life for the writers, and also part of the stock narrative of the colonial encounter. Concerns about identity and conduct remain, however, and are manifested in the production of a series of narratives and anecdotes where the language of consumption hovers between the literal and the metaphorical, sometimes to disturbing effect. The *Annual Register*'s 'Account of the late dreadful Famine in India', for instance, describes the famine's effects on the Anglo-Indian community and their access to food:

> At this time we [that is, British residents] could not touch fish, the river was so full of carcases; and of those who did eat it, many died suddenly. Pork, ducks, and geese, also lived mostly on carnage; so that our only meat was mutton when we could get it, which was very dear.[46]

This catastrophic disruption of the food supply caused by the widespread deaths of Indians is also a reminder of the British role as apex predator of the food chain – the literal, as well as metaphorical, consumers of Indian resources. Arnold argues that famine narratives like this one 'tell us much more about what Europeans think, see, and feel about the assault on their sensibilities and "humanity" than they inform us about Indian experience and suffering'.[47] Arnold's main point – that the focus is on the impact on the British rather than on Indians, the most nearly and strongly affected – is indeed strongly evidenced in this passage. The language and construction of the text, with its striking imagery of the polluted river and fish poisonous to the touch, also suggest that the assault being experienced by the British in this case is transformative: the incorporation of food contaminated with the material bodies of Indians threatens to kill rather than sustain them.

The concerns apparent in this passage recur, in varying forms, throughout the period of this study. At the turn of the century, for instance, the anonymous poet 'S' similarly blurs the boundaries between Indian starvation and contamination of the British food supplies, in the paired poems both titled 'The Famine Relief Officer':

> Whose tents are pitch'd where haunting cries
> Of cholera-stricken workers rise?
> Whose soup and peg are full of flies?
>   The F.R.O.'s.[48]

Even setting aside the extreme circumstances of famine, the categorisation of material as food, and the act of eating, are potentially problematic in any context. Deborah Lupton describes anxieties about food and eating as more or less universally experienced: in material terms, because apparently edible food can be toxic; symbolically, because the boundaries between self and the outside world are being breached in the act of ingestion.[49] In the contact zone of British India – an already liminal space – these anxieties are heightened, and food takes on a greater symbolic weight, though this symbolism is often complex. The returned exile's liking for curry and rice marked him off as an 'Old Indian', as Jos Sedley illustrates on his arrival in Southampton with his 'chests of mangoes, chutney, and curry-powders'.[50]

Paradoxically, the clinging to 'home' ways among the exile community in India also came to be something that set them apart. E. M. Collingham suggests that the grand dinners of eighteenth-century British India became a means of 'celebrating the nabob's Britishness despite his oriental surroundings'. At the same time, however, their 'excessive consumption', including 'spicy Indian food' and alcohol, 'emphasized the danger of corruption inherent in the codes of behaviour current in Anglo-Indian society': to 'celebrate' (in Collingham's phrase) Britishness is also to undermine and imperil it.[51] As eighteenth-century norms regarding the quantity of food to be served, and the mode of serving it, persisted into the nineteenth century in India, while British 'home' fashions changed, this became a point of difference between the exiles and their metropolitan counterparts, alongside the adoption of Indian-influenced foods.[52]

This element of excess – the 'grand dinners' mentioned by Collingham – is frequently remarked upon in the literature of British India. Julia Maitland notes the 'wastefulness of an Indian dinner', complaining: 'Everybody dines at luncheon, or, as it is here called, tiffin-time, so that there is next to nothing eaten, but about four times as much food put upon the table as would serve for an English party.'[53] The emphasis on meat dishes often appears to evoke revulsion in the observer, as in Macnaghten's vision of 'Our heaps of midnight meat to see, / The turkies, hams, and geese; / The saddle, sirloin, round, – oh, me! / And the luke-warm gravy grease'.[54] In these accounts, the amount as well as the condition of the food is repellent; yet, it is sought after by the eaters with an appetite that the writers clearly find, at least, disconcerting. In the paired article and poem titled 'The Supper Call', the author describes with horrified and horrifying satirical excess the meal termed a 'Calcutta Supper': a 'gross, ill cooked, sloppy, vulgar, what-ought-to-be-underdone-overdone-and-what-ought-to-be-overdone underdone, mass of animal victual ... more than enough to exhaust the purses of the rich, and the gastricism of the voracious'.[55] The listed components of this meal run to many lines: 'Eleven oxen (several almost whole), seventeen sheep, twenty-nine turkies, thirty-three geese, seventy-four ducks', and so on through fowls, hams, rabbits, pigs and vegetables including 'ninety-four dishes of boiled potatoes – enough for the seven million lately emancipated'. Upon such 'tons of flesh', the writer comments, 'I have seen you all rushing like a flock of crocodiles' (84). Such excess is presented as a characteristic of the exile community specifically, and contrasted with the 'Bond street' equivalent which is – in equally satirical fashion – described as abundant enough for 'five hundred Ettrick Shepherds'[56] while not being too excessive in appearance for the 'scarcely-tasting ethereal creatures who hover in to partake of that refinement' (84).

As the essay continues along the path of its own lavish hyperbole, the seeking after food acquires added overtones of sexual voraciousness; the writer addresses the male component of the assembly:

ye who have whispered and pressed in the previous waltz or quadrille, shall now presume to stick your faces within four inches of theirs [the female partners], while your internal jaw is still smeared with the inside fat of that rank sirloin; or your fangs' interstices yet unrelieved from the crackling of that porker! And so you will only offer *them* a jelly, or an ice, or a piece of tough blancmange, or a half-buffalo-extracted custard? (85)

In the accompanying poem, the rituals of conversation between men and women are similarly interspersed with offers and exchanges of food items, creating an implicit association of food and sexuality which approaches very near the surface in the final stanzas:

> Such a delicate meal, must make every one feel
> How appropriate it is to the climate;
> And how houris of girls, may save oil for their curls,
> By a dip in the gravies I rhyme at!
> How the turkies and geese, and the wearers of fleece,
> Hogs and beeves, might improve their condition;
> If, like others, they'd bounce all, to his L—ship in C—cil,
> And pray for *this* rite's abolition! (88)

Normative female sexuality is clearly disassociated from food and consumption in this and other texts: here, the girls' hair with its imagined coating of gravy posits a sexualised femininity repulsively mixed with the food they eat. This is a theme reflected elsewhere in this literature. Among the portraits of femininity targeted in *Satires in India*, for instance, Laura is 'lovely as the breathing morn' at all times 'save the Tiffen-hour', when her features are 'all besmeared with Curry – hideous fright! / We turn in terror from the fearful sight'.[57] The 'squeamish Misses' of *The Cadet* live out days that move from the 'well display'd parade' of breakfast through the 'sweets of beer and lemonade' to 'smoking meats' and 'sparkling ale': 'In mix'd confusion men and maidens swill, / And *pious* matrons take alike their fill'.[58] If consumption to excess is problematised for men, it is doubly so for women.

For both sexes, the predominant theme of such texts is the association between consumption and the transformative processes undergone by the British in India. When Tom Raw, protagonist of Charles D'Oyly's *Tom Raw, the Griffin*, newly arrived from Britain, finds himself sitting at table between 'two lean Indians' (in this context, British residents in India) the alienness of the society and the situation finds expression in the food and the language of the company. 'Fish, flesh, and fowl, combine their greasy vapours' on the table, and the conversation also focuses on the fare, as polite phrases are exchanged alongside the items of food to which they refer:

> The conversation, like all table talk,
> Turned on the daintiness of sav'ry dishes,
> On the fat beef and delicate white pork,
> The firmness wonderful of cockub fishes,
> And tarts and puddings cooked up to one's wishes.
> With – 'Let me help you, sir, to this ragout,' –
> 'Did you say loll shraub?' – 'Lord, sir, you're facetious' –
> 'I have the honour to – .' – 'Some of that stew,' –
> 'I like this giblet curry – Pray, ma'am, what say you?'

As Tom Raw listens, vernacular words and phrases infiltrate the dialogue, alienating him further from the conversation and from his interlocutors:

> And, in the pauses – 'Punkah zoor si keencho,
> 'Tis very hot' – 'A gurrum panee bassun,' –
> 'I pledge you, ma'am – Loll shraub – this is white wine – Pshaw!'—
> 'Pray saw you P–l–r as King Richard? – Porsun!
> 'There's too much garlick in these cutlets' – (cursing.)
> Across our hero the two Judges chattered
> Of Moodai, Moodaillahi, and Russoom,
> Which was to him no joke at all – bespattered
> By two full greasy mouths, that more than wordings scattered.[59]

By the end of the passage, the food and the words have become indistinguishable, both unrecognisably revolting to the unfortunate newcomer who finds himself thus overwhelmed by an India which is not simply alien, but which alienates that which should have been familiar and homely: the civilised ritual of the dinner table and its conversation.

Even as the growing numbers of the British community in India, and improvements in transport and preservation technologies, made it possible and economically viable for the British in India to eat in ways less overtly differentiated from those at 'home', food continued to be problematic, and to constitute a threat to British identity and to their well-being, throughout the Victorian period. This was the case mainly because of the material and symbolic transgressions of the interracial boundaries involved in food preparation. Much of the food consumed by Anglo-Indians was purchased in Indian markets, and the preparation of food was carried out by Indian servants. Both kitchen and bazaar (where food was bought) were 'in the Anglo-Indian imagination' unclean places.[60] Manuals such as the *Complete Indian Housekeeper* warned against the 'dirt and slovenliness' of kitchen servants, as well as the 'native's capacity for uncleanliness' more generally, and recommended close oversight of all their activities.[61] The level of anxiety present on this point is reflected in the more-or-less apocryphal anecdotes about Indian hygiene circulating in British memoirs, such as the story of a leper's blanket being used to 'keep warm the dough' for bread.[62] George Graham's memoirs, for example, offer several of these, where the Indians' supposed lack of attention to cleanliness is compounded by the attribution to them of a comic stupidity: the taste of castor oil in the soup is explained by the cook straining soup through the duster used to clean the lamps; and servants serve olives with cream for dessert instead of greengages.[63]

As well as highlighting anxiety over the nature of the food being consumed, these situations also demonstrate a reversal in the normative relationship of power and authority between coloniser and colonised. As Angma Dey Jhala observes, knowledge about the purchase, preparation and preservation of Indian food was the preserve of the (usually male, and usually Muslim) cook in an Anglo-Indian household, with whom the woman of the household was obliged to negotiate, leaving the servant in a position to exert a strong influence over 'what Anglo-Indians ate, how much money was used for food expenses and how food was itself prepared'.[64] Consumption of food, in this context, becomes a performance of weakness, bringing to view the colonisers' lack of control over those vital resources which will be incorporated into their own bodies.

While thus susceptible to contamination in the process of preparation, food could also be transformed by contact with other elements of India. The trajectory of disappointment, where the newcomer to India finds it falls far short of the wealth and luxury he (usually) had anticipated, is frequently marked by the trope of food becoming unappetising or revolting. This is the approach adopted in *Calcutta: A Poem*, a dialogue of two speakers, where the second protagonist ('B') bewails the arrival of the 'ship in evil hour that bore / My jolted frame to India's burning shore!', and dates from this his suffering of the 'bitter torments of a wretched fate; / Deluded, listening to the tales they told, / Lands rich in mines, and rivers streaming gold'.[65] His interlocutor, 'A', casts his experience of India in more ironic mode, but to the same effect: his account of an Indian meal follows a familiar path through the medium of food and its contamination. The 'swinish epicure' calls to 'heap the groaning board / With every taste that orient climes afford' (84). But food is overwhelmed by insects, and consumption ceases:

> On every dish the bouncing beetle falls,
> The cockroach plays, or caterpillar crawls;
> A thousand shapes, of variegated hues
> Parade the table, and inspect the stews!
> To living walls the swarming hundreds stick,
> Or court, a dainty meal, the oily wick,

Heaps over heaps their slimy bodies drench,
Out go the lamps with suffocating stench!
When hideous insects ev'ry plate defile
The laugh how empty, and how forced the smile! (85)

Turtle Soup

At other times, the food in question is conceptually rather than literally unclean, in ways which echo the famine reports, and Burke's speeches, discussed earlier. This becomes particularly notable at the point where foodstuffs generally regarded as delicacies become tainted by association with the wrong part of the food chain, bringing into play what Maggie Kilgour describes as 'an even more charged kind of consumption' – cannibalism.[66]

Bishop Reginald Heber's journal of his travels in India in 1824–5 included a brief anecdote that shocked his Anglo-Indian readers. Heber, who had been in India about six months at this point, writes of eating turtle fished from the river, a tributary of the Ganges. 'There was not, indeed, much green fat', he writes, 'but what there was was extremely sweet and good, without the least fishy taste, and the lean very juicy, well-flavoured meat, not unlike veal.'[67] The idea of eating river turtles was anathema to his compatriots, who were aware that the turtles in their turn derived their food from the Hindu custom of disposing of human remains in the river. Roberts described Heber's meal as 'an act of griffinism [that is, the ignorance of a newcomer] never to be forgotten'.[68] The episode is recalled several times, one anonymous writer saluting Heber with a satirical 'Ode to the Ganges', in which he or she comments that they cannot 'see *why* a prime Ganges turtle, especially after a fine cholera season, should not be ... soup-erlative'.[69] Heber unwittingly set himself beyond the pale of Anglo-India by eating the wrong food – a particularly salient point in a country where food taboos and dietary ritual were significant in differentiating Hindus, Muslims, British and others from one another.

The response to Heber's encounter with the turtle echoes a literary theme of long-standing. The narrative poems of the 1820s frequently chose as their topic what might be called a colonial *Bildungsroman*: the coloniser's trajectory from hapless and naïve newcomer to old campaigner, eventually divested of his romantic fantasies about India, and of most of his fortune, but richer in knowledge. *The Life and Adventures of Shigram-Po* contains several episodes where the putative coloniser's inability to function as such is highlighted through this same ignorance about food and its significance. Tom Shanscrit and his friend Shigram catch a turtle in the course of their journey up the Ganges, cook it, and eat it with relish; only afterwards are they apprised by their servant, Buxoo, of what they have done:

> 'Master, says he; why eat that food,
> Eat *Hindoo* man, dat is not good!'
> Oh picture reader, *nauseous* case,
> What change of features now took place,
> Whilst all in turn, unhappy thing,
> Were seiz'd with *sudden* vomiting!
> Emetics had not made them reach,
> So much, as did poor Buxoo's speech
> . . .
> They now resolved no more to feast,
> On *Hoogly*'s Turtle Soup at least!
> Proceeding on next morn with tide,
> They smelt *unpleasant* fumes long side,
> And looking out Tom chanced to spy,
> A putrid body - - floating bye,
> Each horror struck, with dire dismay
> Shut too [sic] the window, moved away[70]

This 'change of features', whereby the master shows himself to be unmasterful, is a response not to the food that has been eaten, but to the knowledge of its categorisation as taboo. The suggestion is that the riches traditionally associated with India are illusory, that the attempt to consume is ill-fated, leaving, as it does, the coloniser open to criticism and question by his colonised servant. More disturbingly, the attempt to consume leaves the travellers possibly vulnerable to a more radical re-categorisation, not just as failed colonisers but as transgressors – albeit unwittingly and indirectly – against a shared social prohibition on cannibalism.

Reinforcing this point, a similar episode occurs a little later, this time featuring turkeys which are shot with a view to their consumption, and only then discovered to have been miscategorised: they are not turkeys, but vultures. The structure of this episode highlights both the trajectory of disappointment and the process by which the colonisers' positive appreciation of potential food – 'A flock of *Turkies*, oh! conceive their pleasure, / To view at their disposal, such a *treasure*!' – becomes fear and dismay at the thought of being themselves recategorised as food:

> Tom Shanscrit flew to seize upon the birds,
> But picture his surprize, assist me words
> To paint in proper colours his dismay,
> When he discover'd 'midst the slain there lay

A *human body*, oh! with what affright,
Did Tom return from the appalling sight!⁷¹

The repeated trope of the colonisers' 'dismay' at the literal idea of incorporating the material body of the colonised also brings into question the issue of the metaphorical identity of both the body of the nation and the colonising body. The incorporation of the substance of India into the social and political body of eighteenth-century Britain, via the Indianised bodies and attitudes of the returned nabobs, was widely seen as a threat to social order and national identity.⁷² Collingham's study *Imperial Bodies* suggests that India was literally incorporated by British men through a range of social practices, ranging from the use of servants to shampooing, using the hookah, and associating with Indian women. 'By allowing India to infiltrate the norms which governed his relationship with his body every Briton in India engaged in a process which made India his own country', but this was tolerated 'only as long as it did not overwhelm it or make it unrecognisable as an essentially British body.'⁷³ The assimilation, or threatened assimilation, of the Indian body into the body of the Anglo-Indian in these texts is catastrophic: in Tom Shanscrit's 'surprize' and fright, characterised by the narrator as unspeakable ('assist me words'), he has lost the control of his own body that marks the coloniser. Following Peter Hulme's suggestion (made in a slightly different context) that cannibalism, 'the image of ferocious consumption of human flesh', is 'frequently used to mark the boundary between one community and its others',⁷⁴ we might conclude that Tom's misadventure and failure to observe the taboo on cannibalism marks the moment at which his ejection from the community of the British is inevitable, since he has drawn attention to the practices of consumption and oppression within the social rather than the bodily economy that underlie the British presence in India.

Unlike the nabob texts of the eighteenth century, *Shigram-Po* is not a text written from a metropolitan point of view. Although the identity of the author is unclear, the authorial persona created in the introduction to his various works, with their mention of close acquaintance with the civil and military personnel of the East India Company, together with the detailed evocation and in-group jargon of the texts, suggest if not personal experience at least a level of very privileged access that would appear to contra-indicate the kind of distance that produced *Tea and Sugar*, and other similar metropolitan texts.⁷⁵ *Shigram-Po*, by contrast, suggests an unease among those of British India about the underlying justification for, and consequences of, their own presence as colonisers.

This is a theme that further complicates the sharp-edged recollections of Eden in her account of the Rajah of Bhurtpore. 'He is the ugliest and fattest young man I ever saw', she writes. 'A small face that takes up the usual space of the chin, and all the rest is head. He is very black, marked with the small-pox, and can hardly waddle for fat, and is only twenty-one.' The following day, as the 'beautiful fête' given by the rajah begins to drag on, and Eden observes that the presents offered to her and her sister 'were not intrinsically worth the diamond rings we gave in exchange', he takes on a different aspect: 'I fancied the Rajah smelt very strongly of green fat, and as it was past eight, and we are used to early dinners in camp, I thought in my hunger, what a pity it was that we had not brought St. Cloup, who in half-an-hour would have warmed the rajah up into excellent turtle soup.'[76] This encounter, two years after Eden's experience of the famine scenes discussed above, reverses the trajectory conventional to these texts of attraction followed by revulsion, as the rajah's alienating ugliness makes it possible, in antic imagination at least, to reclassify him as a prey animal, and again brings the dynamic of British exploitation of India near to the surface in a disturbingly literal form.

Being Consumed by India

Alongside this problematic representation of the drive to consume, there is also visible in the texts in question a prevalent anxiety about being consumed. Here, again, this phrase is to be interpreted literally: the body of the British coloniser in India is represented as being food for several different entities, from insects to wild beasts. The Bengal tiger which attacked a party of four British men on Saugor Island in 1792, including the son of the former commander-in-chief of the army in India, Sir Hector Munro, caused a frisson of horror across the British press, as an account of the young Munro's fate was widely reprinted. The eyewitness narrative of the victim's 'head ... in the beast's mouth', as the tiger carried him off 'with as much ease as I could lift a kitten', and his death 'in extreme torture' with his 'head and skull ... torn, and broke to pieces', made sensational reading, completed by the remark of another member of the party that he had to be moved, despite his injuries, lest he be 'devoured limb by limb' by the tigers.[77] As the story spread across India, the symbolic resonance of the incident was recognised by Tipu Sultan of Mysore, who commissioned to mark it the famous 'Man-Tiger Organ', a musical instrument in the shape of a red-coated man being mauled by a tiger.[78] The killing finds an echo several times throughout the nineteenth century, as in J. S. Buckingham's anecdote of a night in

Bombay when 'two immense tigers', attracted by 'the scent of so much flesh and blood congregated in a small space', attack one of the party.[79] As a trope of consumption, the killing also makes its way into popular culture in works like F. W. N. Bayley's comic verse narrative *The New Tale of a Tub*. The latter has a tiger attack two greedy 'Bengalese' (of British origin) at their picnic, before being eventually himself trapped in a cask as he pursues them, in a comic reversal of the original situation. The circulation and reiteration of these incidents, whether in tragic or in comic mode, demonstrates the fascination with which the trope of consumption was received.

Roberts's anecdote of an Indian woman being attacked by an alligator suggests the degree of fear and unease which underlies this fascination with the idea of being consumed. 'The Ghaut: An Indian Sketch' was published in the literary annual *Forget-me-not*, accompanying an engraving of a William Daniell painting. The illustration offers a conventional still, posed scene, its composition including palm trees, Indian women carrying water or sitting in picturesque attitudes, and a spire in the background; this is reflected in the narrative's depiction of the view: 'The wide waters of the Ganges seemed formed of liquid topaz, ruby, amethyst, and emerald, as they reflected the crimson, purple, and saffron of the sky, and the vivid foliage of the overhanging groves.'[80] Against this tranquil background, the story told by Roberts is shocking in its abrupt revelation of the danger apprehended by the author and her companions. In the grounds of a European house, the narrator sees 'a party of natives' approaching, and notices 'a female [of] extreme beauty: she possessed those large, soft, melancholy black eyes, so famed in oriental song; and while every lineament was moulded with the regularity of the sculptor's chisel, they were susceptible of the sweetest and tenderest expression'. In the remainder of the anecdote, the narrator's acute focus on the Indian woman is maintained:

> Little regarding the other members of the group, all my attention was directed to the beautiful female. I watched her while dropping the sarree upon her shoulders; she drew down her long black tresses, and, stooping, they streamed upon the water in dark luxuriance. While thus engaged, I perceived what I deemed to be a log of wood floating towards the bathers: in another instant the lovely Hindu, who was the outermost of the group, disappeared, and a loud shriek from her companions, who rushed with one accord to the bank, announced some fatal catastrophe. Scarcely knowing wherefore, I echoed the cry: the sound of my voice brought out the gentlemen and servants from the bungalow, and they hastened to the spot. Knowing nothing of the language, though a witness of the tragic scene, it was some time before I learned the nature of the accident which had befallen the luckless Hindu; the violent gesticulations and loud laments of the survivors announced something

frightful – she had been seized by an alligator, a creature which I had mistaken for a harmless piece of timber; but had I even been acquainted with its precise character, I was at too great a distance to have given the alarm.

Roberts's narrative highlights the narrator's uneasy awareness of her own participation in the scene, both as witness and as failed actor. The accumulation of sentimental detail might be read as an attempt to account for and validate her emotional reaction, as she repeats the description of the victim offered by her host:

'The unfortunate victim,' said he, 'appears to have been the paragon and pride of her village; the only child of aged parents; and, to heighten the calamity which has befallen her, she was tomorrow to have become the bride of a long-betrothed and deserving man, a sepoy, who has journeyed far, on furlough, from his corps to claim her hand, and who has brought with him testimonials of his good conduct from his officers, which have filled the breasts of his relatives and friends with pride and joy.'

The narrator's response to this suggests the importance of storytelling, in whatever form, as a means to come to terms with and normalise the danger made apparent in the episode. Her initial reaction is to emphasise her own fear and its physical manifestations: 'Shuddering, I turned away from the bright river which nursed such fearful monsters in its breast.' Almost immediately, the picturesque mode of the narrative enables the calm of the scene to be restored – 'By the time we had reached the house the darkness of the shrouding night alone was reflected upon its broad waters, and then it seemed, indeed, to wear the hue fitted for the early tomb of the young, lovely, and unfortunate Munna' – but this is a temporary expedient. The resort to narrative as a stabilising force continues for the remainder of the evening, as the company tell one another stories of 'accidents from the fang of the tiger, the cobra capella, and other enemies of the race of man'.[81]

Among these 'other enemies of the race of man' who feature in these texts are insect pests. They do not inspire the same fear or interest as tigers or cobras, but their activities nonetheless are shown to annihilate both symbolic and real elements of the British presence in India. *Tom Raw*, for instance, describes the impact of insects on Government House in Calcutta, its 'marble halls' crowned with paintings in classical style:

But classic taste gave way to the vile white ant.
Whose taste was diametric'ly opposite,
The artist aimed at fame – and he was right o'nt.
The ant t' obliterate his labours quite;
Which party gained the day, it's altered plight
Explains, for not a vestige of it's seen:

> Thus in a few short years, they ate, outright,
> What cost the Bengal Government between
> Seventy and eighty thousand good rupees – I ween.[82] [Punctuation as in the original.]

These images of consumption veer in familiar fashion back and forth between the literal and the metaphorical, often lingering between them. Tom Raw's servants are rhetorically described as 'blood-suckers, arrant leeches', but his face is literally disfigured by the swellings – 'bumps of red and white' – caused by mosquito bites.[83] The thread of disgusted complaint prompted by such events recurs in British writing throughout this period: more than half a century after the account of Tom Raw's miseries, W. T. Webb records a more direct, if ironic, complaint that the colonisers, 'Lords of earth, should furnish food' for the tiger-like, vampire-like mosquitos that afflicted everybody: 'Maiden young and vernal, / Babe or shrivelled colonel, / All alike are spoil for thee, thou imp infernal'.[84] These works imagine the colonising body as powerless and depleted, a trope visible in such comic creations as Colonel Young's poem 'The Mosquito's Song', with its rueful celebration of the swarm's assault on an unwary British sleeper:

> As the lubbard wight doth lie,
> Flushed with heat, and sleep, and ale,
> While our hovering troops assail,
> Juicy English cheek and lip;
> Thus with oft repeated dip,
> In we plunge the sharp proboscis,
> Hunger is the best of sauces,
> And we lack no cookery,
> Griffin-blood, to relish thee![85]

This is the comic version of what is sometimes an entirely serious apprehension of a threat to the integrity of the body. To cite Roberts again, her *Scenes and Characteristics of Hindostan* includes several anecdotes indicative of this fear of being consumed. In one such, a wife goes in search of her missing husband and discovers his body deserted by his servants. 'She soon found', Roberts writes, 'that her utmost strength would be insufficient to repel the daring attacks of hosts of insects, ravenous birds, and savage animals rushing on their prey, or congregating in the neighbouring thickets, awaiting an advantageous moment for attack', so rather than wait for help she digs a grave for him with her hands.[86] In this passage the threat hovers somewhere between real and imaginary – are the predators actually rushing on their prey, or is their presence 'congregating' in the bushes a figment of the distraught wife's imagination? Either way, it makes evident the anxiety accompanying British life in India.

This anxiety intensifies following the rebellion of 1857, as the fate of colonisers who died at rebel hands, and the circulation of narratives of the rape and murder of women, created the figure of a victimised British colonial body.[87] Sumanyu Satpathy suggests this as a context for a reading of the Edward Lear poem 'The Cummerbund: An Indian Poem', the product of a tour of India in 1873–5, where a wilful misuse of the vocabulary of British India is deployed to comic effect.[88] The female protagonist sits on a washerman (dobie), hears admiring comments on her beauty from items of furniture (punkahs), and watches servants (kamsamahs and kitmutgars) come into leaf around her:

> She sate upon her Dobie,
> To watch the Evening Star,
> And all the Punkahs as they passed,
> Cried, 'My! how fair you are!'
> Around her bower, with quivering leaves,
> The tall Kamsamahs grew,
> And Kitmutgars in wild festoons
> Hung down from Tchokis [way-stations] blue.

Comedy takes a dark turn, however, as the woman encounters a cummerbund, or waist-sash:

> She sate upon her Dobie, –
> She heard the Nimmak hum, –
> When all at once a cry arose, –
> 'The Cummerbund is come!'
> In vain she fled: – with open jaws
> The angry monster followed,
> And so, (before assistance came),
> That Lady Fair was swallowed.

Her memorial carries an awful warning to the women of British India, who are urged to 'beware' and stay indoors at night, 'Lest horrid Cummerbunds should come, / And swallow you outright.'[89] The effect of this apparent nonsense is more complex than it at first appears. The invention of the predatory and fearful waist-sash purports to exclude the metropolitan reader, or the newcomer to India, who lacks the required familiarity with the jargon of the colony – though Lear's reputation and previous work as a poet of nonsense might raise a warning flag in this instance. On the other hand, the joke, once understood, also targets the residents of the colony, minimising and rendering ludicrous the fear of bodily defilement and disintegration, as well as the fear of an apparently compliant India which has the capacity to become murderous.

The common theme across texts like these, whose effect is to disempower the coloniser, is the way in which they reverse the political and material hierarchy underpinning the colonial state, presenting the coloniser as oppressed and victimised by the climate, landscape and people of India, without agency or self-determination. In the case of Lear's poem, this might be regarded as the view of an outsider; but the same theme is demonstrably present in the texts written by those writers who are either full participants in the colonial state apparatus – as with Colonel Young – or connected to it by affective and family relations, as in the case of Roberts (whose journey to India was initiated by her sister's marriage to an army officer). Looking across this broader landscape, it might be surmised that such inversions – sometimes comic, sometimes horrific – of the power-structure of colonial India function to dissipate responsibility, not only giving voice to individual colonisers' resentment at the treatment to which they, as individuals, are subjected (for example, Tom Raw), but also implicitly dissociating them from the exploitative elements of the colonial project – positioning them as those who are eaten, rather than those who consume.

The Hunting Cycle

Both these themes – anxiety about consuming and fear of being consumed – come together in one of the most characteristic narratives of British India, the hunting story. Alongside the many accounts of successful hunts and the satisfied accumulation of trophies, there is a smaller subset of narratives where the protagonist is transformed from the consuming subject to the object of consumption, embarking upon a hunt for some wild animal, and instead finding himself its prey.[90]

Tom Raw's attempts at hunting fall into this category, in keeping with his general presentation as a hapless naïf unable to deal with India in any form. Hog-hunting leaves him with his 'ruddy colour changing into blue, / Not knowing, from sheer apprehension, what to do'; and the situation is made worse when the hog turns the tables by charging at him:

> The grunter fell, exhausted, on the sod:
> Tom thought 'twas luck, and then began to perk
> His face up, and roar out, 'Rare sport, by G–d!
> Ha! ha! well done, my boy ! – it would be odd
> If, after this, I could not stick one too.' –

And – at that instant – from his snug abode,
Another monster started into view,
And at poor Thomas with impetuous violence flew.[91]

A tiger hunt, similarly, leaves him at the mercy of his erstwhile prey, as he finds himself trapped on an elephant, the tiger clinging to his howdah and its 'wide and bloody jaws, / Roaring his funeral dirge', while his gun explodes in his hand as he attempts to shoot (237). Tom's luck holds, in the end, as the tiger is eventually overpowered by one of his companions.

J. H. Caunter's satirical poem 'The Cadet' describes the full trajectory of this cycle, from consuming to being consumed: the hunter first 'urges his foaming steed in swift career, / Till gasps the tusked monster 'neath his spear', then eats 'a dinner of the slain boar' with his companions of the chase. At the end of the evening, 'Drunk at the last to bed each rev'ller hies, / And like a fatting hog obscenely lies.' Finally, disgusted with his life and his companions, the hunter dies and is buried, whereupon 'the fell jackal, skulking for his prey, / Scrapes the fresh earth and bears the corpse away'.[92] The movement is from an exultation of the power of the self in the chase, to its egregious augmentation in the consumption scene, to the loss of the self in the material dispersal of the body as it is consumed. This might be regarded as a parallel to a more widely recognised theme in the literature of colonialism: the sexual desire of the coloniser for the colonised 'other', leading to a relationship which involves the real or symbolic danger of the loss of the coloniser's identity or power of self-determination. In Kipling's short story 'Beyond the Pale', for instance, the encounter between Trejago and Bisesa has catastrophic results for both, but Gail Low suggests that the amputation of Bisesa's hands might function as a 'disavowal and projection of Trejago's castration', an act hinted at in the text's reference to a stab wound to the groin.[93]

This theme is particularly prominent where the two kinds of loss of self – sexual and material – occur simultaneously. Thomas Medwin's 'Bengal Yarn', for instance, tells the story of the unfortunate Major B who rescues from a *sati* ceremony and then marries an Indian woman who turns out to be faithless: she absconds with all the property she has had from him; he pursues her into the jungle, and is eaten by a tiger.[94] Both Leask and Chakravarty consider this story – a late self-parody of Medwin's own earlier narratives of interracial romance such as 'Julian and Gizele' – to be an 'anti-romantic' warning against orientalist respect for indigenous culture.[95] It is the form taken by this warning that is notable in the context of this discussion: the Major's sexual desire for Seta, as well as his intellectual attraction to the consumption of and participation in Hindu culture, result in the loss of material possessions and agency, and finally in the disaggregation of the desiring and consuming body.

Trauma and Literary Form

These tropes in the literature of British India are so overdetermined that it is difficult to point to a single source or reason why particular themes find expression in particular literary forms. On the most basic level, the dangers to the material integrity of the body registered in these texts are entirely real and concrete, from the possibility of being attacked by wild animals, to the certainty of being targeted by insects, to the probability of suffering from illness induced by heat, disease or contaminated food. The preoccupation with death, and especially with the chances of dying young, revealed in the memoirs and travel narratives of British writers in India may be, as David Arnold argues, sometimes overwritten for sensational effect; but it is, as he also acknowledges, a genuine concern.[96] It is possible to view the set of experiences that gave rise to these concerns as a kind of ongoing physical and emotional trauma, even while acknowledging that many on the other side of the colonial encounter would contend, with good reason, that their own experience of British activities in India was socially and individually more substantially traumatic.

This analysis draws particularly on the work of Dominick LaCapra, who argues that writing trauma 'involves processes of acting out, working over, and to some extent working through in analysing and "giving voice" to the past – processes of coming to terms with traumatic "experiences", limit events, and their symptomatic effects'.[97] The literature described in this chapter might be read as constituting some of these processes. The reiteration in different modes of a variety of narratives tends towards the rehearsing of an essential preoccupation with damage to the self. This damage takes several forms: injury to the individual's physical body, transformation of the body or dispersal of the unified self. LaCapra also suggests that 'destructive and disorienting events' may produce what he terms 'founding traumas – traumas that paradoxically become the valorized or intensely cathected basis of identity for an individual or a group rather than events that pose the problematic question of identity'.[98] The events he has in mind are cataclysmic social and individual disasters (such as Hiroshima or the Holocaust), but without trivialising those by comparison, it might be argued that the same process – definition of an identity – is observable in the texts discussed here, a response to the much smaller, but relentless, material and psychic assaults sustained by individuals in the colonial state of British India.[99] The version of colonial identity that emerges from these texts is a remarkably consistent one: the protagonists are represented in a dual engagement with India, motivated by a drive to consume and so control and integrate the other within the self; and also by the need to imagine that self as in its turn disaggregated and consumed in the course of the encounter.

In the light of their preoccupation with the theme of a threatened and divided self, these writers' frequent choice of a comic or satirical form may be considered to represent a compensatory assertion of the ego, of the kind suggested by Freud in his late essay, 'Humour'. The proliferating anecdote of contamination (discussed above), where the Indian servant justifies the choice of an inappropriate utensil for preparing food on the grounds that it was already dirty, clearly functions on several levels: it gives expression to the speaker's and the audience's concern about contamination (both material and racial), while simultaneously positioning them as superior to the servant, whose actions are implicitly attributed to stupidity, thereby reinforcing the unequal relationship of coloniser and colonised. An indication of the body's vulnerability is transformed into, in Freud's phrase, an assertion of the 'invulnerability of the ego'. In adopting a humorous attitude, he writes, the 'ego refuses to be hurt by causes in reality, to be obliged to suffer, it insists that the traumas of the outside world cannot get near it, indeed it shows that it sees them only as occasions for the gain in pleasure'.[100]

In cases where the subject of humour is inside rather than outside the British community, a different dynamic may be observed. As these narratives – such as the adventures of *Tom Raw* – do not offer a racially 'other' figure to be thus cast as the target whose stupidity provides the occasion for the self's 'gain in pleasure', the boundaries of the self are redrawn in order to produce, by exclusion, another scapegoat figure. In the episode concerning Bishop Heber's turtle soup, for example, an important point concerns the phrase Roberts uses to describe Heber's gaffe: an 'act of griffinism'. The defining quality of the 'griffin' is his ignorance of the ways of India and the community of British India, a lack of capability that leads him into error and results in his being exploited by India and Indians. The poem 'To a Griffin' underlines the totality of this ignorance, as the griffin is instructed to 'purge from your mind every English-formed notion / Of Ind'. Among these misconceptions is the idea that the British in India live 'in a style of Nabob prodigality', that 'every native / Is either a toady or blood-thirsty caitiff', that 'missionary hardships would move you to pity; / That tigers are common, and ayahs are pretty', that 'sweet English girls, by the P. and O. carried / By hundreds, are no sooner landed than married.' The narrator's voice here becomes the voice of the experienced British resident of India, exhorting the griffin to 'Just drop such ideas in the Suez Canal, sir!'[101]

In 'The Mosquito's Song', similarly, the target of the mosquitos' hunger is 'the ruddy Griffin, / Full of beer and full of tiffin' – in other words, the newcomer whose unwise consumption of too much beer and food leaves him sleeping and vulnerable.[102] In these and other texts, this anxiety over the consumption of the 'wrong' food is deflected by the creation of an internal outsider, a character such as Tom Shanscrit. His consumption of the turtle – eating from the wrong part of the food chain – leaves him open to question and judgement by his Hindu servant, thus precipitating his loss of authority as coloniser; but the comic context of the poem attributes the fiasco to his status as a griffin, lacking in the vital attribute of colonial knowledge. In this way, the in-group, the rest of the British community, or to put it another way the Anglo-Indian 'self', is shielded from the social, moral and political issues around the consumption that sustains, but also compromises, their status as colonisers.

Notes

1. Inchbald, *The Mogul Tale*, pp. 11, 2.
2. See, for instance, Foote, *Nabob* (first performed 1772), and Clarke, *Nabob*.
3. See Lawson and Phillips, 'Our execrable banditti'; Smylitopoulos, 'Rewritten and reused'; Juneja, 'The native and the nabob'; Nechtman, *Nabobs*.
4. Rice, *Nabob*, pp. 48, 66–8.
5. See Touchstone, 'Tea and Sugar'; Foote, *Nabob*.
6. See Bolts, *Considerations on India Affairs*; Verelst, *A View*. The Bolts–Verelst dispute is described in Tuck, 'Introduction', pp. xvii–xxii. See also Sramek, *Gender, Morality*, pp. 28–30.
7. The Earl of Mornington to Henry Dundas, 25 January 1800, Ingram, *Two Views*, p. 218. Mornington began to use his recently acquired title of Marquis Wellesley a few months later.
8. Raven, *Judging New Wealth*, p. 237.
9. Wendeborn, *A View of England*, p. 126.
10. Quoted in Bowen, *Business of Empire*, pp. 15–16; see Walpole to Horace Mann, in *The Yale Edition of Horace Walpole's Correspondence*, ed. W. S. Lewis, vol. xxiii, p. 441; William Cobbett to William Creevey, *The Creevey Papers*, ed. Sir Herbert Maxwell, vol. 1, p. 134.
11. See Marshall, *Impeachment*; Dirks, *Scandal*; Whelan, *Edmund Burke*, among other sources. The theatrical and narrative aspects of the trial are discussed in Suleri, *Rhetoric*, pp. 49–74.
12. Gibbons, *Edmund Burke*, pp. 115, 116.

13. Marshall (ed.), *Writings and Speeches of Edmund Burke*, vol. v, p. 402.
14. Burke, *Works of the Right Hon. Edmund Burke*, vol. 1, p. 334. The context is the parliamentary debate on the Nabob of Arcot's debts, involving accusations of collusion and profiteering against employees of the East India Company.
15. Whelan, *Edmund Burke and India*, p. 210.
16. See, for instance, the arguments put forward by Dirks, *Scandal*, against the account offered by Marshall, *Impeachment*.
17. Whelan, *Edmund Burke*, pp. 59–61.
18. Burke, *Launching of the Hastings Impeachment*, p. 189.
19. *History of the Trial of Warren Hastings*, part vii, pp. 152–3.
20. Sheridan, *Speech*, p. 27. The text is reportage, not a transcript of Sheridan's words.
21. Ralph Broome's *Letters of Simkin the Second*, for instance, were serialised at length in several editions between 1788 and 1791. See my *Poetry of British India*, vol. 1, pp. 23–4, 377.
22. William Dent, 'The Raree Show', 7 February 1788 (BM Satires 7273). There were many such caricatures produced in the course of the trial: see also Gillray, 'Political Banditti assailing the Saviour of India' (11 May 1786), where a grotesquely thin and insect-like Burke fires a blunderbuss at a plump Hastings, whose round shape is echoed by the sacks of gems and rupees attached to the camel on which he rides (BM Satires 7169); and Gillray, 'The Friendly Agent' (9 June 1787), showing Hastings being hanged, his body weighted down by the sacks of rupees and pagodas tied to his feet (BM Satires 7169). Stephens and George, *Catalogue*.
23. The image is complex, and its representation of the trial more generally is beyond the scope of this chapter: see O'Quinn, *Staging Governance*, pp. 178–80.
24. Lawson, *Private Life*, p. 247.
25. Marshall, *Bengal*, pp. 18–20; see also Sharma, *Famine*.
26. Hastings, Letter to the Court of Directors, in Marriott, *Britain in India*, vol. 4, pp. 4–6.
27. Ray, 'Indian Society', p. 514.
28. Davis, *Late Victorian*, p. 33. As Ellen Brinks suggests, famine relief and other forms of intervention also had the effect of expanding British 'arenas of control' (*Anglophone*, pp. 98–9).
29. Bayly, *Rulers*, p. 301; see also Mann, *British Rule*, pp. 177, 182.
30. Sharma, *Famine*, p. 73.
31. R. S. B., 'Records of Bengal, No 1, The Flood of 45', *Mofussilite*, 6 September 1845.
32. Teignmouth, *Memoir of the Life*, vol. 1, p. 25.
33. Graham, *Journal of a Residence*, pp. 69–70.
34. Dunbar, *Poems*, p. 32.
35. Eden, *Up the Country*, 64–5; compare *Romeo and Juliet* V, i.
36. Sleeman, *Rambles*, pp. 195–7.
37. Burt, *Narrative*, pp. 104–5.
38. Burt, *Poems*, pp. 76–9.
39. *Times*, 12 July 1927.

40. Trevor, *Rhymes of Rajputana*, pp. 194–5. See Maloo, *History of Famines*, pp. 118–22.
41. See, for example, Davis's account of Sir Richard Temple's activities in the Deccan in 1877 (*Late Victorian*, pp. 38–40).
42. Quiz, *Grand Master*, p. 13.
43. Qui Hi's riotous living and indebtedness are both characteristic of civil as well as military employees of the East India Company during the early nineteenth century; see Cohn, 'Recruitment', pp. 524–5.
44. See the discussion of this plate in Smylitopoulos, 'A Nabob's Progress', pp. 78–83. Her analysis of the poem covers issues of drinking, debt, and idleness, but not eating.
45. Smylitopoulos, p. 60.
46. 'Account of the late dreadful Famine in India', *Annual Register*, pp. 206–7.
47. Arnold, 'Hunger in the garden of plenty', p. 98.
48. 'S.', 'The Famine Relief Officer (I)', *C. P. Pieces*, pp. 18–21.
49. Lupton, *Food*, pp. 16–17.
50. Thackeray, *Vanity Fair*, p. 532.
51. Collingham, *Imperial Bodies*, p. 29.
52. Raza, *In Their Own Words*, pp. 94–5.
53. Maitland, *Letters*, pp. 36–7.
54. Macnaghten, 'A Sort of Lay Jocund', *Calcutta Magazine*, 1830, p. 253.
55. 'The supper call', *Calcutta Magazine* (February 1831), p. 83. Notwithstanding its satiric exaggeration, the essay is not wholly unrealistic: Steel and Gardiner's *Complete Indian Housekeeper and Cook* (1888) decries the common practice of serving 'a meal of four or five distinct courses . . . when one light *entrée* and a dressed vegetable would be ample' (p. 57).
56. The poet and novelist James Hogg (1770–1835) was also known as the Ettrick Shepherd, a semi-fictional creation whose rural simplicity stands in particular contrast to the excess described here.
57. Henderson, *Satires in India*, p. 51.
58. Caunter, *Cadet*, pp. 11–12.
59. D'Oyly, *Tom Raw*, p. 44. The unfamiliar words are unglossed in the text, thus excluding the metropolitan reader as well as the protagonist.
60. Procida, *Feeding the Imperial Appetite*, pp. 129–30, 137.
61. Steel and Gardiner, *Complete Indian Housekeeper*, pp. 82, 114.
62. See R. Temple-Wright, *Baker and Cook: A Domestic Manual for India* (1893), quoted in Burton, *Raj at Table*, p. 154. These concerns on the part of employers are not confined to India, and in other contexts can be class-based as well as race-based; see, for instance, the reservations expressed about European servants by the New Zealand employers cited in Lawrence, *Genteel Women*, pp. 200–2.
63. Graham, *Life in the Mofussil*, vol. 1, pp. 47–8. The humour in these anecdotes is of the kind posited by C. R. Gruner's 'superiority theory': 'we laugh at the misfortune, stupidity, clumsiness, moral or cultural defect suddenly revealed in *someone else*, to whom we instantly and momentarily feel "superior" since *we* are *not*, at that moment, unfortunate, stupid, morally or culturally defective, and so on' (*Game*, p. 13).

64. Jhala, *Royal Patronage*, p. 89.
65. Majendie, *Calcutta: A Poem*, p. 14.
66. Kilgour, 'Function of cannibalism', p. 239.
67. Heber, *Narrative of a Journey*, vol. 1, p. 116.
68. Roberts, *Scenes and Characteristics*, vol. 2, p. 360.
69. *Parbury's Oriental Herald* vol. 3 (January–June 1839), p. 486.
70. *Life and Adventures*, p. 245.
71. *Life and Adventures*, p. 248.
72. See, for instance, the depiction of the yellowing body of Matthew Mite in Foote, *Nabob*; and Touchstone, *Tea and Sugar*, where a line is drawn between the 'savage band' of Nabobs and 'Britain's famous land' (p. 10).
73. Collingham, *Imperial Bodies*, p. 33.
74. Hulme, *Colonial Encounters*, p. 86.
75. See my *Poetry of British India*, vol. 1, pp. 197–8.
76. Eden, *Up the Country*, pp. 354, 356.
77. *Scots Magazine* (July 1793), p. 360.
78. See de Almeida and Gilpin, *Indian Renaissance*, p. 36.
79. Buckingham, *Autobiography*, vol. 2, p. 351.
80. Roberts, 'The Ghaut', *Forget-Me-Not* (1828), pp. 393–4.
81. Roberts, 'The Ghaut', *Forget-Me-Not* (1828), pp. 394–7.
82. D'Oyly, *Tom Raw*, p. 70.
83. D'Oyly, *Tom Raw*, p. 29.
84. Webb, 'Ode to a Mosquito', *Indian Lyrics*, pp. 69–75. See also his account of the depredations of the white ant, which 'mines and delves with maw voracious' in its consumption of books (164–6).
85. Young, 'The Mosquito's Song. A Calcutta Fragment', *Bengal Annual* (1830), pp. 312–14.
86. Roberts, *Scenes and Characteristics*, vol. 1, p. 279.
87. See Paxton, 'Mobilizing Chivalry'.
88. Satpathy, 'Lear's India', pp. 73–80.
89. Translations in parentheses rely on Yule, *Hobson-Jobson*. See also Ray Murphy's translations in Lear, *Edward Lear's Indian Journal*, pp. 151–2. For Vivien Noakes's more detailed annotations, see Lear, *Complete Nonsense*.
90. For a wider analysis of the hunt in British India, a topic beyond the scope of this chapter, see MacKenzie, *Empire*; Nayar, *English Writing and India*, pp. 132–68; Rajamannar, *Reading the Animal*, pp. 69–128.
91. D'Oyly, *Tom Raw*, p. 213.
92. Caunter, *Cadet*, vol. 1, pp. 147–9.
93. Low, *White Skins / Black Masks*, p. 129. See 'Beyond the Pale' in Kipling, *Plain Tales*.
94. Medwin, 'A Bengal Yarn', in *Ainsworth's Magazine*, vol. 2, 1842, pp. 57–63.
95. Leask, *British*, pp. 167–9; see also Chakravarty, *Indian Mutiny*, pp. 97–8.
96. Arnold, 'Deathscapes', p. 343.
97. LaCapra, *Writing History,* p. 186. The area of trauma theory / studies has burgeoned since the publication of this work, impelled in part by the events of 9/11 (for a recent snapshot, see Buelens et al, *Future*); my analysis here does not pretend to engage with its ramifications, but rather

co-opts its basic principles to address a particular aspect of the British experience of India.
98. LaCapra, *Writing History*, p. 23.
99. The traumatic experiences of individuals during the Indian Mutiny of 1857 might be included in this category of larger disasters, and their impact is discussed in Herbert, *War of No Pity*. My concern here, however, is with the repeated pattern of more minor 'traumas' arising during the British encounter with India.
100. Freud, 'Humour', p. 562.
101. Aliph Cheem, *Lays of Ind*, p. 99. See also the examples of this trope discussed by Roy, *Civility*, pp. 43–6.
102. Young, 'The Mosquito's Song. A Calcutta Fragment', *Bengal Annual* (1830), pp. 312–14.

Part II
Representations of India

Chapter 4

European Nationalism and British India

The representation of Indians, and in particular of Hindus, in literature by British writers underwent a change in the early decades of the nineteenth century. Eighteenth-century stereotypes of the 'mild Hindoo', alien to British ways of thinking because of the 'idolatrous' nature of their religious beliefs, and considered weak for their subjection to the Muslim rulers of the Mughal Empire, gave way to a more complex portrait.[1] This process is influenced by changing British and European ideas about the relationship between individuals and states, as well as by developing British interactions with a wider range of indigenous groups on the Indian subcontinent. Like most of the literature of British India, the texts circulating this set of representations draw on several different sources. One is the mainstream literary tradition of Western Europe (which was also, of course, itself partly shaped by literary encounters with the Orient, or with the 'internal orients' of places like Highland Scotland, in the work of writers such as Scott, Byron and Shelley). Another is drawn from the indigenous traditions of India: the archives of historical, mythological and literary narratives compiled and circulated by British scholars collecting vernacular sources. The third is the writers' lived experience of India, and their apprehension of the particular socio-economic and political forces driving British interactions with and representations of Indians.

In British India, Romanticism's turn to the past had a geographical as well as a historical dimension. The British concept of India as organised on lines similar to those of medieval Europe, and in particular the insistence of influential scholars like James Tod on presenting the 'martial races' of India as feudal societies, meant that the look to history in Romantic-period Europe could become, in India, a view across the landscape.[2] The Highlands of Scotland, for example, are replaced by the mountains of various unspecified but picturesque Indian locations; and while Scott set his action in a Jacobite past, his imitators in British India could plausibly set their bandit romances in their own present day. The Romantic ideal of the primitive is in India found not in the past but in the geographically far reaches of the colonial state.

The difference between the discourses of nationalism in Europe and their equivalent in British India is apparent in some of the poems published in the *Oriental Herald* in the 1820s. The *Oriental Herald* was started in 1824 by James Silk Buckingham, whose record as editor, and partnership with the Bengal liberal reformer Rammohan Roy, co-proprietor with him of the *Calcutta Journal*, are evidence of his personal and professional sympathy with liberal causes.[3] This sympathy underlies the *Oriental Herald*'s publication of works celebrating and endorsing European nationalist enterprise.

'Italy, a War Song', by H.W.J., for instance, is an expression of nationalist fervour, voiced by an unmediated narrator who identifies wholly with the cause of defeating those described as 'tyrant' and 'oppressor':

> But we'll bow to no tyrant's dominion,
> Arise, sons of Italy! on, – and strike home!
> For vengeance is ready, and glory's to come,
> And yet shall the oppressor lie lowly,
> For our cause is the just and the holy.

The poem concludes by drawing a parallel between Italy and the newly formed United States of America, with again no hint that the freedom anticipated is less than desirable:

> A land your sires knew not, beyond the far sea,
> Hath told that yon sun was but made for the free;
> On the night of the slave it hath broken,
> And through Europe it yet shall be spoken![4]

A similarly nationalist work by the same author, 'The Greeks', conveys a comparable message; and the anonymously published 'War Song for Greece' is unequivocal in its encouragement of and demands for nationalist insurrection. 'Unsheath the sword in freedom's cause; / Defend yourselves from despot laws', the Greeks are told; and further, 'Come, arm yourselves! nor longer be / Shackled by Turkish slavery'.[5] In these works, the reader is invited to enter into and share the point of view and the emotions of a narrator who is wholly aligned with the cause being described – the absence of any critical distance within the poem means that a positive effort is required to read against the grain and adopt a sceptical or negative approach to the insurrection so evoked.

In a comparable poem set in India, 'Indian War Song', by contrast, the theme of rebellion is hedged about with multiple formal and thematic devices that have the effect of rendering impossible such unproblematic identification between the reader and the rebel protagonist. The author of the poem is Henry Meredith Parker, a strong supporter of and contributor to the *Calcutta Journal* who was also open to cross-cultural interaction: he included in his social and literary circle the Bengali poets H. L. V. Derozio, who wrote a 'Sonnet to Henry Meredith Parker, Esq', and Kasiprasad Ghosh, who dedicated to him the third canto of his poem, 'The Sháïr'.[6] While Parker could turn a satiric eye on these Indians who tried to enter into dialogue with British or European models of thought, as in 'Young India: A Bengal Eclogue', he was also, particularly at this early stage of his career, capable of an imaginative entry into the mind of those who might be supposed to resent an alien presence in India.[7] 'Indian War Song' was one of the earliest of these 'nationalist' works to appear in the *Oriental Herald*, and reads like a call to arms to rival those addressed to Greece and Italy. As the following extract demonstrates, it is equally stirring in its appeal to the reader to enter into a nationalist cause:

Let the Musulman rise, with his old battle cry,
For the glad hour of freedom and vengeance is nigh;
Let him think on the sceptre his forefathers swayed,
And the might of past ages shall rest on his blade.

Will the fiery rajpoot hear the trumpet that rings
With a nation's appeal to the offspring of kings,
Nor rush to the field, like his proud sires of old,
The vanguard of valour, and guide of the bold?

Sound! sound to horse! hark! the loud clanging hoof
And the neigh of impatience gives gallant reproof;
March! and the trump of our Durrahs shall roll,
Like a fast-moving storm on the infidel's soul.[8]

This work anticipates in several respects the discourse of nationalism developed in the poems discussed above. Several of the religious and ethnic groups on the Indian subcontinent – Muslims, Rajputs and Pindaris – are all invited to unite against the invader; this is accompanied by an appeal to the past (the 'proud sires of old'), a call to martial action and an invocation of the ideal of freedom. The speaker names his enemies as the 'kaffers' who will 'fly to the ships, whence they treacherously came / To rob us of glory, to clothe us in shame' – thus, invaders; and in the central and northern areas of India where the poem is set, British colonisers. The term 'kaffers' is glossed in a note to the poem as 'unbelievers', with the addendum that this is 'a term of reproach mutually applied by Christians, Mohammedans, and idolaters, to the enemies of their respective creeds', a further indication that the poet is willing to entertain the idea of a commonality between the 'Christians' of Western Europe and the Muslims and 'idolaters' of the East.

The speaker of this poem, however, is characterised in such a way as to make reader identification with him at least problematic if not impossible. The introductory note presents the text as having been 'discovered in the cummerbund or sash of a Pindarrie chieftain, who had fallen during a night skirmish between the freebooters and a detachment of our cavalry in India, during the last campaign'. This frame narrative locates the text as the product of a conflict only recently ended: the series of encounters between Pindari raiders (irregular mounted forces drawn from across the Indian subcontinent) and British armies which ended in the Pindaris' defeat by a large army commanded by Lord Hastings in 1817.[9] This conflict widened into the third Anglo-Maratha war (1817–18), which resulted in defeat for the Maratha Confederacy and the consolidation of British power in central India. The 'Pindarrie chieftain' is clearly on the losing side in this encounter, so that his anticipation of nationalist victory is known by the contemporary reader to be hollow even as it is read. The death of the speaker, and the positioning of the text as in some sense one of the spoils of war – taken from the body of a slain enemy – renders the call to nationalist action impotent. While the invitation to the reader to recognise parallels between situations and human responses in Europe and on the Indian subcontinent is implicit in the language of the poem, that reader's response is also confined to the recognition of a historical parallel, not a contemporary one.

Nonetheless, this poem is important, as it indicates that this particular time and place – central and north India in the 1820s and 1830s – is a location of potential, a crucible, in which British perceptions and representations of India were being formed in the context of contemporary politics and conflicts. The imaginative possibilities associated with this region for British writers is apparent in another poem, 'The Rajpoot's Lament', by W. F. Thompson, an employee of the Bengal civil service. Here, the representation of a specifically Rajput identity provides the opportunity for a British writer to develop a portrait of Indian nationalism akin to the pro-independence poems about Greece and Italy discussed above. The work is unusual in the depth of its identification with the Rajput cause, as the protagonist looks back to a golden age of independence and power, and contrasts it to the state of the land in the present time. The ghosts of the 'mighty dead' addressed in the first lines are 'forever fled, / With all the glories of your reign', so that at first reading the poem looks like a narrative of Indian decay. This is not the case, however, as the speaker's dismay at the failure of past greatness, and the inability of those 'shades' to 'guard the right your glory made', is in no sense an acceptance of the current status quo. Rather, his anticipation of the ruin to come is also a protest against the replacement of indigenous power by strangers, those the country 'hath not borne':

> The Cheytrie's pride, the Brahmun's god,
> Shall both be trampled and o'erthrown,
> And the pure land, your footsteps trod,
> Debased by lords to you unknown.
> And will ye sleep, for ever sleep,
> While good men pray and brave ones weep,
> And native honor's latest gasp,
> Is ebbing in the oppressor's grasp?[10]

The identity of these oppressors is not specified in so many words (the British, but also the Mughal invaders before them, might be described in this way). However, the reference to them as 'slaves of slaves, whose god is gold' (382) suggests the intended target might be the East India Company, which started its existence as a commercial trading company and had by the 1830s only just made the transition into a de facto institution of the British government. Regardless of this identification, the important point is the characterisation of the speaker, who is endowed with a selfless dedication to individual and national liberty:

> 'Tis vain, the task is not for me –
> Fly, baseless hope and shadowy throne –
> My country's soul I cannot free,
> I will be master of my own:
> ...
>
> Though ear is deaf and voice is dumb,
> I know the spirit dieth not;
> The ocean sleeps – the storm shall come,
> When I, perchance, shall be forgot;
> Enough for me if freedom's eye
> Shall mark my ashes as they lie,
> And freedom's tardy hand confer
> A wreath on him who died for her. (384)

Despite the conventional trajectory of Thompson's career from Haileybury College to the civil service of the Company and a series of administrative posts in Bengal, he was radically at odds with the thinking of most if not all of his colleagues on the issue of the British colonial project in India. His disaffection with the approach and goals of the British administration is particularly visible in the anonymously published poem *India*, which describes the British as a 'blight' on India, oppressing and victimising its people.[11] The prophetic invocation of the coming storm, in the lines quoted above, is paralleled by the prescient anticipation in *India* of events bearing a remarkable resemblance to the rising of 1857, long after Thompson's own death. In conceiving of a Rajput nationalism developed in opposition to an implicitly British overlording presence, and hinting at the possibility of that rule itself at some stage being cast off, Thompson also gives that nationalism a voice untrammelled by any of the narrative trappings of distance and containment that proliferate in other British ventriloquisms of an Indian consciousness: India's power, the 'mighty dead' of the opening lines, is gone, but the expression of individual desire for liberty by the speaker is neither qualified nor represented as illegitimate.

Alongside this representation and imagination of Indian agency, the work of other British writers constructs a counter-narrative of Indian decline and decay, where a sequential progression from ancient Hindu civilisation to Mughal dominance can be completed with reference to the collapse of the Mughal Empire, and the anticipation of its replacement by British rule. This is the underlying narrative of James Abbott's long poem *The T'hakoorine: A Tale of Maandoo*. This work has its origins in a journey made by Abbott to the ruins of Mandhu, former capital of the Malwa region of northern India, in 1831, when, according to the preface, he heard from local people the legend on which the poem is based. It has, as Abbott claims, its origins in historic events: Baz Bahadur, the Muslim ruler of Malwa during the latter part of the sixteenth century, was famous for his romantic relationship with the Hindu woman Rupmati (or Roope Muttie, in Abbott's version); when he was defeated and had to flee the state, she took poison in order to save herself from capture by his enemies.[12] The poem focuses on the consequences of the Muslim ruler's attraction to his Rajput beloved. 'He strove to win her heart and hand', Abbott writes. 'The first was speedily his, but the splendid lot to which he wooed her could not tempt her to dishonour the sacred race from which she had sprung.'[13] Her father demands that she offer her life as a sacrifice in order to resolve this dilemma, but she is eventually saved by the power of love, channelled through the person of the god of the river Narbudda, who orders the father to relinquish his daughter, and the king to build a palace for her by the riverside (108).

While the main action concludes with the anticipated construction of Rupmati's palace, the poem ends in the ruins of that same palace, as the focus shifts to the narrator, who considers his own presence in the shadow of the past:

> Child of a vanish'd race! what doest thou here?
> Wouldst thou the grim, gaunt tigress for thy mate,
> Or, with the owl, her midnight mopings share,
> Sagest of moralists o'er chance and fate?
> Is not thy couch prepar'd with the great,
> Whom silence curtains in their marble halls?
> Where royal beauty shares thy pillow'd state,
> And murmur'd anthems tremble round the walls,
> As for the mighty dead, some whisper'd requiem falls. (120)

The main impression given here is of the decay of the people whose lives have been chronicled, not only the individuals but their entire society. This theme is further sustained by Abbott's introduction, which locates the work in the context of his own visit to the area of Mandhu, when he saw the 'palace and fountain of Roope Muttie', the inspiration for the poem. His own experience, which he narrates here, mirrors that elegiac conclusion:

> I was at Maandoo during the monsoon, the gloomiest season of the year – when the rain falls night and day in torrents, and the wind sweeps continually over the ruined mountain. I slept in the tomb of Hoshungh Shauh, as being the only building in sufficient preservation to exclude the deluge of rain. Even here, in many places, the water oozes through the roof, and soaking into the walls from above ... In this mausoleum, my candle at night had the faint appearance of a glow-worm, and the intense darkness seemed threatening to smother it, at every moment (xvi–xvii).[14]

What Ina Ferris terms the 'salient ruin features of disintegration and abandonment' are here in abundance: the place is approached 'through a vista of ruined palaces, temples, and tombs', and over the ruins 'in place of plume and lance and banner, the peepul and burgut are waving their glossy foliage, and the wild reed is shooting its fragile stem' (xiii).[15] In a telling image, Abbott refers to Maandoo as being 'now in the desolation of thy widowhood', making an implicit connection between the state of the city, with 'princely palaces ... crumbling to dust, and ... temples falling dome by dome' (xi) and the fate anticipated by its protagonist, who assures her father that the 'widow's double bier' awaits her (70).

This coda is not straightforward, though, and it highlights the ambiguous and complex response of British writers to the notion of Indian autonomy, and the passing of that autonomy. The poem's narrator is aware of his own mortality as well as that of his subjects – the last lines remind him that 'Soon shall thy rest, with theirs, in soundness vie, / And ages, as they roll, unheeded, pass thee by!' (120). Ruins are, famously, problematic for a Romantic-period sensibility that saw them as evidence of the passing of empires, as Shelley's 'Ozymandias' demonstrates with its image of imperial power brought to a 'colossal Wreck' surrounded by nothingness.[16] 'The Romantic ruin is quintessentially the tomb, and the reassuring obsolescence, of the past',[17] Sophie Thomas argues; but for the British, engaged in building their own colonial state, obsolescence can be far from reassuring. The impulse to mark the passing of the ancient kingdoms of Malwa is tied to the need to show British-influenced India replacing it, but it is also a reminder that what would become the British Empire in India is itself transient. The deserted palace of Roope Muttie marks the demise of an indigenous Indian kingdom, but its ruin signals the end of empire.

These aspects of British responses to India – the recognition of commonalities and parallels between West and East, but also their implicit rejection or relegation to the past – are visible throughout the literature of this period. As the examples of Abbott's and Parker's works demonstrate, such representations of India evolve through the writers' personal encounters with the subcontinent, but are also shaped by their experience of metropolitan concerns and literary forms, and by their knowledge of indigenous narratives and versions of history. The three chapters in this section explore some of these representations. Chapter 5 focuses on colonial writers' appropriation of metropolitan models in accounts of Indian criminality. Chapter 6 examines British negotiations with and transformations of episodes in the history and mythology of India. Chapter 7 brings together both of these strands in the literature produced in the period following the Indian Mutiny, as British representations of India responded to a heightened sense of the precarious security of the colonial state after the uprising, and new strands of Indian self-assertion started to emerge towards the end of the century.

Notes

1. See, for example, Sherer, *Sketches*, pp. 55–6.
2. Metcalf, *Ideologies*, pp. 68–78.
3. See Bayly, 'Rammohan Roy', pp. 25–41.
4. H.W.J., 'Italy, a War Song', *Oriental Herald* vol. 17 (April–June 1828), pp. 513–14. The Italian *Risorgimento* had as its aim the unification of Italian states and the independence of Italy from Austrian control. See Seton-Watson, *Nations*, pp. 102–4.
5. H.W.J., 'The Greeks', copied from the *Liverpool Mercury*; and the anonymously published 'War Song for Greece'. *Oriental Herald*, vol. 17 (April–June 1828) pp. 268, 323; see also 'Song of the Young Greek', *Oriental Herald*, vol. 17 (April–June 1828) p. 446. Early nineteenth-century attempts to achieve Greek freedom from Turkish rule (a legacy of

the Ottoman Empire) resulted in the recognition of the independent state of Greece in 1830. See Seton-Watson, *Nations*, pp. 110–14.
6. See *Derozio: Poet of India*, ed. Chaudhuri, p. 264; and Ghosh, *Sháir*, p. 53.
7. Parker, *Bole Ponjis*, vol. 2, pp. 223–8. See also Chaudhuri, 'Young India'.
8. 'C. J.', 'Indian War Song', *Oriental Herald*, vol. 2 (May–August 1824), p. 62. Parker published under several pseudonyms at this time, but most frequently as 'Bernard Wycliffe'; see my *Poetry*, vol. 1, pp. 237–8.
9. See the account of these episodes offered by a near-contemporary historian, Edward Thornton (*Chapters*, pp. 389–433).
10. Thompson, 'Rajpoot's Lament', *Bengal Annual* (1835), p. 382.
11. Thompson, *India*, p. 79.
12. The episode is briefly referenced by John Malcolm (*Memoir*, vol. 1, pp. 39–40).
13. Abbott, *T'hakoorine*, p. 124. The title is a feminine form of the word *thakur* (chief, landholder).
14. Anne Janowitz's observation that the 'mild melancholia' surrounding the ruined castle is generated by 'the emptying out of history' is apposite here: the destruction of Mandhu was a consequence of the complex political history of the region, which saw the Sultanate of Malwa succeeded by the Mughal Empire and then the Maratha confederacy, but this is elided by the narrative, which carries out a direct replacement of Hoshang Shah, one of the early sultans of Malwa, by his successor the British narrator who sleeps in his tomb. See Janowitz, *England's Ruins*, p. 61.
15. Ferris, *Romantic*, p. 105.
16. Shelley, *Poems*, pp. 310–11.
17. Thomas, *Romanticism and Visuality*, p. 66.

Chapter 5

Romantic Heroes and Colonial Bandits

The figure of the bandit hero in the literature of British India has its origins not in India, but in the Europe of the late eighteenth and early nineteenth centuries, as the spread of nationalist movements across the continent gave rise to literary representations by writers such as Schiller, Scott and Byron of the tension and conflict inherent in the opposition between individual and/or national liberty and the maintenance of state or imperial authority. The final episode of the Anglo-Maratha Wars (1817–18) ended with the British exercising direct or indirect control over most of north and central India. Among the consequences was a breakdown in the social and economic order across this landscape: indigenous ruling groups were dispersed, and unemployed soldiers from the East India Company's armies joined increasing numbers of dispossessed or landless people who had no role in the new social organisation.[1] A contemporary observer, W. H. Sleeman, connects this transfer of power directly with increased criminality, writing that 'we [the Company state] do the soldier's work with one-tenth of the number of those who had been employed to do it under the former rule'; leaving those disbanded soldiers with 'nothing which a soldier delights in to do, unless perchance they have turned robbers'.[2] Against this backdrop, the incidence of predatory crime – carried out by bandits, dacoits and thugs – became a problem of policing for the Company, but also an opportunity to widen its sphere of influence by extending that policing into 'native states' where indigenous authorities were accused of sheltering criminal gangs.[3]

The publicity generated by campaigns against thugs and dacoits, first in the Sagar and Narmada territories and later across much of India, brought the problem of banditry, and the figure of the bandit, to public notice from the 1820s onwards.[4] The practice of recording evidence taken from 'approvers' – or informers – and circulating extracts from this evidence in the periodical press focused attention on prisoners' accounts of their own criminal acts. Works such as Sleeman's

Ramaseeana (on thugs) and *Report on Budhuk Decoits* developed a narrative of these criminals as set apart by heredity and religious affiliation from ordinary Indian society, and as uniquely threatening to both that society and British authority in India.

The major work of fiction drawing on this body of colonial knowledge is Philip Meadows Taylor's *Confessions of a Thug* (1839), an account of a thug's career which reflects the narrative form of the depositions taken from prisoners, and which has generated significant critical analysis.[5] As well as being informed by the contemporary discourse on criminality in British India, *Confessions* and other such texts are also shaped by their writers' familiarity with British literary traditions. Taylor uses quotations from canonical authors including Shakespeare and Byron as chapter headings, thereby containing the first-person narrative of the thug Ameer Ali within a 'typological discourse' that constitutes a Western evaluative and interpretative framework.[6] Emma Roberts, similarly, during her tenure as editor of the *Oriental Observer*, prints a first-person account attributed to a thug prisoner, but frames it with her own landscape description drawing on the painterly aesthetic of the picturesque:

> A few words will furnish a sketch of the localities of the places where many of those sanguinary deeds were perpetrated. A wild jungly plain, a village with its mosque or pagoda in the distance, scattered groups occupying the foreground, some cooking, some smoking, others singing to the sound of a drum; baggage piled around with bullocks reclining beside it, and here and there a few ponies picketed. A faint streak of red light bordering the distant horizon, and night falling like a cloud upon the murderers, their victims and the open graves.[7]

A parallel tension between specifically Indian content and metropolitan literary forms is evident in the work of other writers of British India, many of whom developed narratives of colonial criminality within the parameters of representation of the bandit / rebel hero already present in the tradition of metropolitan literature. This chapter examines the use made of the most important of these nineteenth-century metropolitan models – the works of Schiller, Byron and Scott – and the ways in which their depiction of criminality is appropriated and transformed in the Indian context.

Schiller's *Die Räuber* and the Citizen Bandit

The intersection of criminality and the impulse to individual and communal self-realisation lies at the heart of a seminal text of European

Romanticism, Schiller's play *Die Räuber* (1781), which is echoed and transformed in British Romanticism, and thus forms part of the background to Romantic-influenced writers' representation of British India. The play appeared in translation as *The Robbers* in 1792, and this became the version best known in Britain, attracting much critical attention.[8] It was not directly imitated to any significant degree, mainly because it would have been subject to censorship in Britain.[9] Nonetheless, the play, and Schiller's work more generally, were popular and influential: Ewen suggests that it was known and used to differing extents by writers including Byron, Scott, Coleridge, Hazlitt, Wordsworth and Thomas Campbell.[10] Byron's character of Conrad in *The Corsair* has clear parallels with Karl Moor, though Byron did not directly encounter *Die Räuber* until 1814, when he worked on *Lara*.[11]

Apart from its stirring and sensational portrait of the robbers and their leader – which Coleridge found overwhelming, writing that Schiller was a 'Convulser of the Heart', and Moor a 'horrible Wielder of heart-withering Virtues'[12] – the play also brought to its British readers an exploration of a particularly contemporary dilemma: where should fall the limits of the patriarchal authority of a father over his sons; or, metaphorically, the authority and control of a state over its citizens. Franz and Karl Moor's individual rebellions against their father provide evidence of how this form of authority can legitimise despotism, and how its inevitable breakdown fosters the expression of inordinate and illegitimate personal ambition. The ending suggests the possible institution of new values of liberal citizenship: Karl Moor decides that he will sacrifice himself in search of 'atonement'. He achieves this by handing himself in to 'a wretch who labours by the day', so that the man, who supports 'eleven children', should have the reward for his capture – a suggestion that a sense of responsibility to others should take the place of grandiose ambition or desire. Moor's instruction to the robber band to 'Become ... good citizens!' is also relevant here, as is his meditation on his own case: 'Good citizen! And am not I too worthy of that name?'[13] These words suggest that he has become a leader who encourages values of community rather than those of individual gain.

This kind of ending was not available to the writers of British India, for two reasons. One is that the notion of citizenship had no currency there: the British colonial state controlled and protected its Indian subjects. Furthermore, the status and legitimacy of this colonial state was still in question across a large part of the territory of British India, so that the civil and military servants of the East India Company – who made up most of the writers of British India at this time – found themselves materially and by common purpose aligned with the project of sustaining rather than questioning its authority. While the works of these writers often deal with the fundamental tension between individual and state as expressed in *The Robbers*, they approach the bandit figure as mediated through two of the most influential writers of the British tradition, Byron and Scott.

Byron and Scott in India

In British India, as in Britain, both Byron and Scott were widely read and influential authors. Both are high on the list of the 'canonical eight' writers identified by William St Clair, who describes Scott as by far 'the most popular author of the romantic period and later … not only in Great Britain but in English-speaking communities elsewhere'; and notes that *The Lay of the Last Minstrel* inaugurated the long historical verse romance form with its publication in 1805. Byron's *Childe Harold's Pilgrimage* and the *Eastern Tales* sold in large numbers, while *Don Juan* was 'by far the biggest seller of any contemporary literary work during the romantic period' and continued to be read throughout the century.[14] As with Scott, Byron's work also was widely read across Europe, and both became what Diego Saglia has termed 'determining influences' on European Romantic writings on the Orient.[15]

Books and periodicals published in London were widely available to readers in Bengal from the 1820s onward, through lending libraries as well as booksellers.[16] Several studies place Scott and Byron as among the most widely owned and read of those metropolitan imports to British India.[17] Their works also formed part of the mental and cultural apparatus British writers brought to bear on India, inflecting the representations of India they produced. The evidence of this cultural baggage is visible in the most casual of references – Roberts's observation as she stands by the fort of Agra that 'Perhaps Lord Byron himself, when he stood upon the Bridge of Sighs, … scarcely experienced more overwhelming sensations than the humble writer of this paper, when gazing, for the first time, upon the golden crescent of the Moslems, blazing high in the fair blue heavens'; or Emily Eden's observation of the 'native horse' corps displaying their 'manner of fighting' for her benefit that 'Walter Scott would have made some fine chapters out of them' – as well as in the close attention paid to both by commentators such as David Lester Richardson.[18] While these metropolitan models largely shape the representations of India in the works of British writers, the ways in which they are negotiated or transformed illustrate how the writers' participation in or alignment with the colonial project inflects their response to India.

The Byronic Hero in India

Byron's work was an important model for many of the writers of British India. Apart from the many other specific responses to and transformations of Byronic texts evident in this literature, his influence is particularly apparent in works where an Indian protagonist is represented using the model of the criminal or deviant hero.[19] The figure generally termed the 'Byronic hero' – a charismatic, self-willed, solitary individual, both attractive and dangerous – has antecedents preceding Byron himself, and also appears in varying forms in the work of many other authors of the Romantic and Victorian periods and beyond.[20] Peter Thorslev's foundational account has the Byronic hero representing 'a rebellion which asserted the independence of the individual and the primacy of his values not only in the face of society, but even in the face of God'.[21] Byron's own version of this figure often takes the form of the 'noble outlaw' (in Thorslev's phrase), a man self-isolated from the wider society and living in defiance of its values, such as the protagonist of *Childe Harold*:

> But soon he knew himself the most unfit
> Of men to herd with Man; with whom he held
> Little in common; untaught to submit
> His thoughts to others, though his soul was quell'd
> In youth by his own thoughts; still uncompell'd,
> He would not yield dominion of his mind
> To spirits against whom his own rebell'd;
> Proud though in desolation; which could find
> A life within itself, to breathe without mankind.[22]

Other such figures include the protagonists of 'The Giaour', 'The Corsair', 'Lara' and 'The Bride of Abydos'. The bands of outlaws, rebels, or bandits who accompany some of these protagonists, such as Conrad's corsairs or the warlike Albanians encountered by Childe Harold, might also be considered to fall within this category, though they are given group identities rather than presented as fully realised individuals. The followers of Byron within British India translated the noble outlaws of his work into India as dacoit or bandit leaders, many of whom derive most immediately from the characters of Conrad in 'The Corsair' and the eponymous Giaour. The solipsistic, violent protagonists of poems such as 'The Decoit' by Henry Barkley Henderson and 'The Dacoit' by Samuel Sloper share recognisably Byronic characteristics.[23] In many cases, the poems are written in a format avowedly or implicitly derived from Byronic models.

These British Indian versions of the Byronic 'noble outlaw' are both like and unlike their originals for reasons mainly to do with the specific historical and political circumstances of the British experience of India. Against the background of social disorganisation described at the beginning of this chapter, it becomes apparent that there is no room in the literature of British India for the ambiguous dual figure of the criminal who is also a semi-legitimate rebel against an oppressive state authority, such as Conrad becomes in 'The Corsair'. This figure finds an echo in British India, but in a form that alienates him from the reader.

A comparison of 'The Corsair' with a text by Thomas Medwin, one of the writers of British India whose work is strongly influenced by Byron, shows how this alienation is achieved.[24] The opening lines of 'The Corsair' introduce the pirates and their lifestyle in strikingly positive and attractive fashion:

> O'er the glad waters of the dark blue sea,
> Our thoughts as boundless, and our souls as free,
> Far as the breeze can bear, the billows foam,
> Survey our empire, and behold our home!
> These are our realms, no limits to their sway –
> Our flag the sceptre all who meet obey.
> Ours the wild life in tumult still to range
> From toil to rest, and joy in every change.
> . . .
> Oh, who can tell, save he whose heart hath tried,
> And danced in triumph o'er the waters wide,
> The exulting sense – the pulse's maddening play,
> That thrills the wanderer of that trackless way?[25]

The text invites the reader to identify in imagination with the pirates, sharing in the excitement and the freedom of their 'wild life'. Despite the fleeting reference to their 'plunder'd wealth', the pirates, and Conrad their leader, are firmly established as at least partially sympathetic figures before any attempt is made to represent their violent and predatory behaviour. Even then, the account of 'groaning victims and wild cries for life', with Conrad himself a 'glutted tiger mangling in his lair!' is set against their impulse to 'spare the weaker prey' and save the women from the flames.[26]

In Medwin's 'The Pindarees', by contrast, Byron's image of the tiger strikes the keynote of the account, unleavened by any show of chivalric or generous behaviour on the part of the bandits. Rather, they are defined from the start through an emphasis on their self-centred urge to consume, and their inhumanity:

> [They] count their feats of outrage on the way,
> Like tigers dreaming o'er their mangled prey;
> These from their girdled waist drew forth a prize
> Of lettered gold to feast their comrades' eyes;
> Anklets, and armlets, those of women shewed;
> And some of infants, not unstained with blood.

The note to these lines adds the further detail that children's limbs were removed, the easier to take their jewellery. Rather than be inspired to join these bandits, the reader's natural response would be to hope for their defeat, which the text duly supplies: 'Their forces routed and their leader slain'.[27] The ambivalent, romanticised pirates of Byron's source text are reduced to one-dimensional, abhorrent figures.

A similar effect is evident in other transformations of Byron's works, where the 'anti-imperialist views'[28] expressed in poems such as *Childe Harold's Pilgrimage* are absent, or replaced by colonising voices, in the poetry of British India. A case in point concerns Childe Harold's encounter with Albania in Canto II. Several critics have argued convincingly that Byron's account of this episode, based on his own travels in the country, demonstrates his willingness to represent the fierce and wrathful Albanians as 'upholders of individual freedom against the threat of Imperial domination', and the land itself as a location for resistance to 'imperial or colonial' hegemony.[29] As Leask points out, the embedded war song of the Suliotes is particularly significant in this respect, as Byron chooses to avoid equating the Suliotes with criminals (as his travelling companion John Hobhouse did), but rather to focus on their military successes against opponents including French and Russian forces.[30]

Other texts adopt a variant strategy, imagining a colonised voice and presence while simultaneously disempowering it. 'The Decoit: A Fragment' is the product of another British army officer, Henry Barkley Henderson, a close and attentive reader of Byron. 'The Decoit' is preceded by an announcement that it was written 'almost immediately after perusing Lord Byron's Giaour', and an acknowledgement of the 'faint and humble attempts, here made, to imitate [Byron's] style'.[31] The product of these efforts is a very close imitation of Byron's work, from the turbulent hero to the fragmented narrative and the plot turning on the killing of a woman. The tortured anti-hero of the *Giaour* is transferred to an Indian setting and given the name of Omeer, the eponymous 'blood-stain'd, bold decoit' (82). Concealing the fact of his criminality, Omeer lures his beloved Ahmeera from 'country, friends and home, / With him in sin and love to roam' (87). This act proves his downfall: when Ahmeera decides he has been unfaithful to her, the 'slighted maid' seeks out the 'Sahib', or commander, of the armed forces, and gives away the secret of his location (92–3).[32] Omeer is defeated in battle and compelled to take 'shameful flight' (96). He then kills Ahmeera in revenge and surrenders to the Sahib as a prelude to suicide by poison: 'Fearless, unforc'd, myself have come / To ask for death – and meet my doom!' (100). The remainder of the poem reprises the Giaour's final confession to his Abbot: the bandit explains himself to a silent listener, and boasts of his power and pride.[33] He finally commits suicide by drinking poison, in a very Byronic conclusion of power and impotence and damnation combined:

> 'I told the Sahib, his threats were vain,
> E'en now the poison fires my brain;
> I drank as from a madding bowl,
> And ah! it parches up my soul:
> Tott'ring I stand o'er Hell's wide brink,
> No hand to save – I plunge! – I sink! –
> Hold, Hold!' – The murd'rer spake not more –
> He paus'd: for now the drug's fell pow'r,
> In fierce convulsions tore his frame,
> Till death in guilty horror came. (108–9)

Several aspects of 'The Decoit' are characteristic of this group of texts more generally. First, the structure of the work emphasises the power of the bandit, but also emphasises how that power is contained. He speaks at some length, his voice the only one so directly heard in the latter part of the text, and this verbal command of the scene contrasts with the passivity of the voiceless British commander. At the same time, the speaker is contained within a frame narrative; this distances him from the reader, and the narrative voice both places and defines him in the last lines, naming him a murderer and insisting on his guilt. At other times in the poem the reader is similarly discouraged from empathising too closely with Omeer, who is described as a fratricide and a killer of his friend (86–7). Despite his absence from the dialogue of the scene, the British sahib is in some ways a more powerful figure than Byron's Abbot: he acts as Omeer's 'confessor,' listening to his story, but he wields temporal as well as spiritual authority; he stands as the representative of the political and legal order of the British state in India that is stronger for Omeer's downfall. The overall effect is to represent the bandit as a dramatic, psychologically compelling figure, in many ways an intriguing protagonist, but one always contained by the authority of the colonial state.

Similar characteristics are visible in Samuel Sloper's narrative poem 'The Dacoit', which opens on a bandit's wife pining for her absent husband and goes on to describe his criminal life, his eventual defeat and death at the hands of British forces, and her consequent suicide. While the poem celebrates its bandit protagonist's courage and generosity, it falls short of representing him as a heroic or exemplary individual. The framing of the narrative, starting and finishing as it does on the account of the bandit's wife expressing her anguish at his absence and loss, focuses the reader's attention on the human and emotional cost of the bandit's self-centered actions. True heroism in the story is reserved for those who oppose him, the disciplined and gallant British officers and Indian troops who are together referred to as the 'soldiers bearing England's name'.[34]

Other such poems acknowledge the charismatic energy of the bandit figures and the freedom of their lives, but they also focus, like Medwin's work discussed above, on the impact of the bandits on their victims. James Hutchinson's 'The Pindarree' adopts as its model Byron's 'The Destruction of Sennacherib' and echoes its original in content as well as in form: the movement from the vigour of the opening lines to a final image of desolation is apparent in both works. In Hutchinson's poem, the agents of destruction are again Pindaris or raiders. The protagonist's dashing, picturesque strength is emphasised, as is the access to power represented by his 'long spear', and his prancing charger. Their freedom is apparent in the details of their clothing – 'Loose streams to the wind his white-flowing garb' – and their way of life, again reminiscent of Byron's corsairs: 'Their beds are the ground, and their curtains the sky.' By the end, however, the tone has changed, as the poem closes on the image of the ruined village they leave behind, its inhabitants gone:

> All roofless and black is their desolate home
> And their daughters dishonor'd are weeping in vain,
> Nor will glory in youth or in beauty again.[35]

For exile readers, that image of the 'desolate home', 'roofless and black', might be especially potent, making it unlikely that the poem could be read against the grain as a celebration of banditry without a determined and rather perverse effort.

The notable feature, then, of this set of textual transformations of the Byronic hero appears to be the absence of any Byronic sympathy or identification with colonised figures – any trace of what Murray Pittock calls 'fratriotism', or 'the adoption of colonized nations and cultures as a means of expressing reservations concerning the nature and development of empire, of seeing oneself in the other'.[36] Rather, these colonial incarnations of the Byronic hero tend to re-inscribe the boundaries between the colonising self and the colonial other, closing off avenues of identification between reader and colonial subject and resolving the ambiguous criminal / hero of Byron's works to become the criminal object of justice.

Transformations of the Rebel / Outlaw: from Scott to Prinsep

With poems such as *The Lady of the Lake*, and novels such as *Waverley* and *Rob Roy*, Walter Scott used the device of a charismatic male figure to dramatise historical conflict within Scotland, and the Scottish-dominated Jacobite risings of the eighteenth century. In *The Lady of the Lake*, Roderick Dhu embodies the swagger and energy ascribed by Scott to the Highland clans, as he resists submission to the authority of the state represented by King James. Opposed to his anti-authoritarian stance are Ellen Douglas, the object of his affections, and her father, together with Malcolm, Roderick's rival in love, all of whom represent the peaceful conformity to state authority that Roderick himself rejects.[37] While they are willing to accept the rule of King James, Roderick scorns it, telling Malcolm: 'Then mayst thou to James Stuart tell, / Roderick will keep the lake and fell, / Nor lackey, with his freeborn clan, / The pageant pomp of earthly man' (2: xxxv). The action of the poem sets Roderick against the disguised king, James Fitz-James. Before their combat, they are cast as equals:

> And the brave foemen, side by side,
> Lay peaceful down like brothers tried,
> And slept until the dawning beam
> Purpled the mountain and the stream. (4: xxxi)

Roderick rejects James's offer to 'grant [him] grace and favour free' (5: xiii) in return for allegiance, saying that he 'yields not ... to man nor Fate' (5: xiv). His eventual death, from wounds suffered in the ensuing combat, is a necessary contribution to the reconciliation between the different social groups, and the re-establishment of state control and the king's place at the head of the patriarchal order. As Roderick dies in his prison cell, listening to the minstrel's tale of revenge, the last act of the poem culminates with the newly undisguised King James V consolidating his power, pardoning Douglas who was once his enemy, and performing the symbolic marriage of Ellen and Malcolm (6: xxix).

The plot of *Waverley* involves a similar dynamic of social reconciliation brought about by the successful forging of affective relationships between individuals on both sides of the Jacobite / Hanoverian conflict.

The young Englishman Edward Waverley is, despite his Hanoverian father and role as an army officer, a figure who crosses boundaries, as his childhood with his Jacobite uncle and his later encounters with Jacobite Highlanders such as Fergus and Flora MacIvor awaken his sympathy for the Jacobite cause. As with *The Lady of the Lake*, however, the attractive and rebellious Highlanders are absent from the final reconciliation. Having been rejected by Flora, Edward Waverley marries Rose, a moderate Lowlander despite her Jacobite sympathies. Fergus is executed, steadfast to the last in his commitment to 'King James', and Flora travels to exile in France. Their absence at the end of the novel is also a spectral presence that unsettles the apparent stability of the marriage and the resolution. This becomes evident in the notably ironic passage at the conclusion of the novel, when the narrator draws the reader's attention to the painting in the dining room of Tully-Veolan:

> It was a large and animated painting, representing Fergus MacIvor and Waverley in their Highland dress, the scene a wild, rocky, and mountainous pass, down which the clan were descending in the background. It was taken from a spirited sketch, drawn while they were in Edinburgh by a young man of high genius, and had been painted on a full-length scale by an eminent London artist. Raeburn himself (whose 'Highland Chiefs' do all but walk out of the canvas) could not have done more justice to the subject; and the ardent, fiery, and impetuous character of the unfortunate Chief of Glennaquoich was finely contrasted with the contemplative, fanciful, and enthusiastic expression of his happier friend. Beside this painting hung the arms which Waverley had borne in the unfortunate civil war. The whole piece was generally admired.[38]

Saree Makdisi argues that this painting has a complex part in the novel, directing the reader's attention to the romantic history of the novel's main action rather than the compromised and modern present of its conclusion; while at the same time emphasising 'the artificiality of its reconstruction of the past', and thus becoming 'an allegorical restatement of *Waverley*'s own production of the past'.[39] The very complexity of the painting and its construction invites this kind of reading, suggesting that Scott may be disavowing the sentimental narrative of reconciliation by highlighting the mechanics of artistry (albeit painting rather than fiction); and also by leaving the reader with the final image of Fergus and Waverley rather than Waverley and Rose – a concrete memory of a brief moment of male camaraderie when the English soldier moved onto the territory of the Highland rebel / outlaw.

Scott's concept of the difference between a rebellious Highland Scotland and a pragmatic and orderly Britain translates effectively into the context of British India, where the opposition of Highland traditions and the 'settled prosperity' of Britain is replaced by that of Indian lawlessness versus the 'civilising mission' of the colonial project.[40] Augustus Prinsep's poem 'The Dakoit' takes on the iambic tetrameter form of *The Lady of the Lake*, and also Scott's trope of the clash of state authority and rebel insurrection, with a similar narrative device: the journey of a figure of state authority into a rebel stronghold. The narrator, an English soldier, moves alone through a wild landscape to an encounter with an Indian man who announces himself as Choramun the Dakoit. Choramun's first appearance, dramatically illuminated by torchlight, marks him as a figure of brooding danger to rival the 'grim Sir Roderick' of Scott's work:

> On one dark form the lustre fell
> Marking a cloudy brow too well,
> And gleaming on its turban fold
> The Stranger's Hindoo lineage told –
> Folded the arms and fixed the eye
> In some abstract soliloquy –
> The branch has snapt within my grasp –
> He starts! – the falchion in his clasp
> Cleaves the thin air one minute bright'ning
> Darkness with its reflected lightning –
> As fell the Torch's lurid glare
> Upon his face and savage air,
> Might marked the giant limb, and ire
> The eye that flung on me its fire.[41]

The figure bears comparison to Roderick Dhu, with his 'brow of gloom, / His shadowy plaid, and sable plume', and the 'blade of steel' which is his chosen weapon.[42] As well as delineating these physical attributes of the martial hero, Prinsep locates his bandit figure within a complex set of associations. The name recalls a figure from Indian history; the Jats of the Bharatpur region of Agra achieved a degree of autonomy from Mughal rule under their leader Churaman (the more common spelling) in the early eighteenth century. His personal history reflects a larger narrative of the decline of Indian power: in his 'old hall where Rajpoot kings / Sometime had held their banquetings' (345), Choramun tells the narrator of his beginnings as the 'lord of his own mountain land, / With liegemen ready at command' (346). These possessions, however, were lost in the redistribution of power in the aftermath of the Anglo-Maratha wars:

> What time the foiled Mahrattas fled
> Leaving a trail of plundered dead –
> But when the war and chace were ended
> And peace remunerated power

> With rich domains and treasured spoil
> Objects of that ambitious toil –
> Choramun's heart bled for the hour
> When Courts, of whom he held no lease
> Bartered his father's lands for Peace! (346)

Turning to the life of a bandit, he 'swore to live by fire and blood', and did so, gaining the notoriety of 'a Demon fame', until a British force was sent to 'crush the lawless gang at last' (347). In a showdown between them, the bandits are defeated. They escape, taking with them a kidnapped child of one of the troopers (348–9). This English boy, originally destined to be killed, was spared by Choramun, and thereafter regarded by him as his own child, his 'prey and now his pride' (351).

Despite the 'savage air' of Choramun, he does not consider himself to be simply a bandit: the dialogue of his first encounter with the narrator makes clear that the territory of the poem is disputed space, and that the narrator's claim to exercise a lawful authority there is disputed as well. Addressing the narrator as both 'Feringee!' (foreigner, European) and 'Foe!', Choramun prepared to defy him: 'not the Tiger in his den / Fears less the force of skulking men, / than I – Bring up the whole array, / In me thou'lt take no living prey!' (340). The narrator in response claims only the right of hospitality: 'I am a Traveller – lost – alone – / Dost thou the stranger's claim disown / Who seeks in peace thy desert lair?' (341). In this meeting of equals, Choramun is represented as reversing the coloniser's gaze of the earlier passages, first expressing a judgement on the British – 'Thy tribe have speech as fair / And feeble as their moonlike face' – and then on the narrator himself:

> I felt his eye
> Dart on my form its scrutiny,
> And as it rose from heel to brow
> Seeking each hidden nerve to know
> A smile of half contempt and scorn,
> As lightning's winter clouds adorn,
> Lit up his darkened features, when
> He saw me but as other men,
> Not of his own gigantic mould –
> *His* measure of the brave and bold! (341)

In a later interaction, the narrator re-asserts his authority, responding to Choramun's demand 'What art thou, man of the white race?' with a claim to racial dominance: 'my race is here / The Ruler' (342). This tension remains unresolved throughout the poem, as the contest recurs, involving legitimacy as well as power: Choramun boasts of his slaughter of 'your Sircar's oppressive brood / Of Peons'; while the narrator categorises him as 'That Robber of the Rajpoot race, / Who had been outlawed – feared – proclaimed' (342).

This emphasis on Choramun's Rajput heritage marks him out, in the context of the period, as a particular kind of bandit, an elite figure whose predatory behaviour is not always directed at amassing plunder for its own sake, but might be described also as a form of *bhumeawat*, aimed at gaining 'identity, status, and power'.[43] It is evident, also, that Choramun's sense of his own role as heir to the 'Rajpoot kings' in whose hall he dwells is shared by at least some of his compatriots, as the narrator's account of the campaign against him makes clear:

> To crush the lawless gang at last
> The British Hakim boldly passed
> O'er frowning ghaut and rugged waste,
> But there were those in every vale
> Who secret hoped the chase would fail. (347)

Like Fergus MacIvor, the dacoit thus occupies a dual role: outside the law, but possessed of stature and legitimacy in the eyes of his own community, and thus a threat to the authority of the state, rather than – or as well as – an individual predator.[44] As in Scott's version of the encounter with the rebel / bandit, rivalry is temporarily suspended while the intruder is taken in and offered hospitality: Choramun leads the narrator into the ruined hall, 'spread clean rice upon the floor – / And what he least resembled – most / Now was or seemed – the gentle host' (345). Past this point, however, Prinsep's work diverges from the pattern established by Scott. 'The Dakoit' sets up the interaction between coloniser and colonised, but takes their relationship no further. Instead, the remaining passages of the poem focus on the figure of the English boy, while the story of Choramun is hastily and opaquely concluded on the encounter where the narrator observes him in the role of embittered prisoner.

It becomes apparent at this point that Prinsep's version of the colonial landscape is radically simplified and polarised compared with that of Scott. This is true of the form of the text as well as its content: the British narrator / protagonist offers a single account of events, unlike the polyphonic narratives characteristic of Scott's work.[45] The Indian bandit is analogous to Scott's Highlanders, and the narrator ends the story as a Fitz-James-like figure of authority, although his brief period of equivocal sympathy with Choramun aligns him at that earlier point in the text more with Edward Waverley. The missing element in India is the Lowlanders or the moderate Jacobites – figures who can be deployed to bridge the gap between rebellious clans and state authority, in the symbolic marriage of Edward Waverley and Rose Bradwardine. In a parallel turn to romance, 'The Dakoit' supplies such an individual in the English boy who shares a racial identity with the narrator while being able to speak to the dacoit in his own language; but rather than becoming a reconciliatory element, his presence spurs the narrator to take action that has the effect of reversing the redemption that Choramun experienced, reinstating the colonial categorisation of the bandit as criminal. This is made obvious in the final passage of the text, as the narrator encounters Choramun once more, not in his own forest stronghold but on a prison island, where 'India's crimes and guilt's despair / Are crushed or expiated'. A prisoner in irons, at 'toils his crimes condemned him to', Choramun is powerless, subject to the lash of the convict guards and doomed to his own particular hell, as he turns on the narrator 'a scowl of scorn', mingled with 'fiercest, bitterest hate, / Such as on Satan's lips is borne / When man from flames bewails his fate' (352). It is true, of course, that 'The Dakoit' is a shorter and less complex narrative than *Waverley* (and the work of a less accomplished author), but that does not entirely account for the lacuna in the plot, and the abrupt movement from the meeting of equals in the forest to the spectacle of the outlaw criminalised and in chains at the end. This may be attributed instead to a need to resolve the threat to colonial authority in a way that does not simply defeat it, but also negates the fact of its existence.

The role of Scott's work as a model for Prinsep is not simply a function of the former's popularity, but may also draw on the longstanding English categorisation of Scots, and Highlanders in particular, alongside other 'savage' and 'primitive' peoples. This designation positions Scottish men as warlike and ferocious 'expendable troops' in Britain's cause, but also 'immature and unreliable'.[46] By the time of the Mutiny, this image has been modified: the 'Victorian period emphasized both the native qualities of the Celtic Scottish soldier ... and his new-found virtue as a Briton' – that is, courage.[47] Although the Highlanders of Scotland were compared to the 'martial races' of India throughout the period of British rule, the parallels between them clearly go only so far in the colonial mind.[48] The India imagined by Prinsep is a land to be conquered, not shared or won over. This becomes apparent in the landscape represented in 'The Dakoit', which is in some ways directly comparable to that of *Lady of the Lake*, as the protagonist's journey takes him deep into unfamiliar territory, where forest and mountains create a threatening backdrop to his journey. This landscape of India parallels that of Highland Scotland as what Makdisi calls 'a site of difference and otherness': the location for the cultural challenge to, but eventual re-establishment of, British political order.[49] The Indian landscape is more alien, and more threatening to the traveller, than the landscape of Scotland. The narrator hears not eaglets and owlets, as in Scott, but first a wood pigeon and then a tiger. He rouses a cheetah, in an encounter that prefigures that of the main action of the poem, as he faces it, a 'graceful monster couched in ire', and then shoots it: 'I've slain my fearful beauteous foe, / And I may stoop a fang to steal, / Proud trophy of unvaliant skill!' (335) – a bloody and triumphant version of the stag hunt that opens *Lady of the Lake*.

Pittock's reading of Scott emphasises his success in resolving the historical and ongoing tensions between Highland and Lowland Scots, Jacobites and Hanoverians, Scotland and England, by creating what he terms a 'union landscape', based on the material and cultural liminal space of the Border lands. '[Scott's] heroes too, are often psychologically borderers', Pittock argues, 'situated to some extent on both sides of a divide that has been closed by the end of the novel. The ability to cross social and political borders (Waverley, Morton, Latimer, Ivanhoe) is a presage of the disappearance of such borders altogether.'[50] In British India, by contrast, the border between coloniser and colonised is reinforced, rather than frayed or obscured, by Prinsep's account of the landscape of 'The Dakoit', and by the interaction between the protagonists. The ambiguously threatening, but also welcoming, space of the forest and the ruined hall is ultimately replaced by the unequivocally authoritarian space of the prison. The final reappearance of Choramun in this location is thus like that of Fergus MacIvor in the painting, in that he reminds the narrator of his own long-ago encounter with the colonised other, but also unlike: he is not a reminder of the masculine camaraderie of equals, but a reminder of inequality and colonial defeat.

The 'national tale' of India and the Colonial Child

Prinsep's use of the child to gesture towards, and then withdraw, the prospect of the bandit's rehabilitation is also in keeping with a larger trend whereby racial or cultural reconciliation is represented as elusive or unattainable compared to the social reconciliation achieved by marriage in Scott's work. A closer equivalence might be found in Byron's 'Oriental Tales', which, as Stuart Curran points out, end in solitary grief: 'in *The Giaour* the female is murdered, in *The Corsair* and *The Bride of Abydos* she dies of grief, and in *Lara* she is left to mourn'. Curran argues further that 'the only positive, life-sustaining element in these poems is the feminine bower. . . . But the bower is fragile, a sanctuary dependent on the masculine economy whether of sultan or pirate.

And no children are ever born there.'[51] Prinsep provides the dacoit's unlikely 'bower' with a child, albeit one not born there, but stolen; and the promise of redemption offered by his relationship to the dacoit comes to nothing when the child is taken back. In this respect, the poem also reflects the East India Company's policies with respect to orphan children born in India: the small number of those who were 'legitimate and wholly British' were repatriated to Britain, while others were educated and remained in India.[52] In a period when the presence of increasing numbers of white children on the fringes of British society in India was thought by an influential observer, Bishop Cotton of Calcutta, to constitute a threat to colonial authority, the impulse to reinstate distance between coloniser and colonised finds expression in Prinsep's work.[53]

'The Dakoit' lays a sentimental emphasis on the English boy's beguiling innocence, a trait apparent to both the British and the Indian man. As Choramun went to kill him, his mind was changed by hearing 'Of his own language a sweet word / From sweetest voice', and instead he 'reared the beauteous boy / And loved what he could not destroy!' (350). On the day of the narrator's incursion into the forest, a similar response is engendered in him, when the boy interrupts the charged standoff between the two men:

> A voice – a sweet and lisping breath
> Such as may wake a Christian's death –
> A voice – I held my ears to hear –
> 'Twas real – yes, 'twas true – 'twas near! –
> An infant's pleasant voice that came
> From that rude Tower and forest fence
> Like the sweet tones of innocence
> Out from the prison vaults of shame.

The narrator's response is telling: although his situation is 'no scene for woman tears', he says, he 'could not check / The dew that gathered o'er my eyes / With pity – gladness and surprise – / To hear that child so sweetly speak' (343).

The language of such passages of description constructs the boy, despite his gender, as a feminine presence in the text, a 'little angel form arrayed / In all its native beauty' (344). In this, and in the shared affective response of both men to him, he occupies a role in the narrative very close to that of the romantic heroine in Scott's work. Like the romantic heroine, he also becomes a prize to be won, a cause of further contest. The narrator considers himself 'that infant's brother, / For the same country was our mother' (350), and therefore resolves to take him back. At this point, the poem becomes opaque, as the narrator describes at length the importance of the boy to Choramun – his role as 'nursling' of his 'stubborn heart' – but recounts with the utmost brevity the outcome of the encounter: "'Twas hard from that stern savage root / To tear the fair exotic shoot – / From the lone sire, th'adopted son – 'Twas hard to win – but it was won' (351). There this section of the text ends, with no mention of precisely how Choramun was induced to part with the child (although the earlier shooting of the cheetah may provide an indication); and a lapse of 'a score of years' (351) ensues before the later encounter which concludes the narrative.

The pattern of the child as intermediary between coloniser and colonised, and the narrative failure to incorporate this figure into the generic form of the text, is repeated across other texts. In another of Prinsep's works, *The Baboo*, the intermediary child is the mixed-race son of Captain Henry Forester and Dilafroz, an Afghan woman whom he saves from English soldiers attacking her home: 'The English soldiers had penetrated the sacred barrier: they had dared to lay ruffian hands upon me; – but the English chief [Forester] ... was no foul polluter; he saved me from the unmanly grasp of his own men; he chased them from the sanctuary, and, with the generous valour of the truly brave, defended our timid maidens from the approach of further barbarians.'[54] Their 'sweet boy' (1. 148) is described as 'Forester's pride, and the object of much of his affection, notwithstanding that the usages of society, and the world, stamped him as illegitimate, and of inferior caste' (2. 235). Some years later, Forester finds himself hesitating between Dilafroz and the British woman Eva Eldridge. Dilafroz renounces him, goes on pilgrimage with her child, and he marries Eva. On Dilafroz's return after a long absence, the boy is to be 'sent to complete his education in England', so that he may be 'brought up as a sahib, instead of a nuwab' (2. 270). She insists on accompanying him, and the story concludes on the information that it 'required all the influence and authority of Forester ... to prevent her indulgence from effectually counteracting the efforts of his instructors, and defeating the purpose of his education' (2. 271). In this downbeat ending, the focus of the narrative rests on the ongoing struggle over literal or symbolic possession of the intermediary child, thus illustrating the authorial and social difficulties of incorporating such figures into the fabric of British India.[55]

This preoccupation with the colonial child also illustrates another respect in which the literature of British India diverges from its metropolitan counterparts. Katie Trumpener's analysis of the 'national tale' of the early nineteenth century identifies its focus on the 'contrast, attraction, and union of disparate cultural worlds', and notes the pattern whereby 'an English character ... travels to a British periphery, expected to be devoid of culture', but is brought to 'appreciate its cultural plenitude', and settles there, while the narrative ends with 'the traveler's marriage to his or her native guide'.[56] Transferring this idea to nineteenth-century India, it becomes apparent that the 'national tale' does not develop in the same way, because there is no 'nation' of India, but a colonial possession, and the separation required between coloniser and colonised is reflected in the fate of the unions between them. The eponymous heroine of Taylor's *Seeta* does not Indianise the Englishman Cyril Brandon; rather, she is Anglicised by him (see final chapter). The character of McIntosh Jellaludin, in Kipling's 'To Be Filed for Reference', does travel to the periphery of the empire, as the narrator finds him in the 'native quarters' on the edge of the 'Caravanserai'. There is no discovery of cultural treasures, however: the poetry and the classical allusions he refers to in his drunkenness are all from the Western tradition – Rossetti's 'Song of the Bower', Browning's 'Soliloquy of the Spanish Cloister', various ravings in 'Greek or German' – and the 'native woman' whom he calls his wife is not, according to him, 'civilised'. The product of his journey is the 'Book of Mother Maturin', a 'hopeless muddle', and also a reference to the unfinished novel of Kipling's early years that was never finished or published.[57]

Kipling's later novel *Kim* is in some ways a bringing to fruition of that project of representing peripheral Indian life that came to nothing in 'Mother Maturin'. Some material from the earlier text was incorporated in *Kim*, though to what extent is unknown.[58] While the abortive manuscript of 'Mother Maturin' concerned the daughter of an Irish woman sent to England for her education before returning to live in India, *Kim* offers a variation on this theme: the son of Irish parents, born in India, who travels the breadth of India with the lama, encountering a series of representative Indian characters, and coming to terms with his Western racial identity and affective ties to India through his dual achievement of defeating the Russian spies and protecting the lama on his quest for the river of salvation. It is tempting to suggest that this makes *Kim* a late version of a colonial 'national tale', but there is no 'education of the coloniser' involved: Kim is from his first appearance the 'friend of all the world', who has a seemingly miraculous ability to address people from diverse and widely separated ethnic backgrounds in their own languages. His formal education at school, and his informal education through his travels with Mahbub Ali and Hurree Babu, are directed towards making him a more effective spy, not educating him in the cultures of India.

Kim might also be regarded as in some ways a reprise of the narrative of 'The Dakoit' (albeit figuratively rather than literally, as there is no evidence that Kipling was aware of the earlier text). In both texts, a white child is discovered in the care of Indians, and becomes in a sense the object of competition between Indian and British parental figures, as he is 'rescued' from his Indian surroundings in response to what British characters regard as his essential white identity. The much-discussed turn to Buddhism at the end of the novel, where the lama's discovery of his river enables the production of narrative closure through spiritual union, regardless of Kim's unfinished *Bildungsroman*, has the effect of leaving unresolved Kim's dilemma at the point where he is no longer a child.[59] While the overriding theme of the novel is that of co-operation between British and Indians under an ultimately British control, compared to the theme of competition and coercion in 'The Dakoit', the difference between the texts is one of degree rather than substance: the child in both cases is a prize to be saved rather than a symbol of union.

These narratives of encounter with a bandit and recovery of a child signal a dynamic of simultaneous attraction and repulsion between coloniser and colonised, where a brief exploration of the possibility of a sympathetic engagement is quickly and decisively ended with the restoration of both parties to their original roles. The distance between them is indicative of the difficulty experienced by these colonial writers in imagining Indian agency, or envisaging Indian figures as comparable to the attractive or idealised Scots and Irish 'others' of the Romantic-era national tale. The limited nature of their vision becomes apparent when their work is contrasted with that of writers who combined an awareness of the colonial landscape of their own time with a turn to Indian history.

Notes

1. Recent scholarship has focused on this process as a precursor to the East India Company's preoccupation with thugs and other criminal communities during the Victorian period. See Singha, *Despotism*, pp. 176–9.
2. Sleeman, 'On the Spirit', pp. vi–vii.
3. Bayly, *Empire*, p. 174.
4. Rajput bandits (whose motivations were complex and included an element of rebellion against state authority), thugs (religiously motivated ritual murderers and robbers) and dacoits (violent robbers and murderers motivated by economic gain) were distinct categories in the typology of the colonial state, where the distinction between thugs and other criminals, in particular, came to be important in enabling legal action against them. There is extensive scholarship in this area: see Kasturi, *Embattled Identities*, pp. 200–28; Singha, *Despotism*, pp. 168–228; my 'Campaign'; among many other works.
5. See Majeed, 'Meadows Taylor's *Confessions*'; Reitz, *Detecting*, pp. 29–42; Tickell, *Terrorism*, among others.

6. Williams, 'Shadows', p. 488.
7. *Oriental Observer*, 12 June 1831, rpr. in Roberts, *Scenes and Characteristics*, vol. 1, p. 240.
8. Ewen, *Prestige*, pp. 13–15; Willoughby, 'English translations', pp. 297–9. Schiller's work underwent several changes in the course of its first production, including a scaling-back of the social criticism of the original script; and it appeared in several versions and translations in Britain from 1792 onwards (see Sharpe, 'Schiller', pp. 124–5; also Magill and Willoughby, *Schiller's Die Räuber*). The differences between the various editions are in some cases substantial, but they do not materially affect my argument regarding the influence of the text, and especially its charismatic protagonist Karl Moor, on later 'bandit' works.
9. Baker, 'Echo', p. 171.
10. See Ewen, *Prestige* (*passim*); see also Mortensen, 'Schiller', pp. 43–4.
11. Thorslev, *Byronic Hero*, pp. 75–6. The Byronic hero, and his literary antecedents including Schiller's Karl Moor, is discussed by McGann, 'Milton and Byron'.
12. Coleridge, *Collected Letters*, vol. 1, p. 122.
13. Schiller, *Robbers*, pp. 219–20.
14. St Clair, *Reading Nation*, pp. 632, 199, 333.
15. Saglia, 'Orientalism', pp. 471–2.
16. See Gibson, *Indian Angles*, pp. 108–16.
17. See Adams, 'Furnishing'. On Scott's popularity and importance in British India, see Trumpener, *Bardic Nationalism*, pp. 258–9; Scott's work also influenced the poetry of later Indian writers such as the Dutt family (Chaudhuri, *Gentlemen Poets*, p. 143). See also Ann Rigney's analysis of the ways in which Scott's work was 'both recollected and transformed' in successive editions, adaptations, translations and other media (*Afterlives*, p. 20).
18. Roberts, *Scenes and Characteristics*, vol. 2, p. 80; Eden, *Up the Country*, p. 72. See Richardson, *Literary Chit-Chat*; and see also his reprinting of poems by Scott and Byron in the *Calcutta Literary Gazette*.
19. See my essay 'Transformations'.
20. See McGann, *Byron and Romanticism*, pp. 19–35; Elfenbein, *Byron and the Victorians*, Stein, *Byronic Hero*.
21. Thorslev, *Byronic Hero*, p. 172.
22. Byron, *Selected Poems*, p. 418.
23. Both 'decoit' and 'dakoit' appear as alternative transliterations to the more usual 'dacoit' during the nineteenth century.
24. Leask suggests that Medwin's Indian poems might be considered 'mere pastiche versions of Byron's *Eastern Tales*, appropriating Byron's verse couplets as well as elements of character and narrative' ('Anglo-Indian Poetry', p. 66).
25. Byron, *Selected Poems*, pp. 250–1.
26. Byron, *Selected Poems*, pp. 271, 274, 275.
27. Medwin, *Sketches*, pp. 49, 84, 78. This view of the Pindaris is broadly in line with contemporary accounts: John Malcolm likens them to 'swarms of locusts' who 'destroyed and laid waste whatever province they visited' (*Memoir*, vol. 1, p. 428). Malhotra suggests that the poem's positive depiction of 'the military as the agents of law and order' in contrast to the

'savagely cruel and amoral' bandits reflects the 'increasingly militaristic attitudes' of the time (*Making British,* pp. 178–9).
28. Oliver, *Scott, Byron,* p. 135.
29. Oliver, *Scott, Byron,* pp. 142–3.
30. Leask, 'Byron and the Eastern Mediterranean', p. 119; Byron, *Selected Poems,* pp. 118–19.
31. Henderson, *Goorkha,* p. 80.
32. The term 'sahib' by the nineteenth century had come to indicate a British person in a position of authority; the poem describes this figure alternatively as the 'Captain'.
33. Byron, *Selected Poems,* pp. 207–8.
34. Sloper, *Dacoit,* p. 12.
35. Hutchinson, 'Pindaree', *Bengal Annual* (1834), pp. 198–9.
36. Pittock, *Scottish and Irish,* p. 29.
37. Scott, *Lady,* Canto 2: xxxii.
38. Scott, *Waverley,* vol. 3, p. 359. Later editions include a revised, but substantially equivalent, version of this passage.
39. Makdisi, *Romantic Imperialism,* pp. 96–7. The passage, like the novel itself, has been the subject of much critical discussion, which lies for the most part outside the scope of this study.
40. On Scott, see Pittock, *Poetry,* pp. 232–3; the idea of the 'civilizing mission' of Britain in India begins with Christian missionary efforts in the second half of the eighteenth century and draws strength from the Unitarian-inspired reform movement of the 1820s to the 1840s, but has currency throughout the nineteenth century: see Mann, 'Torchbearers'.
41. Prinsep, 'Dakoit', *Bengal Annual* (1831), p. 340.
42. Scott, *Lady,* Canto 2: xiv. There are also clear parallels with the Byronic hero's combination of contemplation and ruthless action – see, for instance, *The Giaour* ll. 235–48, where the protagonist is similarly observed being disturbed from a reverie by a sound, followed by the grasping of a blade (Byron, *Selected Poems,* p. 175).
43. Kasturi, *Embattled Identities,* p. 174. The origins and manifestations of Rajput banditry are complex, as Kasturi's analysis demonstrates: it was partly motivated by 'economic decline', but had other social and cultural components (p. 204).
44. Choramun clearly has much in common with the 'social bandit' described in Eric Hobsbawm's seminal work, although Hobsbawm himself suggested that the caste divisions within Hindu societies militated against the evolution of this figure (*Bandits,* p. 23); this is borne out by Kasturi's analysis (*Embattled Identities,* p. 204).
45. Joshi points out that Scott's work replaces the perspective of an omniscient narrator with those of 'different and differently motivated characters' (*In Another Country,* p. 156).
46. Pittock, *Celtic Identity,* pp. 25–8.
47. Pittock, *Celtic Identity,* p. 43.
48. See Tripodi, *Edge of Empire,* pp. 43–5.
49. Makdisi, *Romantic Imperialism,* p. 98.
50. Pittock, *Reception,* p. 4. See also Pittock's account of how 'Scott's

landscape . . . serves as a Unionist paradigm' ('Scott and the British tourist', p. 162).
51. Curran, *Poetic Form*, p. 143.
52. Hawes, *Poor Relations*, p. 24.
53. Arnold, 'European orphans', p. 110.
54. Prinsep, *Baboo*, vol. 1, p. 142.
55. The ending in this case is the product of an unintended collaboration between Augustus Prinsep and his elder brother Thoby, who finished and published the story after Augustus's death. See Prinsep, 'Three Generations', vol. 2, p. 164.
56. Trumpener, *Bardic Nationalism*, p. 141; this is apparent in *The Wild Irish Girl*, by Sydney Owenson, Lady Morgan (1806) and later novels on the same pattern. Trumpener distinguishes between the national tale, with its geographical movement between 'developmental stages', and the historical novel (as discussed by Georg Lukács), which traces the replacement of one stage by the next (p. 132); 'The Dakoit' falls into the former category (genre notwithstanding), as the narrator's spatial journey into Choramun's territory is also a movement into India's past.
57. Kipling mentions this work in 'To Be Filed for Reference', *Plain Tales*.
58. The writing and the MS versions of *Kim*, and the use Kipling made of 'Mother Maturin' are discussed by Lisa Lewis, 'The Manuscript of *Kim*' (Kipling Society, 2001). <http://www.kiplingsociety.co.uk/rg_lewiskim.htm> (last accessed 23 September 2014).
59. The Irishness, rather than Englishness, of Kim complicates this question to some degree, positioning him as 'in between' coloniser and colonised. See my Introduction, *Kim*, pp. 21–7; Wright, *Ireland, India*, p. 215. Nancy Paxton's analysis of the 'lost child' figure in novels of the late Victorian period focuses on *Kim*, among others (*Writing under the Raj*, pp. 170–8); her observation that these novelists 'imagined children who were temporarily assigned to that intolerable space where mixed-race children were forced to live' might also be applied to the English child of 'The Dakoit', and suggests that 'colonial fears about identity, sex, reproduction, and miscegenation' (p. 165) find expression through this figure in the literature of British India well before the re-emergence of the theme in the 1890s.

Chapter 6

Imagining India through *Annals and Antiquities of Rajast'han*

In looking to narratives drawn from Indian history and legend, British writers found a space – historically distant and/or geographically outside the zone of British direct control – where Indian self-determination could be imagined with less concern for its impact on the contemporary colonial project. One of the most important such resources for writers of the Victorian period was James Tod's *Annals and Antiquities of Rajast'han* (1829, 1832). *Rajasthan* (as I shall refer to it from now on) is one among several important nineteenth-century works on the history of the Indian subcontinent, but is unusually influential both in its own right and as a source text for later writers, both British and Indian.[1] This is partly owing to its subject matter: where Hinduism generally identified ritual purity as its core value and organising principle, Rajputs valued honour; their social organisation and defining narratives were therefore closer to those of contemporary Britain, already familiar with Romantic-influenced ideas of a Western chivalric history.[2] The narrative richness of *Rajasthan* and its colourful vision of India's past also contributed to its impact on British readers and writers.

Tod, an army officer, was first posted to Rajputana in 1805, and set about amassing manuscripts and other sources for the geography, history and folklore of the area.[3] At the outbreak of the third Anglo-Maratha war in 1817, his knowledge and experience proved to be 'of inappreciable value' in the British campaigns.[4] Following British victory over the Maratha confederacy, the princely states of Rajputana signed treaties which bound them to a role of 'subordinate co-operation with the British Government', the payment of revenue, and subjection to British control over their foreign relations.[5] Tod was appointed Agent to the Governor-General in the area then known as the 'Western Rajpoot' states, and remained in post until 1822. During this period, he continued research for *Rajasthan*, a work that had a defining influence on British perceptions, and representations, of the character and history of the people of these regions, and by extension of India more generally.

Rajasthan is a work of several strands, where accounts of the physical geography, history and genealogy of the Rajput states sit side by side with the author's personal narratives of travel and encounters with the area. Its sources include genealogical legends of the Rajput princes, bardic tales of martial heroism, local legends, Brahman temple records and records kept by the Jain communities; it was also shaped by Tod's reliance on the Jain cleric Gyanchandra.[6] It is an encyclopaedic project of accumulation and interpretation totalling over a thousand pages, which resists quick summary.[7] A consideration of the full range of its narratives, and their relationship to the original source material, is beyond the scope of this chapter. Instead, my analysis focuses on some representative examples of how Tod's circulation and framing of episodes in Rajput history were appropriated by later writers in order to develop a narrative of Indian self-determination.

Tod's depiction of the Rajputs is complex and in some respects contradictory, in ways that echo the author's multi-stranded relationship to India. The dedication (to King George IV) reflects his role as servant of the East India Company and by extension of the British state: he describes the 'Rajpoot princes' as 'happily rescued, by the triumph of the British arms, from the yoke of lawless oppression' – the Maratha confederacy – and now constituting 'the most remote tributaries of your Majesty's extensive empire'; but goes on to express the hope that 'this ancient and interesting race' might be restored to 'their former independence, which it would suit our wisest policy to grant'.[8] While this appears to be an example of anti-colonialist advocacy for a Rajput nation, it also operates as an argument for British intervention, Norbert Peabody argues: Tod 'delegitimated the contemporary Rajput polity as "degraded" or "fallen"', enabling the British role in India to be 'recast in a (potentially) paternalistic guise whose goal was to revivify a lapsed local nationality'.[9] In this respect, Tod's role as coloniser inevitably coloured his view of India.

On the other hand, one of the primary achievements of *Rajasthan* was to direct the attention of Tod's readers towards Rajput efforts at self-realisation, as a quest with which they might find themselves in sympathy. Writing of the 'struggles of a brave people for independence during a series of ages, sacrificing whatever was dear to them for the maintenance of the religion of their forefathers, and sturdily defending to death ... their rights and national liberty', Tod implicitly sought readers' agreement that this was 'a picture which it is difficult to contemplate without emotion' (1. xvii). His work also encouraged British readers to identify in other ways with his Rajput subjects. Part of his self-imposed task was to 'endeavour to prove the common origin of the martial tribes of Rajast'han and those of ancient Europe'; and to consider the evidence 'in favour of the existence of a feudal system in India, similar to that which prevailed in the early ages on the European continent' (1.xviii). The inspiration for this endeavour was Henry Hallam's *View of the State of Europe during the Middle Ages*, but Tod rejected Hallam's contention that feudalism was specific to England.[10] Instead, he developed a narrative that positioned Rajput society as parallel with an earlier version of British society, thus inviting readers to consider his Indian subjects as people, if not equivalent to themselves, then at least sharing some characteristics in common. The trajectory of Tod's career reflects the difficulty of accommodating this knowledge of and sympathy with the people of north India within a British colonial state which was growing in power and adopting an increasingly Anglicist approach, stressing reform or Westernisation as goals. In 1822 Tod's responsibilities were curtailed by the colonial government, leading to his eventual resignation; as Freitag suggests, one factor in this may have been his 'reputation for favouring' Rajput rulers.[11]

This contradiction at the heart of Tod's concept of the Rajput nation is visible throughout *Rajasthan*. The emphasis on the feudal structure of Rajput society, and Rajputs' adherence to values of loyalty and martial strength, also has the indirect effect of constituting them as less evolved societies than those of Europe, thus making them easily containable within a larger narrative of Indian subordination and loyalty to a British colonial state.[12] In this discourse, the heroic past of Rajput kingdoms is framed within an overarching narrative of Indian degeneracy that legitimises contemporary British rule. Tod's introduction to *Rajasthan* refers to the Rajputs' 'eight centuries of galling subjection to conquerors totally ignorant of the classical language of the Hindus' (1. ix), and distinguishes between the dynasties that are the subject of his work and the present-day ruling families of Rajputana, who 'owed their present establishments to the progress of the Moslem arms' (1. xvi). By denying these elite groups the 'legitimacy' of long descent, and positioning them instead as a by-product of the Muslim conquest, Tod's narrative avoids representing the British as interlopers on a Rajput sovereignty.

Even while *Rajasthan* creates equivalences between the history of Europe and that of India, Tod's manoeuvre of relegating Rajput national glories to the past is thus a constant dynamic. The comparison with Greece offers a clear sense of Tod's thinking on this issue: referring to the rise of Akber, whom he refers to as 'the first successful conqueror of Rajpoot independence' (1. 324),[13] he describes the lasting and catastrophic effect of his victory on the Rajput people:

> unhappily for Rajast'han, a prince was then rearing, who forged fetters for the Hindu race which enthralled them for ages; and though the corroding hand of time left but their fragments, yet even now, though emancipated, they bear the indelible marks of the manacle; not like the galley slave's physical and exterior, but deep mental scars, never to be effaced. Can a nation which has run its long career of glory be regenerated? Can the soul of the Greek or the Rajpoot be reanimated with the spark divine which defended the kangras [battlements] of Cheetore or the pass of Thermopylae? Let history answer the question. (1. 319–20)

These narrative strategies demonstrate that, despite his sympathetic engagement with his subject, Tod is not describing a culture in which he participates or with which he recognises common identity. His account is compiled from the vantage point of a British colonial administrator, for whom the trajectory of Rajput decay is an enabling part of an implicit justification of British domination in India. If the 'idea of epic', as Herbert Tucker puts it, is to 'tell a sponsoring culture its own story', then Tod's narrative, though it successfully articulates a distinct identity and a set of heroic values for the Rajput peoples, is never just about India: the 'sponsoring culture' is that of the expansionist East India Company's colonial state.[14]

To focus solely on these instrumental uses of Tod's work as colonial historiography is to overlook the impact of its literary quality. It is not simply or even at all a work of history – the introduction asserts that it is rather 'a copious collection of materials for the future historian'. It is dense and inaccessible, with the author being 'less concerned at the idea of giving too much, than at the apprehension of suppressing what might possibly be useful' (1. xix). Readers faced with this mass of aggregate, complex material fell back on narrative, and focused on individual tropes and stories that in their turn made their way into British writing influenced by Tod. The dramatic and engaging stories Tod collected, and his technique of recounting them on an epic scale, have a momentum of their own, so that the briefly delineated lives and desires of individuals derive their significance from their role in the larger narratives of the Rajput peoples. Successive, repetitive accounts of individual heroism and self-sacrifice for causes greater than the self – the community, the nation, family honour – are picked up and used by later writers, both evidencing their impact on these individual readers and setting in motion the process by which the tropes of Tod's vision were popularised and circulated to become part of a wider representation of India.

Tod's Vision of a Rajput Nation

Though *Rajasthan* covers several Rajput states, the section dealing with Mewar, where Tod was stationed as agent from 1818 to 1822, stands first in the book, and provides the source material for most of the adaptations discussed in the latter part of this chapter and the next. Tod's work draws largely on sources from this state, and, as Cynthia Talbot suggests, the book reflects something of the Mewar ruling family's pride in its own history.[15] The Guhilot and Sisodia ruling dynasties of Mewar could claim the prestige of great age, and a record of valorous resistance to Muslim invasion, both reflected in *Rajasthan*.[16] At the period of Tod's arrival, however, the state had fallen into the sphere of influence of the Marathas, and the Rana eventually turned to the Company's government for aid against them. 'To such a pass had the demoralization proceeded', according to a later historian of the nineteenth century, 'that it was evident that Meywar [sic] would have perished in a few years, had not the British Government stepped in to preserve, and raise from the dust, a State, that had undergone so many vicissitudes, and whose Princes and Nobles had given proof, through a long series of ages, of so great heroism and endurance.'[17] Tod's work offers a series of iterations of this trope of Rajput heroism, endurance, and ultimate inability to sustain their own polities, through a narrative of successive episodes where the city of Chitor (the historical capital of the state) came under attack.[18]

The account of the sack of Cheetore (Chitor) in 1303 by the Sultan of Delhi Alla-o-din (Alauddin Khalji), motivated by his desire for the Rajput princess Pudmani (Padmini), indicates some of Tod's envisioned characteristics of the Rajput people.[19] As the Rana watches over his besieged city, the guardian goddess of Cheetore appears to him, demanding tribute: 'I must have regal victims; and if twelve who wear the diadem bleed not for Cheetore, the land will pass from the line.' Eleven of the Rana's twelve sons are sacrificed in turn. The final son obeys his father's command to flee the city, and reaches safety; the Rana himself, 'satisfied that his line was not extinct', now leads a sortie from the city, and the remaining defenders 'with a reckless despair carried death, or met it, in the crowded ranks of Alla'. Before this, 'another awful sacrifice' takes place: 'that horrible rite, the *Johur*, where the females are immolated to preserve them from pollution or captivity':

> The funeral pyre was lighted within the 'great subterranean retreat', in chambers impervious to the light of day, and the defenders of Cheetore beheld in procession the queens, their own wives and daughters, to the number of

several thousands.[20] The fair Pudmani closed the throng, which was augmented by whatever of female beauty or youth could be tainted by Tatar lust. They were conveyed to the cavern, and the opening closed upon them, leaving them to find security from dishonour in the devouring element.

Following these events, Alauddin takes 'possession of an inanimate capital, strewed with brave defenders, the smoke yet issuing from the recesses where lay consumed the once fair object of his desire' (1. 265–6).

The elevated language of the passage, its deployment of an unproblematic narrative of conflict between well-defined opponents, and the use of elite individuals to embody social values and norms all contribute to its effectiveness as a striking illustration of Rajput character. The strongly gendered nature of the protagonists, split between warring men and self-sacrificing women, delineates the borders of gender roles in Rajput society. It also hints at points of correspondence between that society and a Victorian British middle class shaped by the ideological construction of 'separate spheres' for men and women (though here – unusually in Tod's narratives – the Rana's sons are shown to die in a sacrificial rite rather than in combat, a role more commonly associated with women).[21] The reader's sympathy and admiration is invoked in the account of both male and female characters' demonstrated willingness to seek death in the cause of Rajput honour and the defence of the city. A strong claim to mastery of colonial knowledge is made through Tod's demonstration of his own command of his material, both historical – 'The annals state [this episode] to have been in S. 1346 (AD 1290), but Ferishta gives a date thirteen years later' – and also from personal experience: the local guides 'still pretend to point out his trenches; but so many have been formed by subsequent attacks that we cannot credit the assertion' (1. 264).[22] Finally, the narrative arc of heroic resistance and sacrifice leading to the final image of the city in ruins replicates in miniature *Rajasthan*'s core narrative of a Rajput fall from power. While the story of Chitor is central to the history and identity of Mewar state, it thus becomes also a key element of a British narrative of Indian decay.

There was a gap of forty-odd years between the first publication of *Rajasthan*, and the next edition of the text, published in 1873.[23] During this time, the tropes and patterns Tod derived from Indian history were to have a lasting impact on other writers, both directly and by the process of dissemination which saw Roberts's appropriation of episodes from *Rajasthan*, for instance, become a source in turn for her friend Laetitia Landon (see below).

Several writers produced versions of heroic Rajput masculinity that reflect Tod's work. Vincent Tregear's short poem 'The Ancient Rajpoot' succinctly delineates the salient characteristics of Rajput men as they are developed throughout *Rajasthan*:

> His was no heart, I ween, to brook
> Or haughty word, or scornful look;
> But like the snake whose venom'd head
> Is raised in rage at lightest tread,
> His quick revenge fell sure and deep
> On him who raised it from its sleep.[24]

The subject is endowed with the martial traits of pride and combativeness, and also presented as a dangerous enemy. The word 'ancient' in the title serves a familiar dual purpose: it carries the prestige and status of long history, but also locates its subject in the past, echoing Tod's strategy of setting the grandeur of previous Rajput kingdoms against their contemporary counterparts and their 'indelible marks' of subordination.

Other such representations of valorous, though compromised, Rajput heroes include

J. Muir's poem 'The Heroism of Koonbha', which develops this characterisation of both the protagonist Koonbha, and his followers, as the men seek 'their wives, and babes from wrong to shield; / They would not weakly fly, or tamely yield'. The poem describes an incident in the course of a long-ago battle between Rajput and Afghan forces, which pits the 'fierce and high-soul'd valour of Ajmeer' (one of the Rajput states) against the 'art, and fraud, and crooked wile' of the Afghans:

> One heart, one soul, linked all the Rajpoot host, –
> Honour their idol, – loyalty their boast.
> No lukewarm soul sought parley with the foe,
> Too strong their hate – too warm their patriot glow.

Inspired by such qualities, the poem invites the British reader to enter into the nationalistic feeling with the Rajput men: 'Let him whose heart can nurse the Patriot's flame / Revere and cherish Thakoor Koonbha's name.'[25]

The conflict between Rajputs and Muslims is raised again as the occasion for Rajput heroism in Tregear's longer prose narrative, 'The Rajpoot Chieftain', which divides the hero's role in two. In an Afghan-ruled state where Rajputs are on the brink of armed insurgence, Mahabul Singh, a Rajput 't'hakoor', or chief, stages a rebellion, demonstrating both great physical strength and martial determination:

> He was bare-headed, and a slight stream of blood flowed from his broad forehead. He stood with his left foot advanced, his broad shield pressed

close to his breast, and his right arm, which held his bloody sword, was thrown backwards, his hand being on a level with his waist. His countenance expressed cool determined courage, and two bodies at his feet, told how well he had wielded his blade.[26]

Refusing to yield, he adds to the deaths of his enemies the further killing of his own daughter, on discovering that she has been 'dishonoured' by her attackers. This climactic killing of Mahabul Singh's daughter, and other Hindu women, is an act familiar from *Rajasthan*: the man willing to send his sons to their death, and sacrifice his 'dishonoured' daughter, and the other women who sacrifice themselves to save themselves – and thereby their families – from dishonour, are all foreshadowed in episodes such as the sack of Chitor. The landscape of the narrative is changed, however, by the presence of another Rajput leader, Doorga Singh, who is willing to negotiate with the Afghans, and by the depiction of the Afghan ruler himself as an enlightened invader / overlord, who looks forward to an end to conflict, saying 'I am sick of this blood, and would have it stopped . . . every groan is like an arrow in my heart' (210). These elements encode a narrative of the 'colonised' (though the term may not be applicable in its literal sense to the Rajputs of the story) coming to terms with their situation, and with the coloniser. While Doorga Singh's wife takes on the traditional role of seeing him off to the 'battle field' at the start of the action (208), she and his sister both share in the peace his actions of reconciliation, as well as bravery, have brought about in the end. The contrast with the dead of Mahabul Singh's family, and his daughter who has fallen victim to both her enemy and her father, is instructive: this is a Rajput warrior class represented as capable of living in peace under the rule of an outside force. Like Tod before him, Tregear constructs a narrative which glorifies Rajput chivalry, but makes it secondary in the end to the realpolitik of colonial rule.

Female Agency and Sacrifice

While the historiography of Rajputana thus provided British writers from Tod onwards with an image of Indian masculinity that was neither the 'mild Hindoo' nor the criminal bandit, it offered equally transformative possibilities for the representation of Indian women. This is a topic central to the project of colonialism throughout the nineteenth century, underpinned by the view, succinctly expressed by James Mill, that the 'condition of the women' is an indicator of a society's level of 'civilisation'.[27] The stereotypical version of Indian femininity in the first decades of the century was shaped by the prevailing British interest in the rite of *sati*, or widow-burning; and also by the tendency to pair the figure of the predatory bandit (in texts such as those discussed in the previous chapter) with the pitiable figure of his female victim. This is evident in the parallels between narratives of banditry and many *sati* texts, where the division of Indian characters into male figures of predatory masculinity and weak, helpless female figures is common to both. D. L. Richardson's sonnet 'The Suttee', for example, contrasts the 'ruthless throng' who prepare the funeral pyre and the 'exulting cry' of the priest to the 'failing martyr's pleading voice' of the woman who is burning.[28] The extent to which the *sati* rescue and the rescue from bandits become interchangeable is demonstrated in the work of Medwin: in 'The Pindarees', the hero Oswald saves Seta from 'the ruthless ... power' of Zalim the bandit; while another version of the same story published as 'Julian and Gizele' has the heroine saved from the 'crackling flames' of the pyre which awaits her performance of *sati*.[29]

Representations of *sati*, like those of banditry, thus become the occasion for appeals for British intervention. These are sometimes as explicit as the admonition of the missionary William Ward – 'But shall these fires never be put out? Shall these graves still devour the helpless widow? Forbid it, British power! Forbid it, British humanity!' – but sometimes implicit, as in the trope of '*sati* rescue'. Here a widow is saved from her fate by the actions of a British observer, in the manner ascribed to Job Charnock: 'struck by the charms of a young Hindoo female about to be sacrificed for the eternal welfare of her husband', he orders his guards to rescue her. 'They obeyed, and conveying the widow, who happened to be exceedingly beautiful, and not more than fifteen years old, to his house, he took her under his protection, and an attachment thus hastily formed lasted until the time of her death, many years afterwards.'[30]

The trope uniting these narratives of *sati*, and the narratives of banditry discussed above, is the framing of Indian agency as criminal – in the case of predatory masculinity – or absent, in the case of helpless femininity; in both cases, the result is to negate or suppress the possibility of Indian self-determination, and represent British intervention as required to save India from itself. *Sati* and other forms of female self-sacrifice such as the '*Johur*', or *jauhar* (mass immolation of women), associated by Tod with episodes such as Alauddin's attack on Chitor are central to Rajput mythology and identity as these are represented in *Rajasthan*.[31]

In these episodes, Tod takes the figure of the self-sacrificing Indian woman beyond the *sati* debate, and locates it within the context of the culture and society of the Rajput states, both making it integral to Rajput identity and valorising the act of female self-annihilation. In the story of Alauddin's pursuit of Padmini, for instance, Padmini leads her contingent of women into death, rather than being the passive object of destruction by others. The framing of agency in terms of self-sacrifice is clearly problematic: even where physical or emotional coercion of the woman is not an issue, her decision to sacrifice herself is taken in the context of a society where gender inequality limits the available options. The discourse on female self-sacrifice evolves within a set of colonial interactions which, as Spivak's influential argument suggests, have the effect of further depriving of subjectivity the already disadvantaged female subaltern, who is 'more deeply in shadow'.[32] Nevertheless, the concept of willing female self-sacrifice clearly struck a chord with Tod, and with those later writers who looked to his work for their source material, in ways which demonstrate how British concepts of gender roles and identities interacted with colonial representations of India. These interactions are the subject matter of the remainder of this chapter.

By contrast with Tregear's depiction of masculine Rajput strength in 'The Ancient Rajpoot', the subject of his companion poem, 'The Rajpootin', is characterised by her traits of 'mild' and 'gentle' femininity – 'young' in this case suggesting a childlike quality:

> Her form so fair, her look so mild,
> That as she pass'd the ring-dove's nest,
> The gentle bird, to others wild,
> Left not the branch its bosom prest.
> The bounding deer ne'er thought of flight,
> But, where she came, stood still to gaze,
> And met her young eyes, softly bright,
> As calmly as the pale moon's rays.[33]

Unlike her male counterpart, she does not resist becoming the object of the gaze, but accepts it, so innocuous as to be regarded without fear by even the most vulnerable of forest creatures. Her demeanour suggests that she is harmless, and indeed this aspect of her depiction is in keeping with the representation of the helpless *sati* victim who appears many times over in the literature of the nineteenth century.[34] Her association with stillness is deceptive, however. The Rajput woman in Tod's work, and in those texts derived from it, has agency, albeit of a limited and problematic kind. She has the ability to sacrifice herself, and thereby to shape the course of events for her family and wider society; above all, she is an active and desiring subject, not the object of colonial rescue or pity.

Returning to Tod's narratives of the city of Chitor, an instance of such female agency is visible in Roberts's poem 'The Rakhi'. This draws on Tod's work for the custom of a woman giving a man a *rakhi*, or bracelet, which gives him the status of her 'adopted brother' and obliges him to come to her aid should she require it. The woman is this case is the regent Karnavati, who calls on Humayun to come to the aid of Chitor as the city is attacked by Bahadur Shah of Gujarat. Tod's narrative confines itself to a brief account of the fate of the city:

> Combustibles were quickly heaped up in reservoirs and magazines excavated in the rock, under which gunpowder was strewed. Kurnavati, mother of the prince ... led the procession of willing victims to their doom, and thirteen thousand females were thus swept at once from the record of life. The gates were thrown open, and the Deola chief, at the head of the survivors, with a blind and impotent despair, rushed on his fate.

Hemayoon initially responds to the summons of the *rakhi*, but 'instead of following up the spoil-encumbered foe, he commenced a pedantic war of words with Buhadoor, punning on the word "Cheetore"'.[35]

Taking this unedifying account of female sacrifice and male lack of focus, Roberts re-inflects the narrative. Her summary, given in a footnote, has the woman's summons result in instant action: 'In the desperate extremity to which Cheetore was reduced in 1589, the Princess Kurnivati reminded Hemayoon, the son of Baber, and father of Acbar, of his engagement. He quitted his conquests in Bengal, and flew to the rescue of the devoted city.'[36] (The historical figure of Humayun was less prompt in taking action: his reluctance to help the ruling family of Chitor against Bahadur Shah was probably caused by unwillingness to 'aid an unbeliever against an enemy of his own faith'.[37]) As the poem recounts, Hemayoon's actions are in vain:

> He came to the beleaguered walls too late,
> Vain was the splendid sacrifice to save;
> Famine and death were sitting at the gate,
> The flower of Rajasthan had found a grave.
>
> Its warriors perished bravely on the sword,
> Nor stood the feebler sex appalled the while;
> They the dark channel of the tomb explored,
> By the bright blaze of many a funeral pile. (127–8)

Though the actions of both Kurnivati and Hemayoon ultimately result in heroic failure, Roberts's work has the effect of developing a narrative of female agency that is not focused on individual feeling but on acting on behalf of and to the benefit of the larger community – in this case the city of Chitor. Kurnivati does not subsume herself in devotion to a man, but acts, and calls on him to act, in pursuit of her own agenda, seeking her own death only when that project has failed. Spivak points out 'the profound irony in locating the woman's free will in self-immolation',[38] but nonetheless the distinction between seeing the widow as one who willed her own death, and seeing her as a victim to be rescued, is a significant one: the first offers subjectivity and agency, while the second makes her the object of action by others. This is, as Rajan notes, a 'paralysing' dilemma for (as she puts it) a 'concerned feminist analyst'[39] – the phrase describes Roberts well, and may account for her resolution of the dilemma in the image of a sacrificial ending shared by both male and female partners in action.

Another version of the same story, by Laetitia Landon, similarly engages in an appropriation of Tod's work (this time via Roberts) to develop a narrative of female agency, but also foregrounds the interaction of British metropolitan models of femininity – the basic topic of much of Landon's work – with those offered in *Rajasthan*. Landon's poem 'The Raki' focuses on the princess's keeping vigil under siege as she waits for her 'bracelet-bound brother' to return and rescue her and the other women of the city. When he does so, it is too late, as she has already led the women into the cavern of death, and set fire to the funeral pyre. Landon emphasises both Karnavati's lonely wait for her male rescuer, and also her physical appearance: 'Pale and resolved, her noble brow was worthy of a race / Whose proud blood flowed in those blue veins unconscious of disgrace.'[40] She becomes another in a long series of Landon's yearning female protagonists whose role is to enable the author to explore the state of mind of women in relation to and dependent on men.[41] Roberts, on the other hand, does not dwell on Karnavati's appearance or her motivation at this point at all, but sets her in a role of leadership 'at the head of thirteen thousand females' who die together.[42]

Other writers adapting Tod's representation of the Rajput character also developed their narratives in response to the models of gender, and the constraints on femininity, found within British culture. Marianne Postans's *Facts and Fictions, Illustrative of Oriental Character* includes several narratives sourced or adapted from *Rajasthan*, although they are unconvincingly claimed by the author as 'circumstances which fell either under my own observation, or that of friends'.[43] The stories reflect her sense that the 'reading public' of Britain were 'totally uninterested in India' (1. vii), and exhibited 'a very ill-concealed lack of sympathy ... towards the people of the East' (1. viii); they offer sensational accounts of love and death clearly designed to overcome this British indifference, and thus may be considered to be devised with particular attention to British metropolitan norms and expectations.

One such account concerns the life of Jeswunt Sing, Raja of Marwar; its basic plot elements are taken from *Rajasthan* (2. 47–57), and its depiction of Rajput femininity responds to Tod's representation of the nature of Rajput women. In the course of enmity between Jeswunt and the Muslim emperor Arungzéb, the latter summons Jeswunt's son Pirthi Sing to his court, and there receives him warmly. Pirthi Sing is given 'a splendid dress, which, as customary, he put on, and, having made his obeisance, left the presence in the certain assurance of exaltation' (2. 52). Soon afterwards he is taken ill, and 'expired in great torture, and to this hour his death is attributed to the poisoned robe of honour presented by the king' (2. 53).

Postans's version, entitled 'The Rajpoot Bride: A Tale of the Nerbudda', transfers this death to Jeswunt himself, and casts as the perpetrator his queen, Vassanti. The latter figure is represented as a focal point for a wider Rajput identity: 'My father and my husband, murdered by thy hand, my fortress and my faithful friends within thy grasp, one only course remained worthy of a Rajpoot woman' (3. 204). Having watched Jeswunt 'writhing' in the poisoned robe, she turns from his death scene to her own fate: 'Animated by the heroic spirit of her race, she springs from the sculptured parapet, and the deep waters of the sparkling stream receive her fair and unpolluted form, faithful in death to all she loved whilst living' (3. 205). The coda to the story describes a sculpture of the 'monumental symbols used by the Rajpoot people: a warrior mounted, and fully armed; a female hand telling of self-destruction, and an open book, denoting the priestly office' (3. 205). These are explicated as 'wisdom, bravery, and love' – with 'love', by a process of elimination, assigned to the self-destroying female. While this idea of female self-sacrifice as the defining element of Rajput identity is pervasive within *Rajasthan*, Postans's story associates it specifically with companionate love. This element is set at centre stage, over-writing Tod's depiction of the episode as primarily a contest between men and replacing it with an instance of doomed love where the female protagonist's devotion and self-sacrifice is directed towards her family and clan, and to the fulfilment of her identity as a 'Rajpoot woman'.[44] By relocating the story to the private sphere and the realm of the feminine – strongly (though not invariably) associated with feeling, moral virtue and the economic and emotional dependence of women on men – Postans also makes the Rajput woman's self-sacrificial action a personal response to loss and abandonment. In so doing, she evokes the British 'sympathy' for oriental character that her work seeks to bring about, but also diminishes the female agency on which her story depends, re-casting it as an expression of personal despair.

There is also some disquiet evident in these texts about the representation of Indian women and the ways in which they can be seen to parallel or contrast with the roles available to British women. 'The Rajpootni', by Anna Maria Mowatt, is set at the interface between metropole and colony, in the British community in India, where the reader is invited to 'my snug library, with its bright fire, and tempting books – my circle of dear "familiar faces", and last, not least, my Indian garden, filled with English flowers!'[45]

There ensues in this location a conversation between a figure introduced as 'our kind and amusing friend Colonel —', and 'the pretty and lively Fanny, who in spite of being in India, looked so happy, and so English'. She says that she is 'so glad, that I am not a native lady', as 'I do so love to talk, and to hear others talk, and to be treated like a rational being, and give or change my opinions as I like. I could never submit to spend day after day, shut up in a zenana.' The Colonel tells her she is 'quite wrong' in 'thinking so ill of Eve's dark daughters', alludes to the 'respect, the happiness, the freedom, enjoyed by the Rajpoot women' and maintains that the 'influence of the fair Rajpootni, over the prowess of every Rajpoot cavalier, and their power over their husbands, are facts proved by many beautiful anecdotes' (373–5).

The particular anecdote on which the Colonel, or rather the author, chooses to dwell in some detail is one where the 'Rajpootni' does not exercise indirect influence over her husband or 'cavalier', but rather acts directly and on her own account. Mowatt's story of the Queen of Ganore is a close paraphrase, and sometimes a direct copy, of Tod's original: having defended five fortresses against her enemy, the khan, the queen is trapped in her last remaining stronghold, which is then captured. He finds her beauty as alluring as her territory, and demands that she marry him (376).[46] She agrees to do so, and sends him a set of garments and jewels to be worn for the occasion. These turn out to be poisoned: as he dies 'in extreme torture', she tells him that 'you left me no other expedient to escape dishonor', and springs from the battlement to drown 'in the flood beneath' (378). Although Mowatt's story for the most part follows Tod's original with minimal alterations, there is one significant difference between them. The queen's entrance, a prelude to the wedding rite, is described by Tod briefly, through the eyes of the khan: he 'found that fame had not done justice to her charms' (1. 625). Mowatt's version expands this phrase to an entire passage, detailing every aspect of the queen's appearance:

> Though scarcely above the common height, she had the appearance of being much taller; and there was a majesty in the turn of her head, the slope of the shoulder, the breadth of her brow, which showed, she was a queen of Nature's own making. Her long lashes, and exquisitely pencilled brow, gave an additional eloquence to her full black eyes; and her profile, which in a

fine countenance is always so striking and impressive, was purely Grecian: her hair, of the most luxuriant and deepest black, was simply braided over her forehead, reminding the beholder of the highest order of classical beauty; while the upper lip, short and curved, covered the most dazzling teeth, and the full dewy under lip completed her noble and still strictly feminine face. Her throat and bust, were of the justest proportions, and her waist, not the narrowness of constraint, but almost insensibly less, and round as a circle.

The proud Rajpootni saw the effect she had produced on her captor ... (377)

That effect is not described, so that the reader is placed, as in Tod's source-text, in the position of the viewer of the queen, assessing the effect on the khan by their own reaction to it. The predominantly female readership of the literary annuals is thus implicitly joined with the khan in subjecting the Rajput woman to a male gaze that finds her to be a female figure of perfect and 'still strictly feminine' proportions. The focus on the woman's physical attributes – her role as 'a queen of Nature's own making' – effectively distances her from the role of sovereign and commander described in the beginning of the story. Conjoining her physical appearance with the requirement to die to avoid dishonour sets her apart from and makes her 'other' to the British reader – personified in the 'Fanny' of the preamble. The apparent message of the Colonel's account of 'Eve's dark daughters' – his claim that the Rajput woman leads 'a far happier, and certainly a more useful life' than her Western counterparts (375) – is comprehensively negated by a narrative which reduces her to her physical elements and identifies individual purity rather than sovereignty as her defining aspect. The khan dies in his poisoned garments, but the Rajput woman's defeat of him is reduced by Mowatt to a gesture of personal vengeance.

These women writers encountered India in different ways: the lived experience of the subcontinent possessed by Roberts, Postans and Mowatt contrasts with Landon's deployment of images and tropes acquired entirely at second hand. Their differing uses of Tod's work does not, however, align with their experience of India, but appears rather to reflect the level of their engagement with a metropolitan construction of femininity as confined to a private sphere of individual affective and dependent relationships. Roberts's work, here as elsewhere, demonstrates a concern with issues of women's agency in a public sphere, and ability to shape their own destiny in a private sphere, that goes beyond that expressed by her contemporaries.[47]

Women's Agency and Sacrifice: the Story of Kishen Kower

A particular instance of this general narrative of female agency and female sacrifice caught the imagination of many readers. The story of the Udaipur princess Kishen Kower, who died by taking poison in 1809, stands out from other episodes from the archives of north and central India because of its human interest, the clean lines of its narrative, and the way it chimes with existing British responses to India – in particular, with the sensation-seeking pity and horror with which instances of the rite of *sati* were recorded and circulated.[48] Unlike other such episodes, the Kishen Kower narrative was of relatively recent date, and the facts of the case were well known, as it was recorded by several British writers, and also by one of the protagonists, Ameer (or Amir) Khan. The varying versions of what is basically a stable and uncontested narrative produced by a series of British writers offer, therefore, a reflection of the differing responses to India and to Indian women prevalent in the nineteenth century. These narratives also carry information on the writers' views of British India, on women's roles in British and Indian societies more generally, on the relationship between individual and society, and on the relationship between the contemporary present of the writers and the history within which they situate themselves.

The *Asiatic Annual Register* carried among its 'Bengal Occurrences' for November 1810 the news of a 'most important political event', 'the death of the Princess of Oudipore by poison', an event precipitated by the rivalry of two suitors which meant that she could marry neither, and by the consideration that an unmarried daughter would bring shame to her family:

> This lady, it seems, had for some years before been the great source of contention and discord among the Rajpoot States. The family of the Rana of Oudipore being accounted more ancient and honourable than that of any other Hindoo prince, his alliance was naturally sought by the neighbouring potentates of Jaypore and Joudpore, who both aspired to the hand of the princess. The rivalship of these two Rajahs produced a war, in which Scindia, Holkar, Ameer Khan, and all the native chieftains in that quarter, have at one time or other taken a part. The contest, however, has at length been terminated in the manner above related. The poison was administered to the princess by her own aunt, and with the knowledge of her father. Report adds, that the whole scheme was secretly contrived by Ameer Khan; who, finding that the Rana of Oudipore, (now entirely in his power,) was too far engaged to the Jaypore Rajah to retract, and resolved that his own ally, the Rajah of Joudpore should not be disgraced by the triumph of his rival, suggested this expedient, as the only mode of at once settling all their pretensions, and terminating the ten years' war, which this second Helen had excited.

While noting that this was a 'catastrophe ... revolting to human nature', the paper implicitly categorised it as characteristic of oriental barbarity, stating that it 'too closely corresponds with the ordinary course of Asiatic history'.[49]

Tod, who had been stationed in the area at the time, claimed personal direct or indirect acquaintance with the events leading up to Kishen's death:

> I witnessed the commencement and the end of this drama, and have conversed with actors in all the intermediate scenes. In June 1806 the passes of Oodipoor were forced; and in January 1808, when I passed through Jeipoor in a solitary ramble, the fragments of this contest were scattered over its ashy plains.[50]

A detailed account of her fate is included in *Rajasthan*, and Tod's knowledge and possibly his written work (in the process of preparation at this point) also contributed to the version circulated by John Malcolm, who included it in his *Memoir of Central India* (1823).[51] Malcolm's work appears to have served as a direct source for later writers more often than Tod's – *Memoir of Central India* was the first published, and was widely read and further circulated through the publication of extracts in the British periodical press – but does not differ in substance from it.[52] A third version, by one of the protagonists, Ameer Khan, bears out the substance of the British accounts, but did not appear in translation until 1832.[53]

The death of Kishen was not in itself extraordinary, as H. T. Prinsep indicates in his annotations to Ameer Khan's *Memoirs*. He emphasises the political background to her fate:

> In the Policy of Asia a woman's life is but of small account: and more especially so amongst the Rajpoots of Western India, who habitually destroy their female children. . . . The death of the Princess led to the pacification between Jypoor and Joudhpoor, and removed the great source of quarrel and confusion . . . The Princess, according to Rajpoot notions, could have had no other husband, but one or other of the two Rajas, and as neither was possible, death was her only resource.

This categorising of Kishen's life and death as typical of the role assigned to elite Rajput women is underlined when Prinsep makes the point that she is not by any means the only woman to suffer in this way, claiming that a similar episode happened only 'the other day', when a Princess of Bikaneer 'took, or was made to take poison' in 'a necessary consequence' of her planned marriage having been 'broken off by some Court intrigue'.[54] His description of the story told by Tod and Malcolm as 'highly wrought accounts' constitutes an implicit accusation that they are overstating the sensation, pity and human interest of Kishen's plight.[55]

Tod's account of Kishen's death more than merits Prinsep's description. It is rhetorically charged and makes conscious and extensive use of literary and mythological allusions, investing her personal fate with epic significance. 'Kishna Komari [was] . . . like Helen of old, involved in [the] destruction [of] her own and the rival houses' (l. 461); she is compared to the 'dishonoured Virginia' put to death by her 'Roman father', and to the sacrificed Iphigenia, as Tod concludes:

> The votive victim of Jephtha's success had the triumph of a father's fame to sustain her resignation, and in the meekness of her sufferings we have the best parallel to the sacrifice of the lovely Kishna: though years have passed since the barbarous immolation, it is never related but with a faltering tongue and moistened eyes, 'albeit unused to the melting mood'.[56] (1. 463–4)

These parallels are further underlined when he recollects a visit to York Cathedral, in 1823, when both the 'sublime recitation of Handel in "Jephtha's Vow"', and a performance of Racine's *Iphigénie*, 'served to waken the remembrance of [Kishen's] sacrifice'. His quotation of lines from the latter text – apparently 'embodying not only the sentiments, but couched in the precise language in which the "Virgin Kishna" addressed her father' – is offered as proof 'that human nature has but one mode of expression for the same feelings' (1. 465). Tod's insistence on this series of comparisons with religious and classical texts does, as his own remark indicates, have the effect of creating links between the actions and motivations of the Rajputs and those of notable figures from the Western classical tradition. In doing so, his work blurs the self / other divide at the heart of British representations of the *sati* rite, a parallel version of female sacrifice and victimisation. It also has the effect of fictionalising and denaturing the life and death of Kishen, opening up the story for appropriation and recontextualising in the work of others.

Appropriations of the Kishen Kower Story in British Writing

Two opposing movements are visible in the versions of the story produced by later writers, corresponding to the dual aspect of the source material, which both dwells on Kishen's beauty and personal tragedy, and highlights the circumstances of her death as indicative of the politics and cultural concerns of the Rajput people. One version removes the story almost entirely from that political context, instead seizing on and amplifying the reports of Kishen's pitiable end in a manoeuvre which has the effect of making her an idealised version of suffering femininity.[57] The other uses these human aspects of Kishen's fate to construct a version of India as seen through British eyes, which is also an implicit narrative of Britain's relationship with India.

Catherine Richardson's 'Kishen Kower', a typical example of the first category, draws on Malcom's version of the story, which is reproduced in summary form as a note to the poem. The opening address to the protagonist divorces her completely from the political context, by locating responsibility for her death within herself: 'What fatal beauty was your dower! / Through woe and crime's dark cloud, you seem / The angel of some heavenly dream.'[58] The 'immortal pity' which is her fate is the product of her status as attractive victim:

> But oh! to see that sweetest flow'r
> Torn rudely from the shelt'ring stem,
> That fairest face, from regal bow'r
> From an awaiting diadem –
> Whom lovers worshipp'd, nations fought for, laid
> In death's cold arms, by kindred hands betray'd,
> Gives to immortal pity *her* sad lot,
> And transient hour, whose beauty dug the grave
> By thousands wept! but none stept forth to save! (110)

Similarly, Landon's 'Kishen Kower' emphasises the beauty of Kishen herself and her romanticised surroundings of flowers, butterflies and birds: 'the fragile clematis its silver showers flung, / And the nutmeg's soft pink was near lost in the pride / Of the pomegranate blossom that blushed at its side'.[59] She is, the poem states explicitly, to blame for the conflict arising in the state:

> 'There is famine on earth – there is plague in the air,
> And all for a woman whose face is too fair.'
> There was silence like that from the tomb, for no sound
> Was heard from the chieftains who darkened around,
> When the voice of a woman arose in reply,
> 'The daughters of Rajahstan [sic] know how to die.'

That death becomes Landon's central theme by the end of the poem: as her preoccupation with the suffering and abnegation of women overwhelms the text, the bodily pain and process of death become, unusually in this tradition, the main focus:

> The haughty eye closes, the white teeth are set,
> And the dew-damps of pain on the wrung brow are wet:
> The slight frame is writhing – she sinks to the ground;

She yields to no struggle, she utters no sound –
The small hands are clenched – they relax – it is past.
And her aunt kneels beside her – kneels weeping at last.

The poem concludes by referencing itself, in Landon's characteristic mode, with the lines: 'But the heart has her image, and long after years / Will keep her sad memory with music and tears' (24).

Mowatt's 'Kishen Kowur' also emphasises Kishen's doomed beauty, describing her at some length as 'like some lovely flower', 'one of the most perfect of God's created beings', and an exemplar of Rajput physical attractiveness:

> The Rajpoots are a particularly handsome race; but 'Kishen Kowur' was the star of her own peculiar circle. Her sylph-like figure, slightly above the middle height, was graceful in the extreme; while its beautiful proportions were improved by the ample and elegant drapery, ever found in oriental costumes. Her jetty hair, which when unbound, would fall in dark masses to her feet, was generally confined, by a band of pearls, in themselves a Prince's ransom; and her eyes, soft, and intensely dark, were ever, either flashing from the excitement of joy, or when quiet 'swimming beneath the lashes'.

This emphasis on her oriental attributes becomes significant when read alongside the stanza of verse with which the story concludes:

Lo! Here's the fortitude compared,
Which truth and error give –
'Twas but to *die*, the heathen dared;
The Christian, dares to live.[60]

Transforming the preceding story into an account of oriental 'error' versus Western courage, the verse also forces a rereading of the description of Kishen's beauty, commodified by association with the trappings of oriental luxury.[61] The otherness of Rajputana in particular, and the East in general, does not in this context derive from a clash of cultures between West and East, or a mismatch between the traditions of the Rajput states and those of the British colonial presence in India. It is constituted by the physical appearance of the woman who is subjected to the gaze of writer and reader, held responsible for her otherness in their eyes as much as she is responsible for the unfortunate clash of male desires and ideas of honour that led to her death.

A more explicitly politicised appropriation of the story is visible in the works of those writers who are – broadly speaking – more engaged with the British colonial project in India, either as participants or as commentators. Roberts relied on what she termed the 'marketable commodity' of her knowledge of India to sustain her career as a writer, and used the story to draw attention to one of her perennial topics: the treatment of women.[62] With journalistic *savoir faire*, she sets Kishen's death at the climax of a passage concerning female infanticide in the Rajput states, both highlighting the immediacy of the issue and using it to make an implicit case for further British intervention in India:

> In the Rajpoot states, the destruction of female infants was, and it is to be feared still is, common in the highest families, for political reasons. The representations of British residents, and their eloquent appeals . . . have done much . . . towards [its] abolition . . . but there is no law against it, and the tragedy of Kishen Koor, the most cold-blooded murder ever perpetrated by the hand of man, is still recent. The brother of the beautiful victim, slaughtered to secure a state measure, now sits upon the throne of Oodipore . . .[63]

G. Poulett Cameron, whose rank of lieutenant colonel, included on the title page of his book, advertises his alignment with the East India Company's colonial project, makes a similar, but more explicit equation between the circumstances of Kishen's death and the desirability of British intervention in India. 'Kishen Kower: or, the Maid of Odeypoor' expands the sparse narrative of the earlier sources by drawing attention to the political background to the episode. 'Never were the fatal effects of feudal warfare so dreadfully felt by a wretched peasantry as at the period of 18—. The once flourishing country of Rajapootana was almost a desert; the contest was still undecided, and appeared to have the effect of ruining both parties, without determining the superiority of either.'[64] The story is thereafter told in substantial accordance with the pattern established in other texts, until the narrator includes in the concluding passages several references to the colonial state, thus re-inserting Kishen's story into the trajectory of British domination of India:

> The contest between the two Rajahs of Jeypoor and Joudpoor, thus checked by the death of the princess, was effectually concluded by the powerful intervention of the British Government. Ameer Khan was disappointed in the expectations he had formed upon the death of the princess, by the advance of a British force.[65]

That brief reference to the British presence as guarantor of security and good government relegates the internal conflicts of Rajputana to a regrettable past. It also deprives Kishen herself of any agency: others are aware of how she must be sacrificed for the greater good, but she does not enter into or share that thought, and makes her last stand only out of desperation. She plays, in fact, the role of the *sati* woman, whose fate is used to highlight the need for British intervention in India.

H. T. Prinsep's use of the story in the poem 'Kishan Koomaree, Princess of Oodeepoor: A True Tale of Rajwara' is less clearly instrumental, but equally demonstrates a sense of India's treatment of its women as a theme closely connected to the British perception of their role as colonisers. Prinsep, who had earlier translated Amir Khan's account of his own role as advisor to Kishen's father, draws on this as well as the versions offered by Tod and Malcolm, and thus gives more consideration to the political conflict between states as the proximate cause of her death.[66] The weighting of Kishen's individual woman's life against the good of the state becomes the turning point of the action: 'shall the welfare of the whole be sacrific'd for one?' Ameer Khan asks the Rana; and further persuades him that his own life must not be that sacrifice, when the Rana says that he, not his daughter, is 'the guilty one': 'Consider well thy country's good, in what its welfare lies. / A maiden's life is little worth, behind the curtain past, / But thine thy country ill could spare. . .' (71). Ameer Khan's speech is pragmatic, and misogynist, to a degree unparalleled in other versions of the story:

> 'Tis woman's lot to have on earth small influence for good,
> Though woes unnumber'd spring from her, of sin, and crime, and blood.
> I know thy daughter innocent as new-born babe can be,
> But will that save her caste and kin, and keep their honour free? (71)

Her father is finally urged: 'Do thou / What, hadst thou done when she was born, had not been needed now' (72). This last point, a reference to the custom of female infanticide, is notable particularly when set against Tod's insistence that infanticide is 'almost unknown' in this context – it both emphasises the alienation of Rajasthan from British readers, and also diminishes Kishen's agency further: her death is near to foreordained at this stage.[67] As in Roberts, her individual fate has come to stand for a British sense of Rajput, and more generally Indian or oriental, attitudes toward women.[68]

Kishen's death, which takes up the final passages of the poem, goes some way to counter this evacuation of her personal identity, albeit in paradoxical relation to her forced surrender of self. She rejects the attempt to poison her without her knowledge, addressing her father through the servant he has sent to kill her, and claiming ownership of her own death:

> Go, tell my father, 'tis enough! The life that he did give
> He is at all times free to take, – I wish not more to live:
> But wherefore slay me thus by stealth? a princess born and bred,
> A maiden of Seesodee race, should die as she would wed.
> I know I am a sacrifice for him, and for his state,
> And proudly will I meet my death, and deem the glory great. (72)

Her death scene has echoes of the conventional portrait of a *sati* rite, beginning with her being revealed to the public – and the reader – as she 'issues forth, in bridal garments clad', but her last words reaffirm her devotion to her country as well as to the bridegroom of her imagination:

> 'My country asks my life,' says she, 'hand me the poison'd bowl!
> I see a bridegroom up in heav'n, to him I yield my soul:
> And if I leave a spotless name, and honour be its meed,
> Oh! may my country reap the fruit, and glory in this deed!'

Prinsep's text thus creates a space in which the death of a woman can become also an expression of her agency and her capacity for self-determination, enabling her to assert her independent decision to act for the good of her country even as her fate permits India in general to be characterised by its oppression of women in implicit contrast to the traditions of the West.

The tendency, then, in texts of this first half of the nineteenth century is for a nascent idea of Indian nationalist feeling to be entertained briefly, but quickly denied, contained, or so hedged around with narrative boundaries as to be withheld from or inaccessible to the reader. The characterisation of both male and female Indian figures plays a part in this: the Rajput hero and heroine are recognised as validly self-determining – though in gender-determined and circumscribed ways – but located in the past, both in Tod's foundational historiography and in the work of those writers who draw on *Rajasthan*. As the conception of male agency and self-determination oscillates from heroic to criminal, within the corpus of bandit texts, so the idea of female agency is developed using a limited and problematic equation of female self-determination with a freedom to engage in self-sacrifice. All form part of a larger category of narratives of Indian decline, subservience to British authority and need for British protection.

Notes

1. Others include Dow's *History of Hindostan* (1768–72), still current at this period, and John Malcolm's *Memoir of Central India* (1823). As Sreenivasan argues, *Rajasthan* is also 'one of several competing versions' of Rajput history (*Many Lives*, p. 120).
2. Rudolph and Rudolph, *Essays*, p. 179.
3. The political / cultural / historical space of 'Rajasthan' (as opposed to the modern state bearing that name, deriving from the British province of Rajputana) has no very precise boundaries. See Lodrick, 'Rajasthan'.

4. 'Memoir of the Author', in Tod, *Travels in Western India*, vol. 1, pp. xxv–xxvi.
5. Aitchison, *Treaties*. The treaty with the state of Udaipur, or Mewar, (pp. 22–3) is typical.
6. Freitag, 'Serving Empire', p. 112; Talbot, 'Mewar', p. 14. Tod's sources are summarised in *Rajasthan* vol. 1, pp. x–xiv; see also Sreenivasan, *Many Lives*, pp. 137–42; Barnett, 'Catalogue'; and Hooja, 'Tod Collection'.
7. That said, Freitag, 'Tod's *Annals*' offers a valuable account of the work.
8. Tod, *Rajasthan*, n. p.
9. Peabody, 'Tod's Rajast'han', pp. 208–9.
10. Peabody, 'Tod's Rajast'han', p. 198. See also Inden, *Imagining India*, pp. 172–6, on the 'Oriental Feudalism' posited by Tod in *Rajasthan*.
11. Freitag, *Serving Empire*, p. 40.
12. As Bayly points out, the 'romantic stereotyping' of the Rajputs and their 'virtues of honour, independence and loyalty' was also of pragmatic use: 'The need to protect tribal innocence was used to justify the diplomatic and military segregation of areas such as Afghanistan and Rajasthan . . . Areas which had once been major centres of trade and urbanism could thereby be isolated from both indigenous and European capitalism, and the dangerous conflicts to which they might give rise' (*Imperial Meridian*, pp. 154–5).
13. Akber, or Akbar, Mughal Emperor between 1556 and 1605, completed the process of acquiring substantial domination over the Rajput states in 1569.
14. Tucker, *Epic*, p. 13.
15. Talbot, 'Mewar', pp. 15, 29.
16. See Taft, 'Honor and alliance', pp. 232–3. Those aspects of Rajput history that involve co-operation with, rather than resistance to, Mughal rule are less prominent in Tod's work (Lodrick, 'Rajasthan', p. 8).
17. Brookes, *History*, pp. 19–20.
18. During the sixteenth century, Udai Singh moved the capital of Mewar from Chitor to his new city of Udaipur; the kingdom came to be known also by that name, and eventually became the Indian state of Udaipur.
19. The name 'Pudmani' was, as Tod indicates, originally a title ('superlatively fair') for the Sinhalese princess. Nandini Sinha Kapur describes the 'Alauddin-Padminī episode' as 'more bardic lore than historical truth', and suggests that Alauddin Khalji's invasion of Mewar was a tactical manoeuvre to secure trade routes and guard against Mongol attacks (*State Formation*, pp. 65, 134). The history and mythology underpinning this episode, as well as the related events of Kurnavati's appeal to Humayun for aid in opposing Bahadur Shah, and the rescue of the child Udai Singh, are all discussed by R. V. Somani (*History*, pp. 95–101, 186–8, 193–4).
20. The quotation is Tod's, and not further identified.
21. On the ideology of 'separate spheres', see Davidoff and Hall, *Family Fortunes*, a foundational work in this field. Though some recent work contests the explanatory power of the metaphor to offer a comprehensive account of the 'dynamics of nineteenth-century gender politics' (Griffin, *Politics of Gender*, p. 22), it has largely retained its status as a fundamental organising principle of Victorian thought and social structure.
22. The reference is to the Hindu Samvat calendar; re Ferishta, see Dow, *History of Hindostan* (1768–72).

23. Freitag, 'Serving Empire', p. 155.
24. *Bengal Annual* (1834), p. 268. Tregear, of the Indian Educational Department, was killed at Meerut in 1857 (David, *Indian Mutiny*, p. 86), and should not be confused with his son, an army officer of the same name.
25. *Bengal Annual* (1834), pp. 194–8. The incident on which the poem is based is taken from Gleig, *History*, vol. 1, pp. 174–5; Muir's note on sources also directs the reader to 'Todd's Rajpootana' (*sic*); the offhand and general reference suggests that his work was informed by the general trend of Tod's subject matter and approach.
26. Tregear, 'The Rajpoot Chieftain', *Bengal Annual* (1835), pp. 210–11.
27. Mill, *History*, vol. 1, pp. 383–4.
28. Richardson, 'The Suttee', *Oriental Herald* 12 (March 1827), pp. 511–12.
29. Medwin, *Sketches*, p. 64; Medwin, *Angler*, vol. 2, p. 307.
30. Ward, *Hindoos*, vol. 1, p. xlvii; Roberts, *Scenes and Characteristics*, vol. 1, pp. 286–7.
31. This reflects to some degree the organisation of Rajput society, where, as Andrea Major argues, 'Women, marriage and power were integrally linked; matrimonial alliances were important primarily for their ritual symbolic function, through which a ruler's power was constituted and reinforced' (*Sovereignty*, p. 28). It also reflects Tod's interest in Western ideals of heroic sacrifice of women by men – see, for instance, his discussion of the Kishen Kower story, in this chapter.
32. Spivak, *Critique*, p. 274.
33. *Bengal Annual* (1834), p. 268.
34. Such representations constitute one of the broad categories set out in Mani, *Contentious Traditions*. British representations of *sati* are many and various, and do not all conform to this pattern, but even such a nuanced account as that offered by W. H. Sleeman (*Rambles*, vol. 1, pp. 23–44) counterpoints the story of a woman who freely seeks her own death with others of women taken by force to the fire. See Sabin, *Dissenters*, pp. 69–88.
35. Tod, *Rajasthan*, vol. 1, pp. 311–12.
36. Roberts, *Oriental Scenes* (1832), p. 126.
37. Haig and Burn, *Mughul Period*, pp. 22–4. Sharma, *Mewar*, pp. 43–52, describes this episode.
38. Spivak, *Critique*, p. 299.
39. Rajan, *Real and Imagined*, p. 19.
40. *Fisher's Drawing Room Scrap Book* (1834), pp. 17–19. Roberts and Landon were friends of long-standing; Roberts is acknowledged in a note to 'Kishen Kower' (p. 23).
41. Compare, for instance, the protagonists of Landon's other poems 'The Hindoo Girl's Song' and 'Fishing Boats in the Monsoon', *Fisher's Drawing Room Scrap Book* (1836).
42. Roberts, *Oriental Scenes* (1832), note p. 128; the reference is to Tod, *Rajasthan*, vol. 1, p. 311.
43. Postans, *Facts and Fictions*, vol. 1, p. ix.
44. Other Postans stories take a similar theme; see, for instance, 'Aieyla, the Ramooseen' (vol. 2, pp. 199–229).

45. Mrs J. L. [Anna Maria] Mowatt, 'The Rajpootni, or Fire-Side Reminiscences', *Bengal Annual* (1835), p. 373.
46. Compare the opening passages of Tod's narrative (1. 625), which provides Mowatt with her material and phrasing, including the brief reference to the story of the Roman woman Lucretia, whose rape by Tarquin is followed by her suicide.
47. Roberts's interest in Indian women's roles is partly also a concern with gender roles more generally: see her account of 'Bengal Bridals' (*Scenes and Characteristics*, vol. 1, pp. 14–34), and the representation of Mitala's thwarted feminist sensibility in 'The Rajah's Obsequies' (*Oriental Scenes* (1832), p. 58).
48. Tod refers to the woman in question as 'Kishna Komari Baé', the 'Virgin Princess Kishna' (*Rajasthan*, vol. 1, p. 461). The form 'Kishen Kower' was used by John Malcolm, and there are several other variant transliterations. I have retained the original spelling in all quotations, and opted otherwise to follow Malcolm's version, the one most frequently used by later writers.
49. *Asiatic Annual Register*, vol. 12 (1810–11), pp. 49–50.
50. Tod, *Rajasthan*, vol. 1, note p. 463.
51. A substantial portion of *Rajasthan* was written 'as early as 1820–21' (Peabody, 'Tod's Rajast'han', n. 19, p. 196). Malcolm relies on Tod to authenticate several details of the story, though he also claims to have 'visited the court of Odeypoor in March 1821, eleven years after the occurrence of the events I have stated, and possessed complete means of verifying every fact' (see *Memoir*, pp. 340–2).
52. Malcolm, *Memoir*, vol. 1, pp. iv–v. This work is in some respects equivalent to *Rajasthan*, though less encyclopedic in scope, focusing on the Malwa region and the Marathas; see Harrington, *John Malcolm*, pp. 99–127. Koditschek suggests that the difference between Malcolm's version of the 'British Indian romance' and that of Tod lies in the former's 'realist' recognition that the establishment of British authority in India required that indigenous states should be defeated, rather than become part of a 'consensual union with Britain' (*Liberalism*, p. 75).
53. Ameer Khan, *Memoirs*, p. 400. The translator, H. T. Prinsep, sadly omits as 'quite untranslateable' the Persian verses in praise of the princess contained in the original (note p. 296). A long review of this work appears in the *Asiatic Journal*, vol. 18 (November 1835): 226–36; (December 1835): 253–67.
54. Prinsep note to Ameer Khan, *Memoirs*, p. 400.
55. Ibid. p. 400. Malcolm's account bears this out, with its insistence that 'the extraordinary beauty and youth of the victim excited a feeling, which was general in a degree that is rare among the inhabitants of India'; and in the town, 'loud lamentations ... and expressions of pity at her fate were mingled with execrations on the weakness and cowardice of those who could purchase safety on such terms' (*Memoir*, p. 340). Prinsep takes a different line in his own poem based on the story; see below.
56. Compare *Othello* V, ii, 358. In the work of the Roman writer Livy, the schoolgirl Virginia, or Verginia, is put to death by her father to save her from life as a slave, while Agamemnon is commanded by the gods to sacrifice his daughter Iphigenia before the siege of Troy (see *Oxford Classical*

Dictionary). Jephtha is similarly compelled to make good his promise to sacrifice his daughter Iphis (Judges 11).
57. The discussion that follows is confined to texts purporting to offer a version of the story that does not depart in substance from the reported facts of the case. Others used its central motif, transformed to a lesser or greater degree, in the service of different narratives. James Abbott's poem *The T'hakoorine* is one of these (see Abbott, p. 133); another is Marianne Postans's story 'The Chieftain's Daughter: A Tale of Rajpootana', where the progatonist, Komari, is joined in death by her lover Zalim Singh (*Facts and Fictions*, vol. 2, pp. 134–62).
58. Richardson, *Poems*, p. 109.
59. Landon, 'Kishen Kower', *Fisher's Drawing Room Scrap Book* (1834), pp. 21–4.
60. *Bengal Annual* (1834), pp. 363, 365.
61. Compare a similar passage in the work of G. Poulett Cameron, which creates an effect almost grotesque in the way it objectifies and dismantles its subject in the course of setting her within an oriental context: 'It was impossible to conceive of a creature more beautiful, or one who walked in such unparalleled loveliness, – the half opened, rich, full coral lip disclosed two rows of teeth, that rivalled in whiteness the ivory of the desert, or the pearls of Bassein; while her full, large, dark eye excelled in tenderness and expression the antelope of Yemen; her hair falling in clusters of jetty and luxuriant tresses down her neck and shoulders, completed the picture of the Eastern beauty (*Romance*, p. 11).
62. Johnson, *Stranger in India*, p. 165.
63. Roberts, *Scenes and Characteristics*, vol. 1, p. 248.
64. Cameron, *Romance*, p. 1.
65. Amir Khan, a Pindari commander of Afghan origins, was an ally of the Marathas in the early years of the nineteenth century, and came to terms with the British following the Maratha wars in a settlement that gave him the position of Nawab of the state of Tonk. It is in this context that the poem laments the treaty which enabled him to enjoy 'for years the fruits of his villanies [*sic*]' (Cameron, *Romance*, p. 22).
66. Prinsep, *Ballads*, p. 73.
67. Tod, *Rajasthan*, vol. 1, p. 465.
68. The boundaries of 'India' remain conceptually as well as geopolitically indistinct for much of this period.

Chapter 7

Transformations of India after the Indian Mutiny

The Mutiny of 1857 was a watershed in the history of nineteenth-century India, changing how the British in India thought of India, 'home' and their own position in relation to both. This chapter explores the reorientation of British representations of India, first in response to the events of the Mutiny, and later in response to Indian aspirations to self-determination, manifested particularly in the growth of Bengali nationalism towards the end of the century. It also returns to the central themes of the two previous chapters, focusing on the representation of Indian masculine criminality and feminine agency in the literature of the Mutiny, and the engagement with representations of Rajput nationalism in post-Mutiny appropriations of *Rajasthan* by British writers.

In some respects, the literature of the Mutiny takes up and consolidates tropes and themes already firmly established in texts written in the first half of the nineteenth century. Taylor's *Seeta* (1872), for example, recalls some of the themes of the author's first and best-known work, *Confessions of a Thug* (1839). These include the representation of a bandit protagonist and his Indian woman victim, both now viewed through the lens of the Mutiny of 1857 rather than the thug campaigns of the 1830s. *Seeta*, however, is a far less ambiguous novel than *Confessions*, as it reprises, and in doing so resolves, several of the tensions of the earlier work. The ambivalent dual representation of Ameer Ali, the hero of *Confessions*, as both monstrous criminal and sympathetic interlocutor becomes in *Seeta* a one-dimensional portrait of the bandit Azráel Pandé as the villain.[1] The novels are separated by thirty-odd years, but also and most importantly by the action of the Mutiny, which transforms the relationship of the British with India. In effect, the category of Indian hero (male or female) is no longer available to British writers.

It is through the figure of Azráel Pandé that *Seeta* develops a link between the thugs and dacoits of the 1830s and 1840s, and the rebels of 1857. The ritual which precedes his raid on the goldsmith's house, with its ceremonial accoutrements of the axe, the omens of vulture and jackal, and the invocation to Kali, establishes him and his associates as dacoits. The word in this case signifies not simply an armed bandit, but members of one of the hereditary associations of ritual killers which the Thuggee & Dacoity Department of the East India Company had been set up to counter in the preceding decades. The works of T&D officials, particularly W. H. Sleeman's *Ramaseeana* (1836) and its derivatives such as Edward Thornton's *Illustrations of the History and Practices of the Thugs* (1837), had created a sense among both the Company government and the reading public of thugs as inhuman, highly organised and particularly dangerous criminals, an extraordinary threat to the ordinary people of India.[2] As dacoits and other supposedly hereditary criminals by profession began to be thought of and categorised by the colonial state in the same way as thugs, these groups also came to be seen as enemies of ordinary society, set apart by a shared 'language' (Ramasi), and obliged by creed and heredity to prey on the wider community. It is a short step from there to seeing them also as enemies of the state.[3] In identifying such a figure as the rebel Azráel Pandé – fictional uncle to the apocryphal Mungal Pandy who supposedly fired the opening shot of the Mutiny in Meerut – Taylor draws a straight line from the alienated bandit to the nationalist rebel. Azráel Pandé 'laboured mightily in the cause of his religion and his caste'; and is a true zealot, with 'but one thought, one passion of his existence – the destruction of the English'.[4] He is the personification of revolt in his wild sword dance and incantation to Kali, the goddess of the thugs. The failure of the rebellion is foreshadowed in her refusal to answer him: 'Then he stood erect, with his sword stretched out, panting for breath, and his eyes staring into vacancy. "She does not come," he said moodily, as the point of his sword dropped with a helpless action' (332). His eventual death, jointly dealt by the British hero Cyril Brandon and the loyal Indian servant Buldeo, marks the re-establishment of colonial order.

This British order is represented as a version of the salvation of India, the defeat of the rebels a parallel to the earlier defeat of thugs and dacoits. The 'most valuable portions of the population', like Seeta's family, are horrified at the outbreak of Mutiny, and loyal to the British side (315–16). The novel insists on this throughout, as in the account of what happens as soon as British authority is challenged: 'marauders, plunderers, and thieves without number, sprang up in all directions, and there was no more peace abroad' (363). The calm justice of Mr Mostyn as he presides over the trial of Azráel Pandé (83–5) is contrasted to the 'modes of torture' employed to extort money by 'the Rajah and his courtiers' when they take over control (363). By such means the indigenous authority of India is criminalised as well as the main figures of villainy, the rebels. The ambivalent rebel/bandit hero of the pre-Mutiny literature becomes wholly criminalised, with heroism reserved for the representation of British men.

Transformations of Indian and British Women in the Literature of the Indian Mutiny

Seeta also provides an example of the fate of Indian woman characters in this literature. The self-sacrificing heroine undergoes several transformations: her characteristics of devotion to her husband and willingness to die in order to fulfil her assigned social and gender role are co-opted for British women characters. This leaves no space for her in these representations of India, and indeed she is often wholly replaced by British women in novels of the later Victorian period. I shall explore this set of transformations in three works: the poetry of Mary Leslie, *Seeta*, and the turn of the century novel *Jenetha's Venture*, by Colonel Alfred Harcourt.

Mary Leslie's 'Sorrows and Aspirations', a sequence of sonnets, memorialises some of the central characters and episodes of the Mutiny, including the firing of the magazine in Delhi, the siege and relief of Lucknow and the death of its garrison commander Henry Havelock, the massacre of women and children in the 'Bibighar' at Cawnpore, and the apocryphal killing/suicide of Major Skene and his wife as rebel forces overthrew the British garrison at Jhansi. Gibson's succinct summary offers an accurate sense of the work: 'British soldiers are heroes; British women are pitiable victims and noble nurses; and God at the end is entrusted with bringing a Christian future to India.'[5] Leslie's poetry is among the first responses to the events of 1857, and would be of interest for that if nothing else, but my focus here is not so much the content of the Mutiny poetry per se, but the synergies of form and theme apparent between the sonnet cycle and her other poems, collected in the same volume in a section titled 'Legends from India'. The complex resonances developed in this literary relationship make it clear that Leslie is far from being simply the writer of what Gautam Chakravarty terms 'retaliatory fantasies'.[6]

These 'Legends' draw to a large extent on Tod's *Rajasthan*, and are prefaced with two contradictory texts. The first, by John Keats, relegates the legends to the past, in keeping with the narrative of decay established throughout Victorian uses of Tod's work:

> No! those days are gone away,
> And those hours are old and grey,
> And their minutes buried all
> Under the down-trodden pall
> Of the leaves of many years.[7]

The other is Leslie's own 'Prelude', an emotional interrogation of India made in a tone and language surprisingly sympathetic in the light of the sonnets and their message of outrage on behalf of the British victims of rebellion. 'What is this India like? – this gorgeous land, / With her broad, sacred rivers like to seas;' the poem begins, and continues in a recital of the aesthetic and material beauties and wonders of the country (41). The account of 'ruined palaces' and 'cities lying desolate' is a reminder that this is a land in decay; but the poet also anticipates its resurgence. India is a 'trancèd Queen' waiting to be re-awakened (43), while 'We Britons watch beside her, standing girt / As strangers by her streams and in her vales, / And thinking ever of our Island Home' (43). India, in Leslie's vision, will rise again: 'Magnificent in glory; on thy brow / Shall blaze again the jewelled diadem' (45). The events of the Mutiny are recalled only at the close of the poem, when the speaker expresses sorrow rather than bitterness:

> My heart is very mournful, and the tears
> Unshed hang on my eyelids all the day.
> I look upon the redness of the skies,
> And almost deem the antique fable true
> That round the sun the life-blood of the slain
> Gathers in crimson clouds at morn and eve.
> O wretched, frantic India! Why hast thou
> In thy first fevered stirrings seized the sword,
> And plunged it in the hearts of those who stood,
> And watched, and prayed around thee? why hast thou
> Retarded thus the coming years of bliss,
> And caused thy robes thus to be overflowed
> With blood of sinless babes, of brave, true men,
> Of women fair and gentle as the eve?
> Long will it be ere tears of penitence,
> Flowing down silently, blot out those stains,
> And let thy garments whitely droop around! (47)

This anticipation of penitence and a time when Hinduism should be replaced by Christianity is clearly evidence of Leslie's own strong Christian faith, and an expression of belief in the effectiveness and worth of the missionary work she and her family carried out in Bengal.

Leslie's vision of India, then, is founded on the teleology of progress that underlies much of Victorian thought, with this aspect of her work reflected in the constitution of the volume, which seeks to relegate India's legendary past and the recent trauma of rebellion to history even while the poetry dwells on their 'sorrows'. This movement from past to present and future is arrested by the unexpected resonances between the two components of the volume. While the sonnets commemorating the Mutiny, and the poetry based on *Rajasthan*, appear to be widely separated in content and tone, there are points where one echoes the other. 'The Queen of Ganore', for instance, is a re-telling of the eponymous queen's defeat at the hands of a khan, who plans to marry her; she sends him a set of poisoned garments to wear at the wedding, and then throws herself 'over the battlements into the flood beneath', while he dies 'in extreme torture'.[8] Leslie's poem includes passages of direct speech by the queen, who gives voice to the Rajput valorising of honour over life: 'Death is better far than slave-life; than pollution is the grave / . . . Thou art doomed to death, and I am consecrated to the wave!' (72). The poem concludes on her triumphant suicide:

> Still the swift Nerbudda river
> Flows unto the blue sea ever;
> And it bears her on its waters, gliding past each wooded shore,
> With the bridal raiment round her,
> And the rubied crown which bound her,
> Fairest of all India's daughters, Queen heroic, of Ganore! (73)

The motif of the avenging woman appears also in the sonnet cycle, where Leslie alludes to the story of Miss Wheeler, the younger daughter of Sir Hugh Wheeler, British commander at Cawnpore, and his wife Frances, a part-Indian woman. General Wheeler surrendered the city to the rebel commander Nana Sahib on 27 June 1857, in return for safe passage under arms to Allahabad for all under his protection. As they attempted to get into boats for the river journey at Satichaura Ghat, firing broke out on both sides, and the British were overwhelmed. A few men escaped; the rest were killed, along with many women and children. Most of the remaining women and children were taken to the Bibighar, where they were later killed; several others, including Miss Wheeler, were taken from the scene by Indian soldiers. In the immediate aftermath of these events, the story circulated that she killed her captor and his family, and then committed suicide.[9] Leslie addresses her in the name of women more generally, telling her that they 'who mourned . . . The helpless weakness of our womanhood' became 'strong and self-reliant' on hearing her story:

> How thou in midnight's awful solitude,
> While phantoms of the dead around thee stood,

And o'er thee with their sad eyes vainly yearned,
Didst stand, Avenger, by the deep well's brink;
Within thy small, fair hands the dripping blade,
Which thou, with heart unknowing how to shrink,
In thy foe's life-blood hadst most crimson made,
Then plunging in the far down waters sink,
Thy maiden spirit sad but undismayed.[10]

The river which claims the queen is replaced by the well at Cawnpore, but the combination of the avenging woman, the watery death and the woman with her 'honour' unsullied is common to both texts – the 'maiden spirit' of Mary Wheeler paralleled by the queen in her 'bridal raiment'. At a time when the main thrust of British writing on the Mutiny was directed at inscribing boundaries between British and Indians, Leslie's use of an Indian woman as a model for her British heroine is remarkable.

Other echoes of *Rajasthan* are visible throughout the sonnet cycle, as instances of British heroism and sacrifice are referred to in the idiom and register of the Rajput legends. The story of Major Skene's killing of his wife as a prelude to his own suicide, before they should be overcome by rebels, is told in his direct address to her, as he invokes the rhetoric of honour with which Tod recounted the deaths of the garrison at Chitor: 'We fight more for a stainless death than life' (7).[11] During the siege of Lucknow, the group voice of the besieged speaks of the deaths of women and children:

Despair is on us. Though our eyes oft brim
When babe or maiden dies, yet still we say: –
'Thank God! another one has gone away
Before the sea of blood around us swim!' (24)

The defenders of the magazine at Delhi, who stand fast against rebel onslaught until they are likely to be overrun, and then set off explosives in order to destroy the stores of ammunition before they can fall into enemy hands, are addressed in terms that recollect Tod's account of the defenders of Chitor: 'O Dead Ones, gone unto your glorious rest / Amid a hecatomb of slaughtered foes!'[12]

These instances of echo and reflection are not necessarily deliberate or conscious on the part of the writer. Indeed, the occasions when Leslie draws a direct parallel between Rajput and British figures suggests that she is at least wary of equating English and Indians. The poem 'Pertap Singh', for example, seeks for British equivalents to the Rajput hero 'lion-souled Pertap! Rajasthan's Pride'; but the names that Leslie offers are those of Scottish rather than English heroes: 'our Wallace and Bruce, whose high fame / Shall ever abide' (p. 77).[13] The precise tone of this allusion is difficult to read, partly because of the complicated nature of Leslie's own situation: the daughter of a Scottish father, she spent almost all of her life in India.[14] In the sonnet cycle, however, she invokes 'England' and the 'English' fervently throughout; and her earlier patriotic verse generally takes England as its topic, despite the occasional use of terms such as 'Britain' or 'Britannia'. The poem 'Britannia', for instance, has the narrator being shown the book of English history, from King Alfred onwards; and 'The War-Farewell' refers without apparent discrimination to 'England's flag', 'Great Britain's strongest', the 'British Queen', 'Britannia's noble Queen', 'England's monarch' and 'England's throbbing heart'.[15] Scotland is mentioned once only, when she refers in *Sorrows* to the Highland regiment who discovered the bodies of women and children in the Bibighar at Cawnpore (22).

One possible explanation is that Leslie may be using a deliberate equivalence of Rajput heroes with Scottish rebels against English rule, so constructing a Tod-influenced narrative of India as being like Britain at an earlier stage of its history. Or she may be offering Wallace and Bruce as the flower of British heroism, going against the grain of other Mutiny narratives, such as Gerald Massey's 'Havelock's March' (1861), which suggest a hierarchy of civilisation among the components of the British state by making the Highlanders the agents of a bloody and uncivilised British revenge for Indian rebellion.[16] Pittock's suggestion that the distinction between 'Britishness' and 'Englishness' becomes apparent and valuable to the dominant English culture (which otherwise takes them as equivalents) only in 'times of crisis' may be relevant here.[17] The uncertainty is itself telling: as Leslie's work sets out explicit or implicit parallels between Rajputs and Scots, Indians and British heroes, so the categories begin to fragment, blend into one another and lose the clarity of their boundaries. Leslie's vision of an India at peace is also a vision of India westernised and Christianised:

> India's idol fanes
> Shall crumble into dust; her bloody stains
> Fade away silently; her Bramin lore
> Be aye forgotten; Peace shall spread her wings
> Silver-soft over her; dread Caste shall be
> Among the long-departed, perished things;
> And 'mid the joy and blessedness shall He,
> Lord of earth's lords, and King of all earth's kings,
> Commence His reign of glorious majesty! (p. 38)

This is not all one-way traffic, however: Leslie's representations of British figures are also representations of India, and the language of heroism and sacrifice creates affective equivalences between the two even while the content of her work appears to show them most divided.

Post-Mutiny Romances

The blurring of the lines between Indian women and British women in Leslie's poetry can be seen again in the larger corpus of novels written in the years following the Mutiny. Recent scholarship has begun to uncover some of the complexities of this body of representations, pointing to the tendency of Mutiny romance novels to depart from earlier stereotypical images of Indian female victims and British male rescuers, so that the 'Indian helpmeet' intervenes to protect the Anglo-Indian hero, and becomes in doing so also 'a symbolic rival to Anglo-Indian women'.[18] This trend is apparent in *Seeta*, where Taylor sets at the climax of the narrative the eponymous heroine's action of placing her body between the British protagonist Cyril Brandon and a mutineer's spear.[19]

As Indian masculinity becomes further criminalised in the ways discussed at the beginning of this chapter, the focus of the sympathetic female character of Seeta herself moves away from Indian men, and towards her rescuer, Cyril Brandon. The progress of the novel involves her character undergoing a series of transformations, first becoming anglicised, and then being written out of the action altogether, as she is finally replaced by the British woman on whom she had tried to model herself. This is achieved first through Cyril's vision of her, as he imagines her as bridging the gap between European and Indian. As soon as he first has sight of her, his impulse is to recuperate her, rescue her from the category of Indian/other and bring her closer to the European self.

> For a native woman, Cyril Brandon had never seen any one so fair or of so tender a tone of colour. Such, he remembered, were many of the lovely women of Titian's pictures – a rich golden olive, with a bright carnation tint rising under the skin – and Seeta's was like them. One in particular came to his memory like a flash – the wife of the Duc d'Avalos, in the Louvre picture; or Titian's Daughter, carrying fruits and flowers, at Berlin. (61)

Demonstrating his familiarity with and mastery of the culture and aesthetics of Europe, he claims implicitly the right to accord Seeta a place in this category: having named her first a 'native woman', the rest of the meditation is directed at removing that label from her. Their marriage follows, recalling Taylor's own marriage to a woman of partly Indian heritage.[20]

The symbolic journey from India to Europe contained in Cyril's pictorial imagination of Seeta is reflected in the development of her character throughout the novel. She is consistently described as child-like: she is Cyril Brandon's 'pupil' (184), Aunt Ella's 'child' (224), and, dismissively, 'that child' to Mr and Mrs Mostyn (198). Like a child, her role is to be protected and cared for by all around her, as in the scene where she is welcomed by Narendra's household with embraces, music and rituals (228). She learns English, then turns to Christianity in gratitude at Cyril's safe return, when she declares that she will 'go to [God] as a little child'; and afterwards finds Hinduism 'cold and comfortless' (359).[21] She takes as her exemplar Grace Mostyn, who teaches her music and needlework as well as English, and who is described as having 'taken this strange girl to her heart' and 'making her more and more like herself' (319–21). On Seeta's deathbed, however, she remains a liminal character, hovering between Christianity and Hinduism. She explains that 'the Lord is calling me, and I cannot stay'; but as she dies she recites the 'Vedantic invocation to the sun', and 'strange snatches of her Sanscrit prayers were mingled with lines of simple Christian hymns she had learned' (381–3). At this point, she is replaced as heroine, and replaced in Cyril's affections, by Grace, the woman on whom Seeta has modelled her efforts at self-improvement. Cyril marries Grace, and takes over as head of his family on his brother's death; as Pablo Mukherjee observes, this 'restoration of the "pure English" in the romance plot, accompanies that of the pure type of British governance in the political plot'.[22] As Seeta is eventually replaced by a British woman, so India is brought back into the orbit of British rule.

The end of the romance plot, or of Seeta's part of it, is testimony to the limits of the project of anglicising India. As Seeta, the racial 'other', becomes more like Grace, her presence troubles the division and difference between coloniser and colonised. The narrative solution is for her to die, and for Grace to step into her place. In a later work, *Jenetha's Venture* (1899), a different solution is apparent: the narrative forms evolved to describe the heroically self-sacrificing Rajput woman are transferred onto British women. *Jenetha's Venture* is part of the late surge of Mutiny novels in the 1890s, a response to the Ilbert Bill controversy (see below) which raised the spectre of Indians sitting in judgement on British people, as well as a response to the events of the Mutiny.[23] In keeping with the emphasis on 'saving' British women from putative mistreatment by Indian judges during the campaign against the Bill, the novel revisits the narratives of female oppression developed during and after the Mutiny, revising them to replace images of female victimisation with accounts of successful female agency. Like Seeta, the heroine of *Jenetha's Venture* stands against the rebel / criminal villain, but unlike her, she succeeds in defeating him while preserving her own life and her future with the male romantic lead.

Jenetha Wentworth is an English woman, but she also occupies in several ways the narrative space of Rajput women in *Rajasthan* and its later derivatives. She starts the novel in the service of a 'Maharajah', thus being associated with the Rajputs, as her father had been before her.[24] Her first action is an expression of self-will, as she insists on riding with the British hero Ashby and his cohorts. On the road, she falls in love with him, and also realises 'how foolish she had been in undertaking this terrible journey, and what an immense anxiety and trouble she was to those who formed her escort' (77). She leaves, 'risking her life and her very honour', and writes a note for him: 'I will no longer be a burden to you. Go and fight for England. Good-bye' (83). This decision, described as an act of 'heroic self-sacrifice' (94), signals her alignment with the Rajput women of legend, a theme which is immediately taken further when she assumes the persona of the Indian woman Rohni, with the aid of 'a native dress' and 'a bottle of some sort of dye' (109), and travels with her two Rajput attendants who protect her honour fiercely.

Jenetha's association with Rajput womanhood is further recalled with the appearance of the main villain of the novel, the mutineer Alaoodin – his name clearly signalling his identity with the Muslim invader Alauddin, whose pursuit of the Rajput princess Padmini initiates one of the most striking and often-adapted episodes of *Rajasthan* (see previous chapter). The novel remakes him as a low-status rather than an elite figure, 'a fair sample of the low-class Mahommedan who was brought to the surface in the days of the Mutiny' (72); and transfers his interest from the Rajput princess to Jenetha Wentworth, as he becomes 'determined to secure her for himself' (74). When, later in the novel, Alaoodin abducts Jenetha, her response underlines her alignment with Tod's Padmini, as she takes her revolver and resolves that 'alive she would never fall into the hands of the ruffianly crew', but would 'put an end to herself' (255). In the end she saves herself instead, using the butt of the revolver to find a weak spot in the wall and attract the attention of her rescuers. Here the difference between the female agency attributed to the British woman and the Rajput woman becomes clear: the Rajput can only sacrifice herself, while Jenetha can act outside the parameters of Rajput female identity, and save herself, as well as others.

In the sequence of events which brings the novel to a close, Jenetha unites in one character the attributes of both the self-sacrificing Rajput woman and the British woman whose mission it is to save Indian women from predatory Indian masculinity. As the party are about to leave Delhi, she pays a parting visit to a sympathetic Indian princess, and finds herself in a confrontation with her rebel husband, Gholam Khadir, who intrudes upon their conversation and attempts to extort money from his wife. Jenetha promises her, 'I will shoot him if he lays a hand on you' (307), adopting the role of protector of Indian women. After her departure, with the princess's treasure given to her as a gift, Gholam Khadir returns and murders his wife, pursues Jenetha and takes her prisoner. He attacks her, and she resists, telling him 'I am no Hindu woman, but an English girl' (312). Then, in what the text describes as 'the supreme moment', she fires at him, and with 'a great flash of light' he falls dead to the ground (314). Delhi in turn falls to the British, and Ashby sees in the distance the house where Gholam Khadir died, and 'the figure of a girl in English dress clinging to the mast as she ran the Union Jack to the top!' (327). As they draw nearer together, she throws herself in front of him, 'in the desperate hope of saving him from what seemed certain death' from a sniper's bullet (329). Fortunately, both survive the episode.

The trajectory of these texts suggests, then, a process of gradual erasure of the Indian female protagonist. While Leslie's British women take on aspects of Rajput heroines, *Seeta* demonstrates the transformation and then replacement of the Indian heroine by a British woman, and *Jenetha's Venture* finally depicts a British woman who fills the role of Rajput heroine and incorporates her attributes of agency and willingness to sacrifice. These two novels also demonstrate their writers' growing unease with the concept of female agency, whether Indian or British: Indrani Sen points out, for instance, that by the end of *Seeta*, the British woman Grace is faced with 'a prescriptive, exalted model of "Indian" wifely self abnegation'.[25] Sen's broad survey of the fiction of this period identifies 'white female sexuality' as the primary threat to order in British society; and describes this as a response to the gender imbalance of the British population in India, where the relatively small numbers of women give rise to 'a virtual inversion of gender power-relations and an unaccustomed degree of female sexual power'.[26] It is in this context that we might view the trajectory of *Jenetha's Venture*. The text presents her as a figure of power in several respects. As well as wielding sexual power over the male protagonist Ashby – who is relegated to a secondary role for much of the plot – she is also a figure of desire for Indian men, and unlike her predecessors in Mutiny literature, this trait leads not to her death, but to the death of those whose desire for her is a transgression of the racial barrier between them.[27] Her ability to disguise herself – common among male characters of this body of literature, but less so among women – involves the ability to cross gender as well as racial lines, when she successfully adopts the dress of a sepoy (293), and when she confronts Indian men and saves Indian women. Once she has saved Ashby's life, however, she is relegated from romantic hero/heroine to the role of his nurse, and finally leaves India with him. While the novel celebrates her success, it does so uneasily: the agency attributed to British women cannot be historicised or made part of legend as the *Rajasthan* tradition does with Indian female roles, but it is also incompatible with the good order of the British community in India. Though the story of *Jenetha's Venture* is clearly a triumph for the heroine, it also suggests that there is no place in British India for her.

Post-Mutiny Constructions of 'Home' and Colony

During the period 1857–8, mutiny in the ranks of the army and more widespread rebellion across north India threatened the security of the British colonial state. Such traumatic and widely reported events as the killing of women in the Bibighar at Cawnpore, the siege of Lucknow, and the killing of the garrison at Jhansi all contributed to a change in attitudes to India.[28] Sensational media reports focused in particular on the fate of British women and children, and contributed to an initial revulsion and desire for revenge among the British in India. These events were also seen as a justification for the acts of reprisal such as those carried out under the command of Colonel James Neill, when soldiers burned villages and put Indians (in many cases not involved in the conflict) to death by hanging. While this emotional response was, at least initially, shared by the press and public in Britain, both the East India Company as an institution and the actions of individual colonisers were soon assigned some of the blame for the outbreak of rebellion.[29] This is evident, for instance, in the focus on the failures of the British officer corps to maintain control of the army, and to understand the religious and other concerns of their men, in nineteenth-century analyses such as T. R. Holmes's *History of the Indian Mutiny* (1883), which refers to fears among soldiers of forced conversions fostered by the religious zeal of individuals including Lord Canning, governor general at the outbreak of rebellion, and his wife.[30]

The East India Company, which had exerted direct or indirect authority over most of India for the previous century, was replaced in 1858 by government from London, a change accompanied by wholesale reform of the Indian army. Direct rule also entailed a closer monitoring of, and involvement in, the administration of India from Britain. This also led to the colonial government becoming more vulnerable to instability caused by the uncertain nature of British party politics, with policies on Indian affairs susceptible to change at any time in accordance with shifts in the balance of domestic political power.[31]

These events and processes underlie the changes visible in British writers' representations of their experience of India in the latter decades of the century. In the aftermath of Mutiny, there arose an increased social and physical distance between colonisers and colonised.[32] The sense of increasing isolation apparent in the literature of this period is, however, fostered by disaffection with 'home' – at least in its public and political manifestations – as well as with India. Despite the technological advances that enabled faster and safer travel to and from India, and the virtually immediate communication, at least within major centres of population, offered by the telegraph system, the British community in India appears in some respects to be at least as far away from 'home' as in the early decades of the century. This is apparent in the work of writers such as Rudyard Kipling, whose 'Pagett, MP' exults in the plight of the eponymous visitor to India, compelled by personal experience of heat and adversity to reconsider his views on colonisers, and the pseudonymous 'Ram Bux' (discussed in more detail below), whose *Boojum Ballads* offers a succession of complaints about the 'senseless intrusion' of the 'stay-at-home fool' in Britain on the proper business of colonial government.[33]

This development of a sense of the British community in India as separate from and opposed to both India and Britain also involved a growing apprehension of Indian aspirations to self-determination as a threat to colonial dominance. This becomes evident in the representation of such Indians, and particularly the rising middle classes, whose depiction in the work of Kipling and other writers attests to the anxiety provoked by their encroaching onto the previously British space of administration and government. The response to this anxiety often took the form of a bitter attack on Indian aspirations towards self-determination, and in particular on the group most associated with the incipient nationalist movement, the professional classes of Bengal.

Indian men of these classes had long been engaged in an attempt to attain greater autonomy within the colonial state, especially by gaining access to the civil service. While the formal ban on Indians being employed as judges and revenue officials instituted during the tenure of Cornwallis in 1793 lasted only until the 1830s, Bentinck's reforms enabled Indian judges to try only civil cases involving Indian subjects, and Indian employees were confined to the lower ranks of the Bengal civil service.[34] Although the institution of a system of examinations for the Indian Civil Service from 1854 onwards allowed, in theory, Indian men to enter into the higher ranks of the ICS, the experience of those who encountered obstacles created by British individual and institutional prejudice, such as Surendranath Banerjea, indicates that this was not a route open in practice. In the words of Lewis Wolpert, the administration of India became 'even more exclusively British' during the post-Mutiny period.[35] Nonetheless, the development of the Congress movement from the 1880s onward contributed to a growing awareness among the British community of the Indian elite classes as posing a real threat to colonial interests in India.

The British perception of Bengali men (scholarship on this issue, like the source material, has an unfortunate tendency to refer to 'Bengalis' in general, where the argument is clearly relevant to men only) as weaker and less 'manly' than men from elsewhere in India, or from Europe, dates back to the early days of the British encounter with India. Thomas Macaulay's account emphasises these characteristics: Bengali men are 'enervated' by the 'soft climate' and 'accustomed to peaceful avocations':

> Whatever the Bengalee does, he does languidly. His favourite pursuits are sedentary. He shrinks from bodily exercise; and, though voluble in dispute, and singularly pertinacious in the war of chicane, he seldom engages in a personal conflict, and scarcely ever enlists as a soldier. We doubt whether there be a hundred genuine Bengalees in the whole army of the East India Company. There never, perhaps, existed a people so thoroughly fitted by nature and by habit for a foreign yoke.[36]

Mrinalini Sinha's analysis of this stereotype points to a significant change taking place in the last decades of the nineteenth century. Rather than characterising all Bengali men as effeminate, the term is 'used quite specifically to characterise the Indian middle class, or a section of this class identified as *babus*' – whether or not these are geographically located in Bengal itself. Now attached to the category of 'politically discontented middle-class "natives" from all over India', the pejorative appellation of 'babu' comes to signify in particular those whose desire for political agency challenged those 'rights and privileges' previously secured to the British in India.[37]

The 'babu' is a favourite target of 'Ram Bux', whose *Boojum Ballads* constitutes a series of intemperate meditations on the state of India, and the role of British people within it, towards the end of the Victorian period. (In the absence of contextual information on the writer, these poems are read at face value, in keeping with the 'voice' built up across the collection.[38]) In these works, discrete anecdotes or vignettes are used to establish a Bengali group identity, based in this case on such traits as cowardice, self-servingness, physical degeneracy and effeminacy. These individual and racial characteristics ascribed to babus are used to discredit their pretensions to self-determination, and position them as essentially inferior to the British in India. Whereas Rajput martial strength could be celebrated, or at least acknowledged, as part of a narrative of past greatness, the immediacy of the challenge posed by the babu to the British presence and role in India – even though this was not to be realised for another half a century – evoked a scornfully negative response. The babu's aspirations are not only misguided on account of his inability to realise them, but also motivated by base and self-seeking impulses:

> There was a Bengali B.A.
> Who failed to draw government pay:
> So with malice he burned
> And 'patriot' turned
> And reviled the 'Sirkar' night and day![39]

In 'The Bounding Babu: or, Young Bengal' (39–42), the first encounter of the British with India sees them discover the 'latent babu / Digging with a penless hand', suffering the rule of 'moslem tyrants, / Scarcely master of his soul'. Only when the incoming colonisers '[d]rove his moslem master far' does the babu find his voice, quite literally, as imitation of the British points the way to success:

> Left for e'r their fields and jungles –
> Hugli's banks their home became,
> And they learnt our Western lingo,
> Bubbling over with the same.
> Primed with Occidental learning,
> Which they fail to understand –
> Now the new-born *nation*'s ready –
> Now they claim to rule the land.
> . . .
> Armed with pens, they're pressing forward,
> Claiming all a *nation*'s part.
> 'What has Europe now to teach us?
> East and West in *us* you see.
> Liberty's the lesson taught us,
> And we'll now be equal – free!' (39)

The element of excess in this portrait – the babu bubbling over with his newly acquired anglophone voice – and the writer's eagerness to discountenance the claim to national identity and equality both suggest the anxiety that underlies such representations of Bengal nationalism. With heavy-handed irony, the narrative persona, embodying the voice of the British community in India, reports the babu's accusation that the British have ruined India:

> Ne'er cholera and fever
> Raged thus in days of yore,
> Nor famines claimed their millions
> On our once happy shore! (40)

The poem ends with the narrator restating British claims to the moral high ground as well as the upper hand:

> Yes, we'll fight for truth and justice –
> We'll defend ourselves and you,
> And we'll do our honest duty,
> Far as mortal man can do;
> But we'll keep what e'er we've gotten –
> Won with endless blood and gold,
> E'en in spite of all your logic
> And your pen, my babu bold. (41)

The annual meetings of the Indian National Congress from 1885 onwards provided a focal point for this distaste at incipient Indian nationalism. Responding to the meeting of 1888 held in Allahabad (or Prág, as the poem refers to it), 'Young India' positions its subjects somewhere between animals (the 'pack') and unruly children, in one of the conventional metaphors of colonialism:

> A babu pack was run at Prág,
> Our fancy to engage.
> They railed against whate'er exists,
> And called themselves a *'nation,'*
> And said that they were now of age,
> And ripe for agitation.

With sarcastic relish, the narrator anticipates the time when 'babu arms' would 'defend us from the cruel'; while the departure of the British – 'Their rule is o'er' – would enable 'Bharat's children' to enjoy 'what sahibs have won!' (58–9). A more measured, but equally decided, view of the Congress and its contribution to India is expressed by Kipling in 'The Enlightenments of Pagett, MP', published the following year, where the newcomer Pagett is disabused of his 'plausible notions on Indian matters' by a conversation with the long-serving British administrator Orde, who describes it as a 'British contrivance' irrelevant to the lives of Indians, and the ideas held by its supporters as 'directly hostile to the most cherished convictions of the vast majority of the people'.[40]

Another session of Congress, chaired by Dadabhai Naoroji, gave rise to 'Mr Thomas Atkins on the Congress', written in imitation of Kipling, whose *Barrack-Room Ballads* included several dialect verses on the subject of the lives of common soldiers sometimes referred to by the stock term 'Tommy Atkins'.[41] The narrator, using a Kiplingesque demotic register, decries at length the proceedings of congress – a 'congresswaller show, / It's a bally 'umbug sheer' – and the shift of power he sees in India:

> For *honly* t'other day,
> A native give me cheek
> And when I 'it 'im in the eye,
> 'e 'ad me 'fore the beak;
> And though I see 'e checked me –
> I know 'is 'eathen 'bát' –
> The boss, 'e went and fined me,
> And took the nigger's part –
> And then yer talks of justice!
> But what's a cove to do,
> When niggers gives yer impidence,
> Addressin' yer as 'tu'? (201)

The poem also refers to agitators wanting to change the Viceroy's council, and 'cram it full o' natives, / As knows the nigger's ways, / And sack the English gennelmen, / As Inja's trust betrays'.[42] The resentful voice of the text, with its defence of the racial hierarchy that set white British people, of whatever class, above Indians, also echoes the controversy over the proposal in 1883 to enact legislation to enable British residents of India to be tried by Indian judges. Following an intense campaign of protest against a measure which inspired outrage at the idea that Indians might occupy positions of authority over colonisers, the Ilbert Bill was enacted in much-modified form in 1884.[43]

British distrust of 'natives' in positions of power persisted, and may be discerned in works such as Kipling's 'Ballad of Boh da Thone' (1888). This poem reprises the encounter with a bandit familiar in pre-Mutiny texts, but gives it a comic turn, as the role traditionally filled by the British coloniser (the Sahib in *Confessions of a Thug*, the narrator in 'The Dakoit') is given instead to a Babu, Harendra Mukherji. Motivated by the thought of monetary reward, Mukherji sets out in search of the bandit Boh da Thone, and is unexpectedly, albeit comedically, successful. When his convoy comes under attack from the Boh's forces, his cowardly impulse to run away is thwarted:

> The Babu shook at the horrible sight,
> And girded his ponderous loins for flight,
>
> But Fate had ordained that the Boh should start
> On a lone-hand raid of the rearmost cart,
>
> And out of that cart, with a bellow of woe,
> The Babu fell – flat on the top of the Boh!

For years had Harendra served the State,
To the growth of his purse and the girth of his *pêt*

There were twenty stone, as the tally-man knows,
On the broad of the chest of this best of Bohs.

The bandit is crushed to death, and his unwitting killer claims the reward in the conventional 'babu-English' (combining an extensive and elaborate vocabulary with comically misplaced emphasis or mistaking of nuance), explaining that 'Price of Blood / Much cheap at one hundred, and children want food', and signing off with the hope that his interlocutor will 'show awful kindness to satisfy me, I am, Graceful Master, Your H. Mukherji'.[44] The effect is to invite the reader's derision for both the hapless bandit and his oversized nemesis, both far removed from the romanticised portraits of the colonial encounter with the 'other' offered in earlier narratives.

Late Appropriations of *Rajasthan*

In the climate of British anxiety and derision about the prospect of Indian authority and agency that produced these texts, it is perhaps surprising that the accounts of Rajput sovereignty and heroism developed in *Rajasthan* continued to serve as source material and inspiration for writers in the post-Mutiny period. This legacy of *Rajasthan* takes several different forms. Some individual elements of the historical narrative constructed in the work, such as the equation of Rajput social organisation with European feudalism, were rejected by later historians.[45] At the same time, paradoxically, the historiography developed through the work, with its foregrounding of the Rajput states' dynastic and feudal social order, enabled the British tactic of positioning their rulers as 'loyal vassals of the crown' in the aftermath of the 1857 rebellion.[46] As in the pre-Mutiny period, the general tenor of the work, and the individual stories that fill out and add colour to the historiographical framework of *Rajasthan*, proved more influential than the precise nature of Tod's concept of Rajput history. As literature, then, the work informs and shapes a diverse engagement by later writers with the history of Rajputana.

This is particularly the case among Indian poets and playwrights, for whom Tod's work, and that of other writers on Indian history such as Grant Duff and Mountstuart Elphinstone, served as a resource to be used in furthering a nationalist narrative – part of a more general move to produce what Ellen Brinks terms 'a heroic counter-history' to British accounts of India.[47] Rabindranath Tagore and Michael Madhusudan Dutt were among those who recast Tod's accounts of the culture and society of Rajputana, and the heroic episodes of its past, as a contemporary 'call for Indian resistance against the British'.[48] *Rajasthan* was translated many times over into the indigenous languages of India (Joshi notes 'at least ten' in the early 1880s); and associated with a Hindu heritage of courage and patriotism.[49] Tod's work also continued to be used by Western writers into the twentieth century, with a portrait of the man himself as 'savior and protector' of the Rajputs offering a personification of Victorian colonial paternalism. Jason Freitag suggests that such appropriations have the effect of adding to the status of Tod himself and the British government in India, as well as popularising Tod's image of Rajput society.[50]

Looking at some examples of work from the final decades of the century, however, it can be argued that writers such as Kipling, Arnold and Trevor do not so much popularise Tod's own concept of Rajputana as appropriate and transform it in ways that reflect the political context of post-Mutiny British India, and in particular the sense of India as being in decline and in need of British salvation. These texts look back to Tod's representation of Rajasthan, while re-inflecting it as part of an imperial teleology, located on a timeline leading to a 'civilised' and pacified British India where Indian agency is relegated to the past.

The Post-Mutiny Narrative of Indian Decay

Far from glorifying Indian martial activity, Alfred Lyall's poems look back with a qualified nostalgia to the encounter with a rebel/bandit figure of the kind described in the literature of the early nineteenth century. Lyall's own experience of India contributed to the mindset revealed by his poetry: soon after his arrival in India to take up a post as assistant magistrate, he found himself caught up in the events of the Indian Mutiny, and played an active part in a voluntary cavalry corps in Meerut. 'We are exercising unsparing revenge and hang people daily', he wrote during the aftermath.[51] A similar attitude is visible in some of his poetry, which carries out the discursive equivalent of exhibiting captured bandits and rebels for a colonial audience seeking reassurance that insurrection is no longer a threat to British order in India. 'The Old Pindaree' takes as its narrator a former raider now forced to adopt peaceful ways, but resentful of British rule and nostalgic for the traditions and warlike pursuits of his youth. The India represented through his voice is far removed from the romantic past evoked by his account of his parents' exploits:

> My father was an Afghán, and came from Kandahar:
> He rode with Nawáb Amir Khan in the old Maratha war:
> From the Dekkan to the Himalay, five hundred of one clan,
> They asked no leave of prince or chief as they swept thro' Hindusthan;
>
> My mother was a Brahminee, but she clave to my father well;
> She was saved from the sack of Juleysur, when a thousand Hindus fell;
> Her kinsmen died in the sally; so she followed where he went,
> And lived like a bold Patháni in the shade of a rider's tent.[52]

His own life, by contrast, is one of small oppressions suffered in mute rage, from the British man who 'has taken my old sword from me, and tells me to set up a school', to the 'sneaking Baboo, with a belted knave at his heel', whose demand for bribes is a form of robbery alien to him (2). While his plight, his distaste for those 'greedy traders' who used the civil law as a form of exploitation, and his invocation of a martial past caught the imagination of Lyall's readers, the poem is careful to neutralise the potential threat he poses to colonial order, even if that order is less than sympathetic.[53] The final stanza, where the protagonist imagines himself rejuvenated and able to act as he pleases, is resolutely downbeat as the rest of the poem, as he invokes the Pindari leader Cheetoo only to reinscribe him as a symbol of failure:

> And if I were forty years younger, with my life before me to choose,
> I wouldn't be lectured by Káfirs, or bullied by fat Hindoos;
> But I'd go to some far off country where Musalmáns still are men,
> Or take to the jungle, like Cheetoo, and die in the tiger's den. (8)

His own fate, less dramatic, is to resist British authority and control of India in ways that are amusing but ultimately futile:

> Then comes a Settlement Hákim, to teach us to plough and to weed,
> (I sowed the cotton he gave me, but first I boiled the seed)
> He likes us humble farmers, and speaks so gracious and wise
> As he asks of our manners and customs; I tell him a parcel of lies. (3)

Although an old man and a father, his role here is that of rebellious child – his mastery of knowledge, and withholding of that from the district officer, is a form of resistance that relegates him to pointlessness. Compared to Parker's version of the bandit/rebel in 'Indian War Song' (see Chapter 4), the protagonist is still living, but in his powerless state is an even less convincing figure of Indian self-determination. While Parker's Pindari tried (in however unlikely a fashion) to rally all elements of an emerging Indian nation, Lyall's equivalent merely mourns his own predatory past, and so the prospect of a credible Indian nationalism, or successful insurrection against colonial rule, is removed to an even further distance.

The Rajput states in general remained largely quiet during the Mutiny, as their rulers held to the treaties signed forty years before, despite some local uprisings and incidents where bandits made common cause with local rebel leaders in order to take arms against British rule.[54] The history of conflict and antipathy between Rajputs and Muslim invaders meant that there was little support for a rebellion with the Mughal Emperor in Delhi as its figurehead; and British successes against Marathas and Pindaris during the Maratha wars had brought about a peace dividend for the Rajputs. This enabled the British in the post-Mutiny period to develop a narrative of Rajput martial independence sustained within a larger British Empire in India. Lyall's essay 'The Rajput States of India', for instance, remarks on the success of the 'pure-blooded Rajpút clans' in maintaining 'their independence under their own chieftains, and . . . [keeping] together their primitive societies, ever since the dominion of the Rajpúts over the great plains of North-Western India was cast down and broken to pieces seven centuries ago by the Musalmán irruptions from Central Asia.'[55] Rajasthan here becomes a 'primitive' remnant of India's past, its survival both testimony to that long-ago failure of Indians to maintain their own sovereignty and a reminder of the long-standing British claim to have brought stability to an India fragmented and disordered by the collapse of Mughal rule.

Despite this general sense conveyed by Lyall's essay of a British ability to accommodate and celebrate Rajput nationalism, albeit of a limited and denatured kind, his earlier poetic work suggests a different and more anxious view. In two poems written on the topic of Rajput self-determination, an abortive attempt by Rajputs to realise nationalist ambitions is quickly succeeded by their abject surrender. 'Rajpoot Rebels' opens on the sight of 'twenty Rajpoot rebels, / Haggard and pale and thin', who sit on the bank of the Sardah river in Nepal, and consider their plight. Their leader speaks for them:

> From my country driven
> With the last of my haunted band,
> My home to another given,
> On a foreign soil I stand.[56]

Thoroughly defeated, they are characterised by 'listless woe' and 'sunken and weary' eyes, and shivering with cold and disease. Far from displaying the conventional Rajput characteristics of shared purpose, chivalry and honour, they are atomised individuals: 'no one cared for his neighbour, / There was sickness or wounds on all' (25). This point is particularly worthy of note, given Lyall's later insistence that Rajput social organisation is founded on the 'dominion of the clan' and mutual obligation rather than on feudal principles.[57] Rajput martial prowess is no match for that of the 'English foe': 'a sword and a matchlock gun' are powerless against 'the serried line of bayonets bright / A thousand moving like one!' (27) In contrast to *Rajasthan*'s tales of Rajput willingness to sacrifice life to the cause of honour and the kingdom, these rebels anticipate a reluctant yielding to conquest, when they will 'plough with a heavy heart' and try to maintain their lands ''Gainst the usurer's oath, and the lawyer's art', in a world where martial ardour has no place (28). Their leader describes a life of subjection – they will 'cringe like slaves' – endured for 'pay and a morsel of bread'. The final lines appear at first glance to be a version of the chivalric Rajput choice of death over dishonour: 'Our sons may brook the Feringhee's rule, / There is no more life for me!' (28). Set against the detailed imagination of surrender, however, and with no account offered of the death so anticipated, the line is unconvincing. The rebellion of the title is invoked only in the moment of its failure.

From rebel defeat to the invocation of decay and death, another Lyall poem, 'A Rajput Chief of the Old School', with its epigraph 'Moribundus Loquitur' ('the dying [man] speaks'), is a poem that faces two directions. It represents its protagonist as an example of degeneration, the martial attributes associated with Rajput chiefs now deteriorated into old age and weakness. On the point of death, he looks back to 'that summer I rebelled' (39), and to the days of his father's reign; but also forward to a future that holds only subjection. 'Yet the hard world softens, and change is best, / My sons must leave the ancient ways', says the narrator; and an important part of this change is the arrival of the British and the impossibility of resistance to them:

> Eight months my grandsire held the keep
> Against the fierce Maratha hordes;
> It would not stand three winter suns
> Before the shattering English guns. (42)

As he anticipates death, so he also anticipates the ruin of his stronghold: 'these rude old faithful stones . . . / Must rive and moulder'. The prospect of peace and good order is alien to him, and described in terms of stagnation – 'when all the earth is calm / And forts are level, and foes agree / Since feuds must end, to trade and farm, / And toil, like oxen, patiently' (42–3). The tension in the poem derives from the contrast between the heightened, colourful examples of past Rajput life, and the drab reality of the colonial administration; but the former is located decidedly in the past.

In this context, the Rajput chief becomes a mournful figure, his fate serving as both a guarantee of Indian subordination and a memorial to past greatness. The abandoned building that was his palace – a 'desert ruin, choked with sands, / A broken well 'mid trees that fade' (43) – offers a clear echo of Shelley's Ozymandias in its marking of the decay of Rajput nationalism.[58] Lyall's work, then, appears to be motivated by the impulse to valorise Rajput traditions and lament their passing, while at the same time his representation of the Rajputs emphasises the fact that they are of the past, as well as their inability to stand against the British – again denaturing and disavowing Indian agency even while it is apparently being celebrated.

Historicising *Rajasthan* in Late Victorian Poetry

This approach is repeated in the works of George Trevor and Edwin Arnold, each of whom draws on Tod's *Rajasthan* as source material and inspiration for his own writing. Trevor, an army officer and colonial administrator in the Rajput states, published *Rhymes of Rajputana* (1894) towards the end of his career in India. The volume includes some poems on contemporary subjects, but most of it is taken up with incidents from *Rajasthan*. Trevor adheres closely to Tod's narrative, often down to repetition of phrases (see below), but changes the dynamic of the Rajput story within the larger context of British India. This is evident in the series of poems set in Mewar, and recalling Tod's account of Alauddin's successive attacks on Chitor, motivated by desire for the princess Padmini.[59] 'At Chitor' and 'The Suttee of Gorah's Wife' cover two stages of this narrative: 'Padmani the peerless' offers herself as ransom to save her husband as Alauddin attacks Chitor for the first time, but he is eventually freed at the cost of 'perchance eight thousand men', as the Rajput warriors fight 'Like demons, and mowed down [their enemies] like grass'.[60] 'The Suttee of Gorah's Wife' is a vignette from the same event, focusing on Gorah and his nephew Badul who led the Rajput forces. Gorah dies in the assault, and Badul returns to tell the story to his widow, assuring her that 'He spread a carpet of the slain upon / The gory bed of honour', and 'left no foe to dread or praise'. She, with the 'spirit of the Rajput glowing / Within her breast', joins her husband's body on the pyre, and 'with him passed away' (32–5). Much of this dialogue comes straight from Tod, with minimal alteration: for example, Tod's 'to dread or admire him' (1. 262) becomes Trevor's 'to dread or praise' (33).

The narrative framework of the text relocates both the narrative and its source text in the context of a late Victorian reorientation of Tod's work. At the beginning of the first poem, 'At Chitor', the series is presented as the work of a 'local bard ... supposed to be speaking to an English traveller' (27). Despite the connotations of unfamiliarity with the location associated with the role of 'traveller', it is contextualised as information already possessed by the hearer: 'You have heard the story before.' This is a favourite device of Trevor's, repeated several times in the course of the volume.[61] It might justifiably be supposed an example of the poet's lack of imagination, but it is also part of his project of ventriloquising Tod, and through him his sources (here personified and given the veneer of localism and authenticity deriving from an artificial first-person oral narrative), in an orchestrated polyphonic testimony to the glories of a Rajasthan now subsumed into an improved, though less chivalric, colonial British India.

The device of the native informant is used in these poems to present as authentic (that is, indigenous) knowledge a version of Rajput history and mythology that is taken from Tod's work. In 'At Oodeypore', the 'local guide ... supposed to be addressing an Englishman who is in a boat fishing' tells his listener how the 'tribes and customs' of the region 'have all been revealed / By Tod Sahib – was there ever such a man?' His further relaying of information to the Englishman is prefaced with the phrase 'You know', signifying that the knowledge he offers is generated from and already possessed by the British. Interspersing his lore with instances of British improvements – 'The Durbars (that's the chiefs) have frequently / Troubles with Thákurs, which, at one time quelled / By arms, the British Government / Now settles' – he ends by offering to 'show you all / The local sights'; these are further examples of the British influence: 'the city, the Victoria Hall / And Lansdowne Hospital'.[62]

This narrative of colonial knowledge and colonial civilisation of India is further developed throughout the volume. The final poem in the 'Chitor' series, 'The Third Sack and After', describes a process of fragmentation: 'times soon changed. / Rajwarra tore her entrails; our own fiefs / And vassals blossomed into minor chiefs, / Servants of Delhi' (46). Into this new landscape, the arrival of the British is presented first almost in passing, as 'thro' Chitor men came from Inglistan' (47), and then as a kind of salvation for Rajasthan. While the speaker laments lost opportunities – 'What glory might have fallen on the land / And made the lotus of our love expand / Had only Rajasthan remained allied!' – the period of Maratha dominance is passed over in a subclause, as the speaker moves back to prophesise that which has already happened. 'We could not see', he says:

178   *Representations of India*

> That Chitor would look down with helpless eyes
> On the Mahratta camped beneath her walls,
> Thirsting to spoil the jewels and bright halls
> Of Oodeypore: and that his robberies
>
> Would last a century and leave Méwar
> Beggared of almost all but her past fame –
> Till the red coats and the white faces came,
> And once again uprose her fortune's star. (48–9)

This 'fortune's star' does not signify a resurgence of the former status of Rajasthan, but its reappearance in the guise of a British protectorate. 'The Mayo College', dated 1890, uses the foundation of the eponymous college by the then Viceroy, the Earl of Mayo, 'for the education of the chiefs and nobility of Rajputana' to draw an explicit comparison between the past state of Rajasthan and the benefits of British rule, culminating in the school's motto, 'Let there be light':

> The history of Rajwarra reeks with war;
> But since then came the long, long reign of peace
> And ordered law is growing governor,
> With fruits of knowledge yielding rich increase. (12–13)

The scope of the British 'civilising mission' is further extended in 'Infanticide' to encompass the issues of infanticide and *sati*, both represented as belonging to the distant past, and both now the occasion for a narrative of colonial salvation and Indian gratitude:

> But the strong hand that quenched the death of flame
> Is reverenced throughout the land, and shame
> Now clings to relics of a country's pride –
> What relic worse than girl-infanticide? (111–12)

The theme of Indian reverence for the coloniser is maintained in 'Dixon Sahib', which celebrates a colonial administrator in the same rhetorical tone as the heroes of old Rajasthan: in the headnote to the poem, the eponymous Colonel Dixon is described as having 'ruled over' several of the Rajput states; after his death, his name is 'a household word in both districts, and his tomb at Beawur is still an object of veneration and pilgrimage'. He 'reigned serene', the narrator recounts, 'Till the great Mutiny. That broke his heart.' The outbreak of rebellion is distanced from Dixon's subjects, 'thousands' of whom mourned his death: 'people still describe / His deeds with love and wonder; near and far / They speak and date from time of "Dixon Sahib".'[63] By these strategies of parallelism and ventriloquism, Trevor's work transforms the legends of 'old' Rajasthan into a prelude to a more dynamic narrative of British order and patriarchal control.

Compared to Trevor's detailed and contextualised accounts of Rajput legends, the poems of Arnold are vignettes, brief sketches of single episodes which appear to invite a sentimental response to an instance of feminine courage or sacrifice. He, like Trevor, uses the device of a British narrator who elicits a story by dialogue with an indigenous informant. In 'A Rajpût Nurse', this storyteller, Vittoo, tells of how Môti is appointed wet nurse to the motherless baby son of the Rana of Joudhpore, and suckles him alongside her own child. When the palace is invaded by the Rana's enemies with the aim of killing the boy, she quickly switches the clothes worn by the children:

And laid her own dear offspring, her flesh and blood on the floor,
With the girdle of pearls around him, and the cap that the King's son wore;
While close to her heart, which was breaking, she folded the Râja's joy,
And – even as the murderers lifted the purdah – she fled with his boy.[64]

The invaders are taken in by the deception and her own child is put to death as she flees.

Though Arnold locates the story in Jodhpur (Marwar), it derives from an episode in *Rajasthan*'s Annals of Mewar, when, in Tod's words, a 'Rajpootnee of the Kheechee tribe, her name *Punna*, or "the Diamond"', saved her charge Oody Sing, then 'about six years of age', in parallel circumstances, resulting in the death of her own son. *Rajasthan* continues Punna's story at some length, narrating her continuing care for the prince as she ensures that he finds refuge and acts on his behalf until her testimony sees him restored to his true identity.[65] Udai Singh (1540–72), the boy in question, was head of the Sisodia ruling family of Mewar and foremost in status among all the rulers of Rajputana; his defeat and the sack of his city of Chitor by Akbar in 1567 marked the overwhelming superiority of Mughal power in north India.[66] His childhood rescue and return to power is thus an event of great significance, but Arnold treats it simply as human interest, erasing the complex machinations of Rajput state politics in order to end the poem with a fictional instance of apparently pointless sacrifice, as the nurse commits suicide.

Another poem of Arnold's, 'The Rajpoot Wife', similarly focuses on feminine devotion and sacrifice, and uses it to tell a story of Rajput defeat. The plot is based on the life of Suraj Dev, a Dogra ruler of Jammu.[67] Abdool Shureef Khan invades Rajput territory and takes prisoner the Rajah Soorj Dehu, holding him in an 'iron cage', and ordering that he should 'die in torment, or live a Mussulman'.[68] Refusing to undergo conversion, he eventually succumbs to torture. His wife Neila disguises herself in the sari of a dancing girl and sings to her husband as he dies, then performs the erotic 'dance of the bee' in order to gain access to Shureef Khan. Having stabbed and beheaded him, she performs *sati* on the pyre where her husband burns.

The action of the poem is again distanced from the reader by a frame narrative – where the bardic narrator is requested to 'sing something, Jymul Rao' – and tied to the present day of the listeners, though not the readers:

> And vain of village praise, but full of ancient days,
> He begins with a smile and with a sigh –
> 'Who knows the babul-tree by the bend of the Ravee?'
> Quoth Gunesh, 'I!' and twenty voices, 'I!' (101)

In this way, the story is represented as part of the local colour of India, bound up with the parochialism of 'village praise' and the nostalgia of 'ancient days'; it also deploys the local knowledge of the bard's audience to associate the events of Rajput legend with the everyday lives of contemporary Indians. Removed from its context in the history of Rajasthan, the episode is used to represent India as timeless, enthralled by its past and rehearsing a narrative of failure: the final lines of the poem depict the Rajputs carrying away 'the ashes of dead kinsmen' (112), calling into being again the trope of Indian decay.

It will be apparent that the tenor of British responses to India evident in the representations discussed in this chapter is generally one of disengagement, notwithstanding the close attention to some aspects of the subcontinent visible in individual texts. Across the range of writers and genres discussed, the tendency is to flatten and distance the politics and history of Indian nationalism, whether Rajput or Bengali. The valorised portraits of Indian women accessed through *Rajasthan* are co-opted or anglicised, while the uneasily recognised agency of Indian men is wholly criminalised or derided as unmanly. Even as *Rajasthan* began to constitute, in the works of indigenous writers, the basis of a narrative of Indian self-realisation, the post-Mutiny works of British writers form a counter-narrative, one which emphasises colonial domination and Indian subjection.

Notes

1. Several critics have addressed the uneasy dynamic of sympathy and repulsion between the protagonist, the imprisoned thug Ameer Ali, and the Sahib who hears his story. Tickell offers an overview of work in this area (*Terrorism*, pp. 46–8).
2. The colonial state's treatment of thug criminals was designed to further this

perception of their role as 'other', extending to the method and representation of their execution: see my 'Staging Criminality'.
3. See Singha, *Despotism*; see also Lloyd, 'Bandits'. It has been argued that Taylor's earlier work *Confessions of a Thug* goes some way towards representing the thugs as 'a proto-nationalist insurgent group' (Tickell, *Terrorism*, p. 53; see also Mukherjee, *Crime*, pp. 109–10); Majeed, without going to these lengths, suggests that *thagi* was perceived by Taylor as 'a "system" which both necessitated and mirrored the countersystem of East India Company rule' ('Meadows Taylor', p. 89).
4. Taylor, *Seeta*, pp. 250–1.
5. Gibson, *Indian Angles*, p. 199.
6. Chakravarty, *Indian Mutiny*, p. 109.
7. Leslie, *Sorrows*, p. 39. See Keats, 'Robin Hood'; the parallel between the English legendary figure, now 'sleeping in the underwood' of history, and those of *Rajasthan* is immediately apparent (*Poems*, p. 133).
8. Leslie, *Sorrows*, p. 69; the quoted words are from the headnote to the poem, an extract from Tod's work. See *Rajasthan*, vol. 1, p. 625.
9. Later versions of the story had the protagonist converting to Islam in order to marry her captor/rescuer. Many details of this episode remain unclear, including the name of the woman involved: contemporary reports referred to 'Mary', while General Wheeler's daughters were named Margaret Frances (probably the woman in question) and Eliza. See Hibbert, *Mutiny*, pp. 194–5; Sharpe, *Allegories*, pp. 71–3.
10. Leslie, *Sorrows*, p. 12.
11. Compare Tod's account of the *jauhar* at Chitor during the siege by Alauddin, as the fire awaits 'whatever of female beauty or youth could be tainted by Tatar lust' (*Rajasthan* vol. 1, p. 266). Captain Alexander Skene, political agent at Jhansi, his wife Caroline and their two daughters were killed alongside the rest of the British garrison of the fort on 8 June 1857 after they had surrendered to rebel forces. An apocryphal version of events, current at the time, had Skene shoot his wife and then himself. See Herbert, *War of No Pity*, pp. 149–51.
12. Compare Tod on the city's last offensive against Alauddin, when the Rana gathers 'his devoted clans, for whom life no longer had any charms, they threw open the portals . . . and with a reckless despair carried death, or met it' (*Rajasthan*, vol. 1, p. 266).
13. Rana Pratap Singh (reigned 1572–97) successfully resisted the Mughal conquest of Mewar at a time when other Rajput states were making terms. See Talbot, 'Mewar', pp. 20–2.
14. Gibson, *Indian Angles*, p. 200.
15. Leslie, *Ina*, pp. 219–28; 258–64.
16. Metcalf's account of the role of Scotland in the 'British imagination' at this period suggests some of the complexity of this issue: 'Scotland had much in common with the Punjab, with the result that the "sturdy" Highlander, much like the Sikh, was invested with a distinctive martial ability' (*Imperial Connections*, p. 73); see also Streets, *Martial Races*. The equation of Scottish Highlanders with the 'people of India' dates back at least to the work of James Mill, whose account is pejorative to both (*History*, vol. 5, p. 524).

17. Pittock, *Celtic Identity*, pp. 104–5.
18. Tickell, *Terrorism*, p. 122; see also Kapila's discussion of the evolution of the post-Mutiny romance away from the 'rescue' trope (*Educating Seeta*, p. 12).
19. Taylor, *Seeta*, p. 377.
20. Such cross-cultural unions were not common after the 1830s. These relationships were structurally unequal, as Durba Ghosh points out: the female partner had no claim to social recognition from British 'familial networks', or legal recognition by the East India Company (*Sex and the Family*, p. 30). See also Kapila, *Educating Seeta*, pp. 23–51; Hawes, *Poor Relations*, pp. 1–20.
21. Kapila's wider study of Taylor's work makes the point that the process of Seeta's education and domestication might be regarded as a fictional parallel to Taylor's own political and administrative 'coercion' of the Rani of Shorapur, with whom he dealt in his role as Political Agent at Shorapur in the 1840s (*Educating Seeta*, pp. 112–16).
22. Mukherjee, *Natural Disasters*, p. 129.
23. See Paxton, 'Mobilizing chivalry', pp. 19–21; Sharpe, *Allegories of Empire*, pp. 89–91.
24. Harcourt, *Jenetha's Venture*, p. 55.
25. Sen, *Woman and Empire*, p. 130.
26. Sen, *Woman and Empire*, p. 80.
27. The idea of a consensual sexual encounter between an Indian man and a European woman is normally absent from works of this kind: in Bhupal Singh's wide-ranging overview, examples of fiction dealing with the 'marriage of an English girl with an Indian' are taken from the early twentieth century (*Survey*, pp. 171–9).
28. Streets, 'The Rebellion of 1857', pp. 11–12. The events and repercussions of the Mutiny have been subject to extensive historical analysis, and a detailed consideration is beyond the scope of this chapter. Hibbert, *Great Mutiny* remains the standard modern overview; see also David, *Indian Mutiny*.
29. Jenny Sharpe discusses the circulation of atrocity narratives founded on the (largely) imagined rape and torture of women (*Allegories*, pp. 61–73); such narratives were soon acknowledged to be 'fraudulent', but continued to influence public response and discourse (Herbert, *War*, p. 70). On British reprisals, see the account of J. W. Sherer, a contemporary observer, of the aftermath of this campaign (quoted and discussed in Sharpe, *Allegories*, pp. 76–9); and compare Gerald Massey on Neill's subordinate Major Renaud, whose actions are noted with an apparently blasé approval: 'Renaud hung his dangling dead, with but short time for shrift, / He caught them on their way to hell, and gave them there a lift' (*Havelock's March*, p. 21).
30. Holmes, *History*, pp. 77–9.
31. See Moore-Gilbert, *Kipling and 'Orientalism'*, pp. 69–78, which reads Kipling's Indian fiction in the light of these changes in the society of British India.
32. Collingham, *Imperial Bodies*, p. 165.
33. Kipling, *Complete Verse*, pp. 20–1 (the poem was first collected in *Departmental Ditties* (1886)); Ram Bux, 'Tempora Mutantur' in *Boojum Ballads*, pp. 240–50; see also 'Britons, Babus, and Viceroys' (pp. 62–4).

34. See Sramek, *Gender, Race*, pp. 109–13.
35. Wolpert, *History*, pp. 246, 251–2.
36. Macaulay, 'Review', p. 318.
37. Sinha, *Colonial Masculinity*, p. 16.
38. 'Ram Bux' is a conventional Hindu name, sometimes used at this time as a generic reference to a common soldier, as in the *Times of India*'s reference to British and Indian troops as 'both Thomas Atkins and Ram Bux Sepoy' (3 February 1892, p. 4). I am unconvinced by Willard Oxtoby's suggestions re the etymology of the name (*Experiencing India*, p. 88). The volume offers no information as to the writer's identity, though some 'Ram Bux' poems appearing in the *Times of India* may be written by the same person (see 'Conjugal Rights', 24 August 1895, p. 5; 'Fulmen Olympicum', 8 June 1895, p. 4).
39. Ram Bux, 'The B.A.', *Boojum Ballads,* p. 38. 'Sirkar' in this context indicates the British administration.
40. Kipling, *Under the Deodars*, pp. 189, 190, 216. The story was usually omitted from later editions of this collection, but an annotated text is available in Radcliffe, *New Readers' Guide* to Kipling's work at <http://www.kiplingsociety.co.uk/pagett.htm> (last accessed 27 December 2014).
41. See, for instance, 'Tommy' and 'Oonts' in Kipling, *Complete Verse*, pp. 318, 325–6.
42. Ram Bux, *Boojum Ballads*, pp. 200–3.
43. See Sinha, *Colonial Masculinities*, pp. 33–63; Kolsky, *Colonial Justice*, pp. 97–103. The unfolding of the Ilbert Bill controversy, and its intersection with the work and attitudes of the young Rudyard Kipling (then a journalist on the Allahabad *Pioneer*) and his parents Alice and Lockwood Kipling, are discussed in Havholm, *Politics*, pp. 19–41.
44. Kipling, *Complete Verse*, pp. 202–9. The poem first appeared in *Barrack-Room Ballads*. Mukherji's success, ludicrous and accidental though it is, contrasts with the abject failure of the 'babu' in Kipling's better-known later story, 'The Head of the District', where a Bengali administrator flees in panic when faced with insurrection among the tribesmen of a frontier region (*Life's Handicap*).
45. See, for instance, Lyall, *Asiatic Studies*, pp. 211–12.
46. Rudolph and Rudolph, 'Writing', pp. 274–5.
47. Brinks, *Anglophone*, p. 38; she argues that Toru Dutt and others were 'wresting control' of the archives of ancient Indian epics and folktales from 'European Orientalists' (p. 39).
48. Peabody, 'Tod's Rajast'han', p. 217; see also Chaudhuri, *Gentlemen Poets*, pp. 145–50, and the comprehensive analysis of later iterations of the legend of Padmini offered by Sreenivasan, *Many Lives*.
49. Joshi, *In Another Country*, pp. 50, 270 n. 30; see also Sreenivasan, *Many Lives*, pp. 168–70.
50. Freitag, *Serving Empire*, pp. 158, 161; see Gabrielle Festing, *From the Land of Princes* (1904). Though Freitag describes this group of texts as 'late-nineteenth century', they date mainly from the first decades of the twentieth century, with the exception of Trevor's work discussed below.
51. Quoted in Durand, *Life*, p. 72.
52. Lyall, *Verses*, pp. 4–5.

53. J. H. Rivett-Carnac, who published the poem for the first time in the *Central India Times*, c. 1864, describes it in retrospect as 'one of the most picturesque and faithfully descriptive pieces in Anglo-Indian literature'; and one of which 'hardly any educated person in [India] has not heard' (*Many Memories*, pp. 131–2).
54. Kasturi, *Embattled Identities*, p. 204. See also the detailed account of events in Mewar state offered by Bakshi and Sharma, 'Rising of 1857', and the memoir of Lieutenant-General Showers, political agent in Mewar during 1857–8, who pauses during his narrative of 'A Missing Chapter of the Indian Mutiny' to recount the story of Alauddin's invasion of Chitor in search of Padmini, in a version based on Tod's work (pp. 54–65).
55. Lyall, *Asiatic Studies*, p. 182.
56. Lyall, *Verses*, pp. 24, 25.
57. Lyall, *Asiatic Studies*, p. 210.
58. Compare Shelley, *Poems*, pp. 310–11.
59. See Tod, *Rajasthan*, vol. 1, pp. 262–4.
60. Trevor, *Rhymes*, pp. 29–31.
61. See also 'Rajah Karan Singh of Bikanir', where 'A bard of Bikanir is supposed to be speaking to an Englishman' (Trevor, *Rhymes*, p. 83); and 'The Rahtores: At Jodhpore' where 'A local bard is supposed to be addressing an English traveller' (59).
62. Trevor, *Rhymes*, pp. 21–6. The 'Notes' included in the volume are extracts from Tod's work; the introduction claims *Rajasthan* as a source for most of the poems (vii), and also cites Walter Scott as precedent for the literary device of having a local guide address the reader (viii).
63. Trevor, *Rhymes*, p. 11. Lieutenant Colonel Charles George Dixon (1795–1857), was credited with the economic development of the kingdom of Marwar. See Mulvany, *Story of Mairwara*; Dixon, *Sketch of Mairwara*.
64. Arnold, *Lotus and Jewel*, pp. 181, 183, 185.
65. Tod, *Rajasthan*, vol. 1, pp. 315–17.
66. Richards, *Mughal Empire*, pp. 25–7.
67. See Smyth, *History*, p. 236. Charak, *Short History*, describes a 'local tradition' of legend surrounding Suraj Dev, which includes the elements of his capture, imprisonment and 'choice between Islam and death' as in Arnold's version (pp. 55–6).
68. Arnold, *Indian Poetry*, p. 104.

Afterword: Reading India

The boundary between lived experience and discursive representation, inherent in the formal division of this book, is in practice neither clear-cut nor sustainable, though it serves its purpose as an organising principle. Looking at individual writers' representations of India, what comes over time and again is the complexity of what they perceive: that is, their sensory engagement with the materiality of India is both shaped by their previously formed expectations, and overlaid with their knowledge of the responses of others. Their expression of these perceptions is equally complex, formulated as it is in negotiation with existing metropolitan, colonial and indigenous tropes and genres.

Such intricate processes are apparent throughout the versions of India discussed in this book, but perhaps especially so in those texts dealing with the issue of *sati*. The combination of a sensational event (to which the writer may or may not be a direct witness), and the need to interpret that event within a framework of conflicting and intertwining ideas of gender, cultural and racial norms and expectations, creates a situation where both writer and implied reader invest the representation with multiple layers of social and emotional significance. The three examples following demonstrate some of these complexities.

One of the earliest poems written by Emma Roberts soon after her arrival in India, 'The Suttee', is a conventional narrative of the *sati* woman as victim. Suleeni's 'pensive sorrow' is evidence of her reluctance to perform the rite, but she is represented as subject to persuasion, if not coercion, from both religious figures and family members, while 'a fearful warning' deters her from incurring the scorn of 'all that she holds dear'. The final stanza adopts a passive narrative voice, recounting actions without ascribing them to human agency, thus setting Suleeni and those who surround her apart from their contemporary social context and into an ongoing timeless present:

> And now the flame upspringing,
> Mounts onward to the skies,
> And brazen gongs are ringing
> To drown the victim's cries.
> The last red volume flashes –
> And that once blooming bride,
> A blackened heap of ashes,
> Floats down the Ganges' tide.[1]

This poem, unusually, was not collected in either edition of *Oriental Scenes*, even when Roberts revised the second edition to be entirely composed of India-related material and added to it the other such works she had written during her time in India. She included instead another, later poem on the same topic: 'The Rajah's Obsequies'.

Among the distinguishing features of the latter poem is its use of a doubled female figure rather than the single protagonist of 'The Suttee'; and its technique of embedding within the narrative an instance of first-person address by each woman, the Rajah's two wives who both offer their differing reasons for performing *sati*. The elder bride, Mitala, explains her decision to undergo 'these most unholy rites' by reference to her role as a woman in a patriarchal society – 'too weak to break my sex's bands' – and her subjection to 'lordly man's controul', which extends 'beyond the grave' to force her to accept either death, or the degraded life of an 'outcast – reft of queenly state – / A beggar, lost, despised and desolate'.[2] The other, unnamed wife's song makes a claim to the agency which Mitala considers herself to be lacking, as she posits her death as a sacrifice freely offered (in accordance with some Hindu scriptures) to bring about her husband's salvation.[3]

> Lord of my soul! I yield my breath
> To snatch thee from the chains of death;
> I claim the privilege divine,
> Which makes thee more than ever mine!
>
> Yes, to my thrice blessed hands 'tis given
> To ope the saffron gates of heaven;
> I bring, beloved, a boon to thee,
> A pure and bright eternity. (55)

The speaker of these lines is portrayed by Roberts as 'the youngest (and perchance the bride / Preferred for her retiring charms)' (54); and her demeanour as she joins her deceased husband suggests that, 'In some blest trance she seems to be, / Or day's delicious reverie' (57). Despite these possible suggestions of naïvety or intoxication by one of the drugs given to women to enable them calmly to face the flames, the poem offers the song as the product of a 'voice divine' (54) – a reference to the tradition that held a *sati*'s last words to be prophetic. In that context, the younger wife's claim that her death is deliberate, willed and with purpose requires to be taken seriously. Taken at her own valuation, she is not the bemused victim of coercion seen in 'The Suttee', and in many other contemporary works on *sati*, but a woman in possession of agency.

It is impossible to identify any single reason for the difference between these texts. Roberts had seen more of India at the time of writing 'The Rajah's Obsequies' (though there is no indication that she witnessed a *sati* rite at any point); she had access to, and made use of, the poetry and paratextual notes on *sati* produced by H. L. V. Derozio; she was developing commonalities between the lives of colonised and colonising women, and possibly responding to metropolitan debates over women's property rights.[4] She was also reading widely in the history of India, with special attention to women's lives – another poem, 'The Sacrifice', is identified as having its origins in 'the third volume of Dow's Hindoostan'. This work, according to Roberts, 'abounds with records' of women 'ready to sacrifice themselves, either for the purpose of allowing their male relatives to retreat with honour, or to disappoint the victor of his promised prey, when they were about to perish in unequal fight'.[5] The stories of these women may underlie the transformation of Suleeni into the purposeful figure who claims the right to carry out by her self-sacrifice the momentous action of bringing her husband to salvation. However explained, Roberts's return to and revision of the topic of *sati* shows her drawing from and participating in several different colonial and metropolitan discourses on contemporary and historical views of individuals' socially determined roles.

At mid-century, another British poet, Henry George Keene, wrote 'Tomb of the Suttee', a meditation on a monument and the woman commemorated by it. The text depicts her as both a victim alienated from her own society – ''midst a jostling crowd / Of self-applauding saints and minstrels loud, /And loveless friends exulting in her part' – and a heroine: 'one with more than manhood's might who strove, / And conquered death by learning how to die'. It represents her going to her death with a final 'calm delight', and masks her burning with the 'flames that, odorous and bright, / Rise canopied with smoke'. The frame narrative distances her, and the act of *sati*, from the writer and the reader. This is apparent not only in references to the monument overgrown through the passage of time, but also in the narrator's interactions with his wife, who appears with him at the start and end of the poem. The concluding lines are in her voice:

> We gaze tonight
> Upon her tomb, I and my fair-haired wife;
> She – not unequal, should love bid her dare –
> As home we turn, asks, 'Does not duteous life
> Make truer martyrdom, and sight more fair
> For men and angels, than one blank hour of despair?'[6]

The gender relationships here contrast, but also reflect, those of the rest of the poem: the British woman is imagined as asking a question – albeit rhetorical – of her husband, but in doing so positioning herself as an object of the gaze of 'men and angels', and relegating the Indian woman's end to something that is not even an act, but an endurance, 'one blank hour of despair'. The poet's imagined encounter with the 'other', evolved from a tradition of colonial representations of *sati*, becomes the occasion for constructing an implicit racial and gender hierarchy in his own present day.

Towards the end of the Victorian period, Rudyard Kipling's several accounts of the deaths of Rajput kings in *Letters of Marque* include a brief reference to a *sati* performed by a dancing girl, who by doing so 'stole a march in the next world's precedence and her lord's affections, upon the legitimate queens', the king's wives. The narrator makes a point of directly referencing *Rajasthan* (Kipling read Tod's work on this journey), with the remark that she had followed the dead 'to use Tod's formula, "through the flames"'.[7] That anecdote takes second place, however, to the story of how a contemporary king made common cause with the British political agent to remove himself to a secure location on the eve of his death. This is necessary because:

> there was a fear that his womenkind should, on his death, going mad with grief, cast off their veils and run out into the streets, uncovered before all men. In which case, nothing, not even the power of the Press, and the locomotive, and the telegraph, and cheap education and enlightened municipal councils, could have saved them from *sati*, for they were the wives of a King'. (83–4)

The 'Englishman' (the traveller / Kipling's narrative persona) asks 'why a frantic woman must of necessity become *sati*', and feels 'properly abashed when he was told that she *must*. There was nothing else for her if she went out unveiled deliberately. The rush-out forces the matter. And indeed, if you consider the matter from a Rajput point of view, it does' (85). The vatic repetition leaves the question of rationale unanswered, and the dynamic of the episode uninterrogated. Underlying it, however, is the story, once more, of Alauddin and Padmini, when his predatory intent towards Chitor is expressed in terms of his demand to possess her, or at least to 'have sight of her legendary beauty'.[8] Buried under the imagery of irrational femininity, and the sceptical listing of the benefits of a colonial civilising mission, the encounter of coloniser and colonised is expressed once again in terms of the male gaze and male control of women.

These accounts demonstrate the extent to which lived experience, for these colonial writers, is itself discursive, drawing from an accumulated tradition of literary representation which permeates what appear on the surface to be transparent narratives of an encounter with India. They also show, conversely, how colonial images of Indian lives and landscapes are also reflections of their writers' own socially constructed expectations and preoccupations. The process of reading and writing India is multivalent, involving the implicit or explicit representation of 'home' as well as colony; and these writers' project of representing India involves simultaneously exploring the constitution of the colonial self.

Notes

1. Roberts, 'The Suttee', *La Belle Assemblée* (1 February 1830), p. 74. The poem is datelined Etawah, May 1829.
2. Roberts, *Oriental Scenes* (1832), p. 60.
3. The 'Petition of the orthodox Hindu community of Calcutta against the Suttee Regulation' (1830) argues that 'Hindoo widows perform [*sati*] of their own accord and pleasure, and for the benefit of their husband's soul and their own' (quoted in Mani, *Contentious Traditions*, p. 51). Mani's discussion shows the British understanding of *sati* as permitted or endorsed by Hindu scripture to have been arrived at within a context of the colonial production and codification of knowledge by means of the interrogation of pundits on their interpretations of an extensive, complex and often contradictory body of sacred texts (pp. 32–40).
4. See my 'India and Women's Poetry', pp. 193–4; Gibson, *Indian Angles*, pp. 94–7.
5. Roberts, *Oriental Scenes* (1832), p. 167; see Dow, *History of Hindostan* (1812), vol. 3, pp. 110–13.
6. Keene, *Ex Eremo*, pp. 81–3.
7. Kipling, *Letters of Marque*, p. 86. The text is from Letter VIII, written from Udaipur (Mewar) and first published in 1888. The episode of the dancing girl later became the basis of a poem, 'The Last Suttee' (*Complete Verse*, pp. 189–92).
8. Tod, *Rajasthan*, vol. 1, p. 263. Kipling retells the story (*Letters of Marque*, pp. 109–10).

Bibliography

Periodicals Cited

Agra Ukhbar
Ainsworth's Magazine
Annual Register
Asiatic Journal
Asiatic Observer: or, Religious, Literary, and Philosophical Miscellany
Asiatic Annual Register
Asiatick Miscellany
Bengal Annual
Bengal Herald
Bengal Hurkaru
Bengal Weekly Messenger
Calcutta Courier
Calcutta Gazette / Government Gazette
Calcutta Journal
Calcutta Literary Gazette
Calcutta Magazine
Calcutta Magazine and Oriental Museum
Calcutta Monthly Register
Calcutta Quarterly Magazine and Review
Calcutta Review
Ceylon Gazette
Delhi Gazette
East India United Service Journal
Eastern Miscellany
Edinburgh Review
Englishman
Fisher's Drawing Room Scrap Book
Forget-Me-Not
Government Gazette (Colombo)
Government Gazette (Madras)
Hicky's Bengal Gazette; or, Calcutta General Advertiser
India Gazette
Indian Observer
John Bull
Kaleidoscope

La Belle Assemblée: or, Bell's Court and Fashionable Magazine
Literary Gazette (London)
Literary Souvenir
Madras Comic Almanac
Madras Literary Gazette
Madras Male Asylum Herald
Meerut Universal Magazine
Mofussilite
Monthly Review
Orient Pearl
Oriental Herald
Oriental Magazine and Calcutta Review / Quarterly Oriental Magazine, Review and Register
Oriental Magazine; or, Calcutta Amusement
Oriental Miscellany
Oriental Observer / Oriental Literary Observer / Oriental Observer and Literary Chronicle
Parbury's Oriental Herald and Colonial Intelligencer
Quarterly Review
Scots Magazine
Times (London)
Times of India
Trifler
United Service Gazette and Literary Chronicle
Weekly Examiner: and, Literary Register

Other Works Cited

Abbott, James, *The T'hakoorine: A Tale of Maandoo* (London: Madden, 1841).

'Account of the late dreadful Famine in India', *The Annual Register, or A View of the History, Politics, and Literature, for the Year 1771*, xli (1772): 205–8.

Adams, Matthew (2006), 'Furnishing the colonial mind: Book ownership in British India, 1780–1850,' <http://www.ehs.org.uk/events/academic-papers-2006.html > (last accessed 31 August 2014).

Adburgham, Alison, *Women in Print: Writing Women and Women's Magazines from the Restoration to the Accession of Victoria* (London: Allen and Unwin, 1972).

Agnew, Éadaoin, 'Relocating domesticity: Letters from India by Lady Hariot Dufferin', in Julia Kuehn and Paul Smethurst (eds), *Travel Writing, Form, and Empire: The Poetics and Politics of Mobility* (London: Routledge, 2009), pp. 95–107.

Aitchison, C. U., *A Collection of Treaties, Engagements and Sanads Relating to India*, vol. III (Calcutta: Government of India, 1932).

Aliph Cheem [Walter Yeldham], *Lays of Ind*, 2nd series (Bombay: Times of India office, 1873).

Ameer Khan, *Memoirs of the Puthan Soldier of Fortune, the Nuwab Ameer-ood-Doulah Mohammud Ameer Khan*, compiled in Persian by Busawun Lal, trans. and ed. H. T. Prinsep (Calcutta: Military Orphan Press, 1832).

Anderson, Benedict, *Imagined Communities: Reflections on the Origin and Spread of Nationalism* (London: Verso, 1991).

Arnold, David, 'Deathscapes: India in an age of Romanticism and Empire, 1800–1856', *Nineteenth Century Contexts* 26.4 (2004): 339–53.
Arnold, David, 'European orphans and vagrants in India in the nineteenth century', *Journal of Imperial and Commonwealth History* 7.2 (1979): 104–27.
Arnold, David, 'Hunger in the garden of plenty: The Bengal Famine of 1770', in Alessa Johns (ed.), *Dreadful Visitations: Confronting Natural Catastrophe in the Age of Enlightenment* (London: Routledge, 1999), pp. 81–111.
Arnold, Edwin, *Indian Poetry*, 6th edn (London: Kegan Paul, Trench, Trübner, 1891).
Arnold, Edwin, *Lotus and Jewel* (Boston: Roberts, 1887).
Baker, George M., 'An echo of Schiller's *Räuber* in England', *Modern Language Notes* 26.6 (1911): 171–2.
Bakshi, S. R. and S. K. Sharma, 'Rising of 1857 and Mewar', in *Mewar Rulers and the British* (New Delhi: Deep & Deep, 2000), pp. 153–89.
Bannatyne, Colin. 'The Indian press', *Blackwood's Edinburgh Magazine* 12.67 (1822): 133–9.
Barnett, L. D., 'Catalogue of the Tod Collection of Indian manuscripts in the possession of the Royal Asiatic Society', *Journal of the Royal Asiatic Society* April (1940): 129–78.
Bayley, F. W. N., *The New Tale of a Tub* (London: Orr, 1847).
Bayly, C. A., *Empire and Information* (Cambridge: Cambridge University Press, 1995).
Bayly, C. A., *Imperial Meridian: The British Empire and the World 1780–1830* (Harlow: Longman, 1989).
Bayly, C. A., 'Rammohan Roy and the advent of constitutional liberalism in India, 1800–1830', *Modern Intellectual History* 4.1 (2007): 25–41.
Bayly, C. A., *Rulers, Townsmen and Bazaars: North Indian Society in the Age of British Expansion 1770–1870* (Cambridge: Cambridge University Press, 1983).
Bhabha, Homi K., *The Location of Culture* (London: Routledge, 1994).
Birkenhead, Lord, *Rudyard Kipling* (London: Weidenfeld & Nicolson, 1978).
Bolts, William, *Considerations on India Affairs*, 3 vols (London: Dodsley, 1772–5).
Bose, A., 'The verse of the English "Annuals"', *The Review of English Studies* 4 (n.s.) 13 (1953): 38–51.
Bowen, H. V., *The Business of Empire: The East India Company and Imperial Britain, 1756–1833* (Cambridge: Cambridge University Press, 2006).
Brinks, Ellen, *Anglophone Indian Women Writers, 1870–1920* (Farnham: Ashgate, 2013).
Brookes, J. C., *History of Meywar* (Calcutta: Baptist Mission Press, 1859).
[Broome, Ralph], *The Letters of Simkin the Second, Poetic Recorder of All the Proceedings, Upon the Trial of Warren Hastings* (London: Stockdale, 1791).
Brown, Samuel Sneade, *Home Letters, Written from India between the Years 1828 & 1841* (London: Roworth, 1878).
Buckingham, James Silk, *Autobiography*, 2 vols (London: Longman, 1855).
Buelens, Gert, Sam Durrant and Robert Eaglestone (eds), *The Future of Trauma Theory: Contemporary Literary and Cultural Criticism* (London: Routledge, 2014).
Buettner, Elizabeth, *Empire Families: Britons and Late Imperial India* (Oxford: Oxford University Press, 2004).

Burke, Edmund, *Works of the Right Hon. Edmund Burke*, intro., Henry Rogers, vol. 1 (London: Holdsworth, 1837).
Burke, Edmund, *The Writings and Speeches of Edmund Burke, Vol. VI: India: The Launching of the Hastings Impeachment 1786–1788*, ed. P. J. Marshall (Oxford: Clarendon Press, 1991).
Burke, Edmund, *The Writings and Speeches of Edmund Burke, Vol. V: India: Madras and Bengal 1774–1785*, ed. P. J. Marshall (Oxford: Clarendon Press, 1981).
Burt, Thomas Seymour, *Narrative of a Late Steam Voyage from England to India via the Mediterranean* (Calcutta: Medical Journal Press, 1840).
[Burt, Thomas Seymour], *Poems: Consisting of Tales from the Classics, the Exile's Return, the Delights of India and Miscellaneous Pieces* (London: Hayman Bros., 1853).
Burton, David, *The Raj at Table: A Culinary History of the British in India* (London: Faber, 1993).
Byron, Lord, *Lord Byron: Selected Poems*, ed. Susan Wolfson and Peter J. Manning (London: Penguin, 2005).
Cameron, G. Poulett, *The Romance of Military Life: Being Souvenirs Connected with Thirty Years' Service* (London: Cox, 1853).
Carrington, Charles, *Rudyard Kipling: His Life and Work* (1955) (Harmondsworth: Penguin, 1986).
[Caunter, John Hobart], *The Cadet*, 2 vols. (London: Jennings, 1814).
Chakravarty, Gautam, *The Indian Mutiny and the British Imagination* (Cambridge: Cambridge University Press, 2005).
Chanda, Mrinal Kanti, *History of the English Press in Bengal 1780–1857* (Calcutta: K. P. Bagchi, 1987).
Charak, Sukhdev Singh, *A Short History of Jammu Raj* (Pathankot: Ajaya Prakashan, 1985).
Chaudhuri, Brahma, 'India' in J. Don Vann and Rosemary VanArsdel (eds), *Periodicals of Queen Victoria's Empire: An Exploration* (Toronto: University of Toronto Press, 1996).
Chaudhuri, Rosinka, *Derozio, Poet of India* (New Delhi: Oxford University Press, 1998).
Chaudhuri, Rosinka, *Gentleman Poets in Colonial Bengal: Emergent Nationalism and the Orientalist Project* (Calcutta: Seagull, 2002).
Chaudhuri, Rosinka, '"Young India: A Bengal Eclogue": Meat-Eating, Race and Reform in a Colonial Poem', *Interventions* 2.3 (2000): 424–41.
[Clarke, Richard], *The Nabob: or, Asiatic Plunderers* (London, 1773).
Cohn, Bernard S., 'The recruitment and training of British civil servants in India 1600–1860', in *An Anthropologist among the Historians and Other Essays* (Delhi; Oxford: Oxford University Press, 1987), pp. 500–53.
Coleridge, Samuel Taylor, *Collected Letters of Samuel Taylor Coleridge*, 6 vols, ed. Earl Leslie Griggs (Oxford: Clarendon Press, 1956–71).
Collingham, E. M., *Imperial Bodies* (Cambridge: Polity, 2001).
Cronin, Richard, Alison Chapman, and Antony H. Harrison (eds), *A Companion to Victorian Poetry* (Oxford: Blackwell, 2002).
Cronin, Richard, *Romantic Victorians: English Literature, 1824–1840* (Gordonsville, PA: Palgrave Macmillan, 2002).
Curran, Stuart, *Poetic Form and British Romanticism* (Oxford: Oxford University Press, 1986).

David, Deirdre, *Rule Britannia: Women, Empire, and Victorian Writing* (Ithaca, NY: Cornell University Press, 1995).
David, Saul, *The Indian Mutiny: 1857* (London: Penguin, 2003).
Davidoff, Leonora and Catherine Hall, *Family Fortunes: Men and Women of the English Middle Class 1780–1850* (London: Hutchinson, 1987).
Davis, Mike, *Late Victorian Holocausts: El Niño Famines and the Making of the Third World* (London: Verso, 2001).
de Almeida, Hermione and George H. Gilpin, *Indian Renaissance: British Romantic Art and the Prospect of India* (Aldershot: Ashgate, 2005).
Delanougerede, J. F., *Wuzeerally: A Dramatic Fragment and Other Poems* (Calcutta: Artha Vanijya Gabesana Mandir, 1836).
Dirks, Nicholas B., *The Scandal of Empire: India and the Creation of Imperial Britain*. (Cambridge, MA: Harvard University Press, 2006).
Dixon, C. G., *Sketch of Mairwara* (London: Smith, Elder, 1850).
Dow, Alexander, *The History of Hindostan*, 3 vols (London: Walker, 1812).
Dow, Alexander, *The History of Hindostan, from the Earliest Account of Time to the Death of Akbar; Translated from the Persian of Mahummud Casim Ferishtah* (London: Becket and de Hondt, 1768–72).
[D'Oyly, Charles], *Tom Raw, the Griffin* (London: Ackermann, 1828).
Dunbar, John, *Poems* (Calcutta: Thacker & Spink, 1853).
Durand, M., *Life of the Right Hon. Sir Alfred Comyn Lyall* (Edinburgh and London: Blackwood, 1913).
Eden, Emily, *Up the Country: Letters Written to Her Sister from the Upper Provinces of India* (London: Bentley, 1867).
Elfenbein, Andrew, *Byron and the Victorians* (Cambridge: Cambridge University Press, 1995).
Elwood, Mrs Colonel [Anne Katharine], *Narrative of a Journey Overland from England*, vol. 2 (London: Bentley, 1830).
'English in India,' *Calcutta Review* 1.1 (1844), pp. 1–41.
Erickson, Lee, *The Economy of Literary Form: English Literature and the Industrialization of Publishing, 1800–1850* (Baltimore and London: Johns Hopkins University Press, 1996).
Erickson, Lee, 'The market', in Richard Cronin, Alison Chapman and Antony H. Harrison (eds), *A Companion to Victorian Poetry* (Oxford: Blackwell, 2002), pp. 345–60.
Ewen, Frederic, *The Prestige of Schiller in England 1788–1859* (New York: Columbia, 1932).
Ferris, Ina, *The Romantic National Tale and the Question of Ireland* (Cambridge: Cambridge University Press, 2002).
Festing, Gabrielle, *From the Land of Princes* (London: Smith, Elder, 1904).
Finkelstein, David and Douglas M. Peers, '"A great system of circulation": Introducing India into the nineteenth-century media', in Finkelstein and Peers (eds), *Negotiating India in the Nineteenth Century Media* (Basingstoke: Macmillan, 2000), pp. 1–22.
Fleming, Alice Macdonald, *Trix: Kipling's Forgotten Sister*, intro. Lorna Lee (Peterborough: Pond View, 2004).
Foote, Samuel, *The Nabob* (London: Colman, 1778).
Freitag, Jason, *European Expansion and Indigenous Response, Volume 5: Serving Empire, Serving Nation: James Tod and the Rajputs of Rajasthan* (Boston, MA: Brill, 2009).
Freitag, Jason, 'Tod's *Annals* as archive and history', in Giles Tillotson (ed.),

James Tod's Rajasthan: The Historian and his Collections (Mumbai: Marg, 2007), pp. 86–97.
Freud, Sigmund, 'Humour', in Adam Phillips (ed.), *The Penguin Freud Reader* (London: Penguin, 2006), pp. 561–6.
Ghose, Indira (ed.), *Travels, Explorations and Empires, Vol 6: India* (London: Pickering & Chatto, 2001).
Ghose, Indira, *Women Travellers in Colonial India: The Power of the Female Gaze* (Delhi: Oxford University Press, 1998).
Ghosh, Durba, *Sex and the Family in Colonial India: The Making of Empire* (Cambridge: Cambridge University Press, 2006).
Ghosh, Kasiprasad, *The Sháïr and Other Poems* (Calcutta: Scott, 1830).
Ghosh, Priyali, 'David Lester Richardson (1801–1865): A Romantic Anglo-Indian' (PhD thesis, Canterbury Christ Church University, 2009).
Gibbons, Luke, *Edmund Burke and Ireland: Aesthetics, Politics, and the Colonial Sublime* (Cambridge: Cambridge University Press, 2003).
Gibson, Mary Ellis (ed.), *Anglophone Poetry in Colonial India, 1780–1913* (Athens: Ohio University Press, 2011).
Gibson, Mary Ellis, *Indian Angles: English Verse in Colonial India from Jones to Tagore* (Athens: Ohio University Press, 2011).
Gilmour, David, *The Long Recessional: The Imperial Life of Rudyard Kipling* (London: Murray, 2002).
Gleig, G. R., *The History of the British Empire in India* (London: Murray, 1830).
Graham, George, *Life in the Mofussil, or, the Civilian in Lower Bengal*, 2 vols (London: Kegan Paul, 1878).
Graham, Maria, *Journal of a Residence in India* (Edinburgh: Archibald Constable and Company, 1812).
Griffin, Ben, *The Politics of Gender in Victorian Britain: Masculinity, Political Culture, and the Struggle for Women's Rights* (Cambridge: Cambridge University Press, 2012).
Gruner, Charles R., *The Game of Humor: A Comprehensive Theory of Why We Laugh* (New Brunswick, NJ: Transaction, 1997).
Haig, Wolseley and Richard Burn, *The Cambridge History of India, Vol. IV: The Mughul Period* (Cambridge: Cambridge University Press, 1937).
Harcourt, A. F. P., *Jenetha's Venture: A Tale of the Siege of Delhi* (London: Cassell, 1899).
Harrington, Jack, *Sir John Malcolm and the Creation of British India* (Basingstoke: Palgrave, 2010).
Havholm, Peter, *Politics and Awe in Rudyard Kipling's Fiction* (Aldershot: Ashgate, 2008).
Hawes, Christopher J., *Poor Relations: The Making of a Eurasian Community in British India, 1773–1833* (Richmond: Curzon, 1996).
Heber, Reginald, *Narrative of a Journey through the Upper Provinces of India*, 2 vols (London: John Murray, 1828).
Hemans, Felicia, *Records of Woman* (Edinburgh: Blackwood; London: Cadell, 1828).
[Henderson, Henry Barkley], *The Goorkha and Other Poems* (Calcutta, 1817).
Henderson, Henry Barkley, *Satires in India* (Calcutta, 1819).
Herbert, Christopher, *War of No Pity: The Indian Mutiny and Victorian Trauma* (Princeton: Princeton University Press, 2008).

Hibbert, Christopher, *The Great Mutiny: India 1857* (London: Allen Lane, 1978).
The History of the Trial of Warren Hastings, Esq. (London, 1796).
Hobsbawm, Eric, *Bandits* (1969) (London: Weidenfeld & Nicolson, 2000).
Hofkosh, Sonia, *Sexual Politics and the Romantic Author* (Cambridge: Cambridge University Press, 1998).
Holmes, T. Rice, *A History of the Indian Mutiny*, 5th edn (London: Macmillan, 1904).
Hooja, Rima, 'The Tod Collection of Indian manuscripts at the Royal Asiatic Society', in Giles Tillotson (ed.), *James Tod's Rajasthan: The Historian and his Collections* (Mumbai: Marg, 2007), pp. 70–9.
Hulme, Peter, *Colonial Encounters: Europe and the Native Caribbean, 1492–1797* (London: Methuen, 1986).
Inchbald, Elizabeth, *The Mogul Tale: or, The Descent of the Balloon* (London, 1788).
Inden, Ronald, *Imagining India* (1990) (London: Hurst, 2000).
Ingram, Edward, *Two Views of British India: The Private Correspondence of Mr Dundas and Lord Wellesley: 1798–1801* (Bath: Adams & Dart, 1970).
Janowitz, Anne, *England's Ruins: Poetic Purpose and the National Landscape* (Oxford: Blackwell, 1990).
Jhala, Angma Dey, *Royal Patronage, Power and Aesthetics in Princely India* (London: Pickering & Chatto, 2011).
Johnson, George William, *The Stranger in India: or, Three Years in Calcutta* (London: Colburn, 1843).
Joshi, Priya, *In Another Country: Colonialism, Culture, and the English Novel in India* (New York: Columbia University Press, 2002).
Juneja, R., 'The native and the nabob: Representations of the Indian experience in eighteenth-century literature', *Journal of Commonwealth Literature* 27 (1992): 183–98.
Kapila, Shuchi, *Educating Seeta: The Anglo-Indian Family Romance and the Poetics of Indirect Rule* (Columbus, OH: Ohio State University Press, 2010).
Kapur, Nandini Sinha, *State Formation in Rajasthan: Mewar during the Seventh–Fifteenth Centuries* (New Delhi: Manohar, 2002).
Kasturi, Malavika, *Embattled Identities: Rajput Lineages and the Colonial State in Nineteenth-Century North India* (New Delhi and Oxford: Oxford University Press, 2002).
Keats, John, *Keats, Poems Published in 1820*, ed. and intro. M. Robertson (Oxford: Clarendon, 1909).
Keene, H. G., *Ex Eremo: Poems Chiefly Written in India* (Edinburgh and London: Blackwood, 1855).
Kilgour, Maggie, *From Communion to Cannibalism: An Anatomy of Metaphors of Incorporation* (Princeton: Princeton University Press, 1990).
Kipling, Rudyard, *Barrack-Room Ballads and Other Verses* (Leipzig: Heinemann and Balestier, 1892).
Kipling, Rudyard, *Departmental Ditties and Other Verses* (Lahore: Civil and Military Gazette Press, 1886).
Kipling, Rudyard, *Kim* (London: Macmillan, 1901).
Kipling, Rudyard, *Letters of Marque* (New York: Caldwell, 1899).
Kipling, Rudyard, *The Letters of Rudyard Kipling, Volume 1 1872–89*, ed. Thomas Pinney (Basingstoke: Macmillan, 1990).
Kipling, Rudyard, *Life's Handicap* (London: Macmillan, 1891).

Kipling, Rudyard, *The Light that Failed* (London: Macmillan, 1891).
Kipling, Rudyard, *Plain Tales from the Hills* (Calcutta: Thacker, Spink, 1888).
Kipling, Rudyard, *Rudyard Kipling: The Complete Verse* (London: Kyle Cathie, 2002).
Kipling, Rudyard, *Something of Myself and Other Autobiographical Writings*, ed. Thomas Pinney (Cambridge: Cambridge University Press, 1990).
Kipling, Rudyard, *Under the Deodars* (London and Boston: Edinburgh Society, 1909).
Koditschek, Theodore, *Liberalism, Imperialism, and the Historical Imagination: Nineteenth-Century Visions of a Greater Britain* (Cambridge: Cambridge University Press, 2011).
Kolsky, Elizabeth, *Colonial Justice in British India* (Cambridge: Cambridge University Press, 2010).
Kopf, David, *British Orientalism and the Bengal Renaissance: The Dynamics of Indian Modernization, 1773–1835* (Berkeley: University of California Press, 1969).
LaCapra, Dominick, *Writing History, Writing Trauma* (Baltimore: Johns Hopkins University Press, 2001).
Lamb, W., 'Reeling in the strathspey: The origins of Scotland's national music', *Scottish Studies* 36 (2013): 66–102.
Laurie, W. F. B., *Sketches of Some Distinguished Anglo-Indians with an Account of Anglo-Indian Periodical Literature* (London: W. H. Allen, 1887).
Lawrence, Dianne, *Genteel Women: Empire and Domestic Material Culture, 1840–1910* (Manchester: Manchester University Press, 2012).
Lawson, Charles, *The Private Life of Warren Hastings* (London: Swan Sonnenschein, 1905).
Lawson, P., and T. Phillips, '"Our execrable banditti": Perceptions of nabobs in mid-eighteenth-century Britain', *Albion* 16.iii (1984): 227–30.
Lear, Edward, *The Complete Nonsense and Other Verse*, ed. Vivien Noakes (London: Penguin, 2006).
Lear, Edward, *Edward Lear's Indian Journal: Watercolours and Extracts from the Diary of E. Lear, 1873–1875*, ed. Ray Murphy (London: Jarrolds, 1953).
Leask, Nigel, *British Romantic Writers and the East: Anxieties of Empire* (Cambridge: Cambridge University Press, 1993).
Leask, Nigel, 'Byron and the Eastern Mediterranean' in Drummond Bone (ed.), *The Cambridge Companion to Byron* (Cambridge: Cambridge University Press, 2004), pp. 99–117.
Leask, Nigel, *Curiosity and the Aesthetics of Travel Writing, 1770–1840* (Oxford: Oxford University Press, 2002).
Leask, Nigel, 'Towards an Anglo-Indian poetry? The colonial muse in the writings of John Leyden, Thomas Medwin and Charles D'Oyly', in Bart Moore-Gilbert (ed.), *Writing India, 1757–1990* (Manchester: Manchester University Press, 1996), pp. 52–85.
Leslie, Mary E., *Ina, and Other Poems* (Calcutta: Newman, 1856).
Leslie, Mary E., *Sorrows, Aspirations and Legends from India* (London: John Snow, 1858).
Lewis, Lisa (2001), 'The Manuscript of *Kim*' (Kipling Society) <http://www.kiplingsociety.co.uk/rg_lewiskim.htm> (last accessed 23 September 2014).
Lewis, W. S. (ed.), *The Yale Edition of Horace Walpole's Correspondence* (New Haven, CT: Yale University Press, 1937–83).
Life and Adventures of Shigram-Po (Calcutta, 1821).

Lloyd, Tom, 'Bandits, bureaucrats and Bahadur Shah Zafar: Articulating sovereignty and seeing the modern state effect in the margins of colonial India, c. 1757–1858', in Crispin Bates (ed.), *Mutiny at the Margins* (New Delhi: Sage, 2013), pp. 1–24.
Lodrick, Deryck O., 'Rajasthan as a region: myth or reality?', in Karine Schomer, Joan L. Erdman, Deryck O. Lodrick, Lloyd I. Rudolph (eds), *The Idea of Rajasthan: Explorations in Regional Identity* (Manohar: American Institute of Indian Studies, 1994), vol. 1, pp. 1–44.
Low, Gail Chiang-Liang, *White Skins / Black Masks: Representation and Colonialism* (London: Routledge, 1995).
Lupton, Deborah, *Food, the Body and the Self* (London: SAGE, 1996).
Lyall, Alfred C., *Asiatic Studies: Religious and Social*, 2nd edn (London: Murray, 1884).
Lyall, Alfred C., *Verses Written in India* (London: Kegan Paul, Trench, 1889).
[Macaulay, T. B.], Review of Sir John Malcolm's *Life of Lord Clive*, *Edinburgh Review* (January 1840), pp. 295–361.
MacKenzie, John M., *The Empire of Nature: Hunting, Conservation and British Imperialism* (Manchester: Manchester University Press, 1988).
Magill, C. P., and L. A. Willoughby, *Schiller's Die Räuber: Ein Trauerspiel* (Oxford: Blackwell, 1949).
Maitland, Julia Charlotte, *Letters from Madras, During the Years 1836–1839* (1843), ed. Alison Price (Otley: Woodstock, 2003).
Majeed, Javed, 'Meadows Taylor's *Confessions of a Thug*: The Anglo-Indian novel as a genre in the making', in Bart Moore-Gilbert (ed.), *Writing India 1757–1990* (Manchester: Manchester University Press, 1996), pp. 86–110.
[Majendie, William Henry], *Calcutta: A Poem* (London: Stockdale, 1811).
Major, Andrea, *Pious Flames: European Encounters with Sati, 1500–1830* (Delhi: Oxford University Press, 2006).
Major, Andrea, *Sovereignty and Social Reform in India: British Colonialism and the Campaign against Sati, 1830–1860* (Abingdon: Routledge, 2010).
Makdisi, Saree, *Romantic Imperialism: Universal Empire and the Culture of Modernity* (Cambridge: Cambridge University Press, 1998).
Malcolm, John, *A Memoir of Central India*, 2nd edn, 2 vols (London: Kingsbury, Parbury, Allen, 1824).
Malhotra, Ashok, *Making British Indian Fictions 1772–1823* (Palgrave, 2012).
Maloo, K., *The History of Famines in Rajputana (1858–1900 A.D.)* (Udaipur: Himanshu Publications, 1987).
Mani, Lata, *Contentious Traditions: The Debate on Sati in Colonial India* (Berkeley and London: University of California Press, 1998).
Mann, Michael, *British Rule on Indian Soil: North India in the First Half of the Nineteenth Century* (New Delhi: Manohar, 1999).
Mann, Michael, '"Torchbearers upon the path of progress": Britain's ideology of a "moral and material progress" in India', in Harald Fischer-Tiné and Michael Mann (eds), *Colonialism as Civilizing Mission: Cultural Ideology in British India* (London: Anthem, 2004), pp. 1–26.
Marchand, Leslie Alexis, *The Athenaeum: A Mirror of Victorian Culture* (Chapel Hill: University of North Carolina Press, 1941).
Marriott, John, and Bhaskar Mukhopadhyay (eds), *Britain in India, 1765–1905, Vol. 4: Cultural and Social Interventions* (London: Pickering & Chatto, 2006).

Marshall, P. J., *Bengal: The British Bridgehead: Eastern India 1740–1828* (Cambridge: Cambridge University Press, 1987).
Marshall, P. J., 'British immigration into India in the nineteenth century', in P. C. Emmer and M. Mörner (eds), *European Expansion and Migration: Essays on the Intercontinental Migration from Africa, Asia, and Europe* (New York: Berg, 1992), pp. 179–96.
Marshall, P. J., *The Impeachment of Warren Hastings* (Oxford: Oxford University Press, 1965).
Marshall, P. J., 'The white town of Calcutta under the rule of the East India Company', *Modern Asian Studies* 34.2 (2000): 307–31.
Massey, Gerald, *Havelock's March and Other Poems* (London: Trubner, 1861).
Maxwell, Herbert (ed.), *The Creevey Papers* (London: John Murray, 1903).
McGann, Jerome, *Byron and Romanticism*, ed. James Soderholm (Cambridge: Cambridge University Press, 2002).
McGivering, John, 'Notes to "The Moon of Other Days", by Rudyard Kipling' (21 February 2011), at <http://www.kiplingsociety.co.uk/rg_moon_other1_p.htm> (last accessed 31 August 2014).
McLaren, Martha, *British India and British Scotland* (Akron: University of Akron Press, 2001).
Medwin, Thomas, *The Angler in Wales*, 2 vols (London: Richard Bentley, 1834).
Medwin, Thomas, *Sketches in Hindoostan, with Other Poems* (London: Ollier / Simpkin and Marshall, 1821).
Metcalf, Thomas R., *Ideologies of the Raj* (Cambridge: Cambridge University Press, 1997).
Metcalf, Thomas R., *Imperial Connections in the Indian Ocean Arena, 1860–1920* (Berkeley: University of California Press, 2007).
Mill, James, *The History of British India*, 2nd edn, 6 vols (London: Baldwin, 1820).
[Money, Robert Cotton], *Journal of a Tour in Persia, During the Years 1824 & 1825* (London: Tcapc, 1828).
Moore-Gilbert, B. J., *Kipling and 'Orientalism'* (London: Croom Helm, 1986).
Moore-Gilbert, Bart (ed.), *Writing India* (Manchester: Manchester University Press, 1996).
Mortensen, Peter, 'Robbing *The Robbers*: Schiller, xenophobia and the politics of British Romantic translation', *Literature and History* 11.1 (2002): 41–61.
Mukherjee, Upamanyu Pablo, *Crime and Empire: The Colony in Nineteenth-Century Fictions of Crime* (Oxford: Oxford University Press, 2003).
Mukherjee, Upamanyu Pablo, *Natural Disasters and Victorian Empire: Famines, Fevers and the Literary Cultures of South Asia* (Basingstoke: Palgrave, 2013).
Mulvany, Henry William, *The Story of Mairwara: or, Our Rule in India* (London; Longmans, 1868).
Nair, P. Thankappan, *Hicky and His Gazette* (Kolkata: S&T Book Stall, 2001).
Nayar, Pramod K., *English Writing and India, 1600–1920: Colonizing Aesthetics* (London: Routledge, 2008).
Nechtman, T. W., *Nabobs: Empire and Identity in Eighteenth-Century Britain* (Cambridge: Cambridge University Press, 2010).
ní Fhlathúin, Máire, 'The campaign against thugs in the Bengal press of the 1830s', *Victorian Periodicals Review* 37.2 (2004): 124–40.
ní Fhlathúin, Máire, 'India and women's poetry of the 1830s: Femininity

and the picturesque in the poetry of Emma Roberts and Laetitia Elizabeth Landon', *Women's Writing* 12.2 (2005): 187–204.
ní Fhlathúin, Máire (ed.), *Kim*, by Rudyard Kipling (Peterborough, Ontario: Broadview, 2005).
ní Fhlathúin, Máire (ed.), *The Poetry of British India*, 2 vols (London: Pickering & Chatto, 2011).
ní Fhlathúin, Máire, 'Staging Criminality and Colonial Authority: The Execution of Thug Criminals in British India', *Nineteenth Century Theatre and Film* 37.1 (2010): 23–32.
ní Fhlathúin, Máire, 'Transformations of Byron in the literature of British India', *Victorian Literature and Culture* 42.3 (2014): 573–93.
Oliver, Susan, *Scott, Byron and the Poetics of Cultural Encounter* (Basingstoke: Palgrave, 2005).
O'Quinn, Daniel, *Staging Governance: Theatrical Imperialism in London, 1770–1800* (Baltimore and London: Johns Hopkins University Press, 2005).
Owenson, Sydney, *The Wild Irish Girl: A National Tale* (London: Phillips, 1806).
Oxford Classical Dictionary (Oxford University Press, 2012), <http://www.oxfordreference.com> (last accessed 23 December 2014).
Oxtoby, Willard G., *Experiencing India: European Descriptions and Impressions 1498–1898* (Toronto: University of Toronto Library, 1998).
Parker, Henry Meredith, *Bole Ponjis*, 2 vols (London: Thacker, 1851).
Parker, Mark, *Literary Magazines and British Romanticism* (West Nyack, NY: Cambridge University Press, 2001).
Paxton, Nancy L., 'Mobilizing chivalry: Rape in British novels about the Indian uprising of 1857', *Victorian Studies* 36.1 (1992): 5–30.
Paxton, Nancy L., *Writing under the Raj: Gender, Race, and Rape in the British Colonial Imagination, 1830–1947* (New Brunswick, NJ: Rutgers University Press, 1999).
Peabody, Norbert, 'Tod's Rajast'han and the boundaries of imperial rule in nineteenth-century India', *Modern Asian Studies* 30.1 (1996): 185–220.
Peers, Douglas M., 'Colonial knowledge and the military in India, 1780–1860', *Journal of Imperial and Commonwealth History* 33.2 (2005): 158–80.
Pittock, Murray, *Celtic Identity and the British Image* (Manchester and New York: Manchester University Press, 1999).
Pittock, Murray, *Poetry and Jacobite Politics in Eighteenth-Century Britain and Ireland* (Cambridge: Cambridge University Press, 1994).
Pittock, Murray, *The Reception of Sir Walter Scott in Europe* (New York: Continuum, 2006).
Pittock, Murray, 'Scott and the British Tourist', in Gerard Carruthers (ed.), *English Romanticism and the Celtic World* (Cambridge: Cambridge University Press, 2003).
Pittock, Murray, *Scottish and Irish Romanticism* (Oxford: Oxford University Press, 2008).
Plotz, John, 'The first strawberries in India: Cultural portability in Victorian Greater Britain', *Victorian Studies* 49.4 (2007): 659–84.
Postans, Marianne, *Facts and Fictions, Illustrative of Oriental Character*, 3 vols (London: Allen, 1844).
[Prinsep, Augustus], *The Baboo: and Other Tales Descriptive of Society in India*, 2 vols (London: Smith, Elder, 1834).

[Prinsep, Henry Thoby], *Ballads of the East, and Other Poems*, by H. T. P. (London: Longman, 1846).
Prinsep, Henry Thoby, Preface and annotations, *Memoirs of the Puthan Soldier of Fortune, the Nuwab Ameer-ood-Doulah Mohammud Ameer Khan*, compiled in Persian by Busawun Lal (Calcutta: Military Orphan Press, 1832).
Prinsep, Henry Thoby [the younger], 'Three Generations in India, 1771–1904)', 3 vols, BL MSS EUR C.97, British Library.
Procida, Mary A., 'Feeding the Imperial appetite: Imperial knowledge and Anglo-Indian domesticity,' *Journal of Women's History* 15.2 (2003): 123–49.
Quiz, *The Grand Master; or, Adventures of Qui Hi? in Hindostan. A Hudibrastic Poem in Eight Cantos* (London, 1816).
Radcliffe, John (gen. ed.), *The New Readers' Guide to the Works of Rudyard Kipling* <http://www.kiplingsociety.co.uk/rg_index.htm> (last accessed 14 December 2014).
Rajamannar, Shefali, *Reading the Animal in the Literature of the British Raj* (Basingstoke: Palgrave, 2012).
Rajan, Rajeswari Sunder, *Real and Imagined Women: Gender, Culture and Postcolonialism* (1993) (London: Routledge, 2003).
Ram Bux, *Boojum Ballads* (Bombay: Tatva-Vivechaka Press, 1895).
Raven, James, *Judging New Wealth: Popular Publishing and Responses to Commerce in England, 1750–1800* (Oxford: Clarendon, 1992).
Ray, Rajat Kanta, 'Indian society and the establishment of British supremacy, 1765–1818' in P. J. Marshall (ed.), *Oxford History of British Empire, Vol. 2: The Eighteenth Century* (Oxford: Oxford University Press, 1998), pp. 508–29.
Raza, Rosemary, *In Their Own Words: British Women Writers and India 1740–1857* (New Delhi: Oxford University Press, 2006).
Reitz, Caroline, *Detecting the Nation: Fictions of Detection and the Imperial Venture* (Columbus, OH: Ohio State University Press, 2004).
Rice, Mrs, *The Nabob: A Moral Tale* (London: Harris, 1807).
Richards, John F., *The Mughal Empire* (Cambridge: Cambridge University Press, 1995).
Richardson, David Lester, *Flowers and Flower-Gardens . . . With an Appendix of Practical Instructions . . . Respecting the Anglo-Indian Flower-Garden* (Calcutta: 1855).
Richardson, David Lester, *Literary Chit-Chat, with Miscellaneous Poems and an Appendix of Prose Papers* (Calcutta: D'Rozario, 1848).
Richardson, David Lester, *Literary Leaves*, 2 vols (London: W. H. Allen, 1840).
Richardson, David Lester, *Literary Recreations* (London: W. Thacker, 1852).
Richardson, David Lester, *Selections from the British Poets from the Time of Chaucer to the Present Day* (Calcutta: Baptist Mission Press, 1840).
Richardson, Mrs G. G. [Catherine Eliza], *Poems* (Edinburgh: Cadell, 1828).
Rigney, Ann, *The Afterlives of Walter Scott: Memory on the Move* (Oxford: Oxford University Press, 2012).
Rivett-Carnac, J. H., *Many Memories of Life in India, at Home, and Abroad* (Edinburgh and London: Blackwood, 1910).
Roberts, Emma, *Oriental Scenes, Dramatic Sketches and Tales, with Other Poems* (Calcutta: Calcutta Depository, 1830).
Roberts, Emma, *Oriental Scenes, Dramatic Sketches and Tales, with Other Poems*, 2nd edn (London: Edward Bull, 1832).

Roberts, Emma, *Scenes and Characteristics of Hindostan*, 2nd edn, 2 vols (London: W. H. Allen, 1837).
Roy, Anindyo, *Civility and Empire: Literature and Culture in British India, 1822–1922* (London: Routledge, 2005).
Rudolph, Susanne Hoeber and Lloyd I. Rudolph, *Essays on Rajputana: Reflections on History, Culture and Administration* (New Delhi: Concept, 1984).
Rudolph, Susanne Hoeber and Lloyd I. Rudolph, 'Writing and reading Tod's *Rajasthan*: Interpreting the text and its historiography', in J. L. Gommans and Om Prakash (eds), *Circumambulations in South Asian History: Essays in Honour of Dirk H. A. Kolff* (Leiden: Brill, 2003), pp. 252–82.
Ruin: A Familiar Tale of the East (Calcutta: Scott, 1820).
S., C. P. *Pieces* (Allahabad: Pioneer Press, 1899).
Sabin, Margery, *Dissenters and Mavericks: Writings about India in English, 1765–2000* (Oxford: Oxford University Press, 2002).
Saglia, Diego, 'Orientalism', in Michael Ferber (ed.), *A Companion to European Romanticism* (Oxford: Blackwell, 2005), pp. 467–85.
Saha, Subhas Chandra, *Indian Renaissance and Indian English Poetry* (London: Sangam Books, 1998).
Said, Edward W., *Culture and Imperialism* (London: Vintage, 1994).
Said, Edward W., *Orientalism* (1978) (London: Penguin, 2003).
Said, Edward W., 'Reflections on Exile', in *Reflections on Exile and other Essays* (Cambridge, MA: Harvard University Press, 2000), pp. 173–86.
Satpathy, Sumanyu, 'Lear's India and the politics of nonsense', in Roderick McGillis (ed.), *Children's Literature and the Fin de Siècle* (Westport, CT: Praeger, 2003), pp. 73–80.
Schiller, Friedrich, *The Robbers: A Tragedy* (London: Robinsons, 1792).
Scott, Patrick, *Oriental Musings* (London: James Fraser, 1840).
Scott, Walter, *The Lady of the Lake: A Poem*, 2nd edn (Edinburgh: Ballantyne, 1810).
Scott, Walter, *Rob Roy* (Edinburgh: Constable, 1818).
Scott, Walter, *Waverley: or, 'Tis Sixty Years Since*, 3 vols, 4th edn (Edinburgh: Constable, 1814).
Sen, Indrani, *Woman and Empire: Representations in the Writings of British India (1858–1900)* (Delhi: Orient Longman Private, 2002).
Seton-Watson, Hugh, *Nations and States: An Enquiry into the Origins of Nations and the Politics of Nationalism* (London: Methuen, 1977).
Seymour-Smith, Martin, *Rudyard Kipling* (London: MacDonald, 1989).
Shakespeare, William, *The Complete Works*, ed. Stanley Wells and Gary Taylor (Oxford: Oxford University Press, 1988).
Sharma, G. N., *Mewar and the Mughal Emperors (1526–1707 A.D.)* (Agra: Shiva Lal Agarwala, 1962).
Sharma, Sanjay, *Famine, Philanthropy and the Colonial State: North India in the Early Nineteenth Century* (Delhi: Oxford University Press, 2001).
Sharpe, Jenny, *Allegories of Empire: The Figure of Woman in the Colonial Text* (Minneapolis: University of Minnesota Press, 1993).
Sharpe, Lesley, 'Schiller and the Mannheim National Theatre' *Modern Language Review* 100.1 (January 2005): 121–37.
Shelley, P. B., *The Poems of Shelley: Volume 2: 1817–1819*, ed. Kelvin Everest and Geoffrey Matthews (1989, 2000) (Abingdon: Routledge, 2014).

Sherer, Moyle, *Sketches of India for Fire-Side Travellers at Home*, 3rd edn (London: Longman, 1825).
Sheridan, R. B., *The Speech of R. B. Sheridan, Esq. on Wednesday, the 7th of February, 1787, in Bringing Forward the Fourth Charge Against Warren Hastings, Esq. Relative to the Begums of Oude* (London: J. French, 1787).
Showers, Charles Lionel, *A Missing Chapter of the Indian Mutiny* (London: Longmans, 1888).
Singh, Bhupal, *A Survey of Anglo-Indian Fiction* (London: Oxford University Press, 1934).
Singha, Radhika, *A Despotism of Law: Crime and Justice in Early Colonial India* (Delhi: Oxford University Press, 2000).
Sinha, Mrinalini, *Colonial Masculinity: The Manly Englishman and the Effeminate Bengali in the Late Nineteenth Century* (Manchester: Manchester University Press, 1995).
Sleeman, N. H. [W. H. Sleeman], *On the Spirit of Military Discipline in our Native Indian Army* (Calcutta: Bishop's College Press, 1841).
Sleeman, W. H., *Ramaseeana, or a Vocabulary of the Peculiar Language Used by the Thugs*, 2 vols (Calcutta: Military Orphan Press, 1836).
Sleeman, W. H., *Rambles and Recollections of an Indian Official* (London: Hatchard, 1844).
Sleeman, W. H., *Report on Budhuk, Alias Bagree Decoits, and Other Gang Robbers by Hereditary Profession; and on the Measures Adopted by the Government of India for Their Suppression* (Calcutta: Bengal Military Orphan Press, 1849).
Sloper, Samuel, *The Dacoit and other Poems* (London: Simpkin, Marshall, 1840).
Smylitopoulos, Christina, 'A Nabob's Progress: Rowlandson and Combe's *The Grand Master*, a tale of British Imperial excess, 1770–1830' (PhD Thesis, McGill University, Montreal, July 2010).
Smylitopoulos, C., 'Rewritten and reused: Imaging the nabob through "upstart iconography"', *Eighteenth-Century Life* 32.2 (2008): 39–59.
Smyth, G. Carmichael, *A History of the Reigning Family of Lahore, with Some Account of the Jummoo Rajahs* (Calcutta: Thacker, 1847).
Somani, Ram Vallabh, *History of Mewar* (Jaipur: Ranka, 1976).
Spivak, Gayatri Chakravorty, *A Critique of Postcolonial Reason: Toward a History of the Vanishing Present* (Cambridge, MA; London: Harvard University Press, 1999).
Spry-Leverton, Jeffery (ed.), 'The Spry Letters', 1985, BL Photo Eur 308, British Library.
Sramek, Joseph, *Gender, Morality, and Race in Company India, 1765–1858* (New York: Palgrave Macmillan, 2011).
Sreenivasan, Ramya, *The Many Lives of a Rajput Queen: Heroic Pasts in India c. 1500–1900* (Seattle: University of Washington Press, 2007).
St Clair, William, *The Reading Nation in the Romantic Period* (Cambridge: Cambridge University Press, 2004).
'Starting a Paper in India', *Household Words* (n.s.) 1.29 (1853): 94–6.
Steel, Flora Annie, and Grace Gardiner, *The Complete Indian Housekeeper and Cook*, ed. and intro. Ralph Crane and Anna Johnston (Oxford: Oxford University Press, 2011).
Stein, Atara, *The Byronic Hero in Film, Fiction and Television* (Carbondale: Southern Illinois University Press, 2004).

Stephens, F. G. and George, M. D. (eds), *Catalogue of Political and Personal Satires preserved in the Department of Prints and Drawings in the British Museum* (London, 1870–1954).
Streets, Heather, *Martial Races: The Military, Race and Masculinity in British Imperial Culture* (Manchester: Manchester University Press, 2004).
Streets, Heather, 'The Rebellion of 1857: Origins, consequences, and themes', *Teaching South Asia* 1.1 (Winter 2001): 85–104.
Suleri, Sara, *The Rhetoric of English India* (Chicago and London: University of Chicago Press, 1992).
Sullivan, Alvin (ed.), *British Literary Magazines, Vol. 2: The Romantic Age* (Westport, CT; London: Greenwood Press, 1983).
Taft, Frances H., 'Honor and Alliance: Reconsidering Mughal–Rajput Marriages', in Karine Schomer, Joan L. Erdman, Deryck O. Lodrick, Lloyd I. Rudolph (eds), *The Idea of Rajasthan: Explorations in Regional Identity* (Manohar: American Institute of Indian Studies, 1994), vol. 2, pp. 217–41.
Talbot, Cynthia, 'The Mewar Court's Construction of History' in Joanna Williams (ed.), *Kingdom of the Sun: Indian Court and Village Art from the Princely State of Mewar* (San Francisco: Asian Art Museum – Chong Moon Lee Center for Asian Art and Culture, 2007), pp. 12–33.
Taylor, Philip Meadows, *Confessions of a Thug* (London: Bentley, 1839).
Taylor, Philip Meadows, *Seeta* (1880) (New Delhi: Asian Educational Services, 1989).
Teignmouth, John, *Memoir of the Life and Correspondence of John Lord Teignmouth* (London: Hatchard, 1843).
Thackeray, William Makepeace, *Vanity Fair: A Novel Without a Hero* (London: Bradbury & Evans, 1849).
Thomas, Sophie, *Romanticism and Visuality: Fragments, History, Spectacle* (London and New York: Routledge, 2008).
[Thompson, William Francis], *India: A Poem* (London: Priestley, 1834).
Thornton, Edward, *Chapters of the Modern History of British India* (London: Allen, 1840).
[Thornton, Edward], *Illustrations of the History and Practices of the Thugs* (London: Allen, 1837).
Thorslev, Peter, *The Byronic Hero: Types and Prototypes* (Minneapolis: University of Minnesota Press, 1962).
Tickell, Alex, *Terrorism, Insurgency and Indian-English Literature, 1830–1947* (London: Routledge, 2012).
Tod, James, *Annals and Antiquities of Rajast'han, or the Central and Western Rajpoot States of India* (London: Smith Elder, 1829–32).
Tod, James, *Travels in Western India* (London: Allen, 1839).
Touchstone, Timothy, *Tea and Sugar, or, the Nabob and the Creole* (London, 1792).
Trevelyan, George Otto, *The Competition Wallah* (London: Macmillan, 1866).
Trevor, G. H., *Rhymes of Rajputana* (London: Macmillan, 1894).
Tripodi, Christian, *Edge of Empire: The British Political Officer and Tribal Administration on the North-West Frontier 1877–1947* (Farnham: Ashgate, 2011).
Trumpener, Katie, *Bardic Nationalism: The Romantic Novel and the British Empire* (Princeton: Princeton University Press, 1997).
Tuck, Patrick, 'Introduction', *The East India Company, 1600–1858*, vol. 3 (London: Routledge, 1998), pp. v–xxv.

Tucker, Herbert F., *Epic: Britain's Heroic Muse 1790–1910* (Oxford: Oxford University Press, 2008).
Venn John and J. A. Venn (eds), *Alumni Cantabrigienses, Volume 2: From 1752 to 1900, Part 4: Kahlenberg-Oyler* (1951) (Cambridge: Cambridge University Press, 2011).
Verelst, Harry, *A View of the Rise, Progress, and Present State of the English Government in Bengal* (London, 1772).
Ward, William, *A View of the History, Literature, and Mythology of the Hindoos: Including a Minute Description of Their Manners and Customs, and Translations from Their Principal Works*, 3 vols (London: Kingsbury, Parbury, and Allen, 1822).
Webb, W. T., *Indian Lyrics* (Calcutta: Thacker, 1884).
Wendeborn, Fred. Aug., *A View of England towards the Close of the Eighteenth Century* (c. 1786) (Dublin: Sleater, 1791).
Whelan, Frederick G., *Edmund Burke and India: Political Morality and Empire* (Pittsburgh: University of Pittsburgh Press, 1996).
White, Daniel, *From Little London to Little Bengal: Religion, Print and Modernity in Early British India, 1793–1835* (Baltimore: Johns Hopkins University Press, 2013).
Williams, Robert Grant, 'Shadows of Imperialism: Canonical typology in Taylor's *Confessions of a Thug*', *Dalhousie Review* 72.4 (1993): 482–93.
Willoughby, L. A., 'English translations and adaptations of Schiller's *Robbers*', *Modern Language Review* 16.3–4 (1921): 297–315.
Wolpert, Stanley, *A New History of India*, 6th edn (New York: Oxford University Press, 2000).
Wright, Julia M., *Ireland, India and Nationalism in Nineteenth-Century Literature* (Cambridge: Cambridge University Press, 2007).
Yule, H., *Hobson-Jobson: A Glossary of Colloquial Anglo-Indian Words and Phrases, and of Kindred Terms, Etymological, Historical, Geographical and Discursive*, ed. W. Crooke (London: J. Murray, 1903), at <http://dsal.uchicago.edu/dictionaries/hobsonjobson> (last accessed 31 August 2014).

Index

Abbott, James, 100
 The T'hakoorine, 100–2, 153n57
Agra Ukhbar, 14
Alauddin Khalji, Sultan of Delhi, 131, 150n19, 163; *see also* Chitor
Aliph Cheem (pseud.), 'To a Griffin', 86
Amir Khan, Nawab of Tonk (Ameer Khan), 153n65
 Kishen Kower and, 142, 147, 148
 Memoirs, 143, 152n53
 'The Old Pindaree' (Lyall), 173
Anderson, Benedict, 3, 9
Annals and Antiquities of Rajast'han (Tod), 128–30, 132
 Edwin Arnold and, 179–80
 classics, allusions to, 144
 Rudyard Kipling and, 188
 legacy of, in post-Mutiny India, 171–2
 Mary Leslie and, 159–60
 Marianne Postans and, 138–41
 Rajput self-sacrifice as theme of, 132, 135–6
 Emma Roberts and, 136–7
 Vincent Tregear and, 133, 136
 George Trevor and, 176–8
 see also Chitor; Kishen Kower
Arnold, David, 70, 85
Arnold, Edwin
 'The Rajpoot Wife', 179–80
 'A Rajpût Nurse', 179
Asiatic Observer, 12
Asiatick Miscellany, 10–11

babu(s), Bengali, 167–71, 173
bandit(s), 5
 'The Ballad of Boh da Thone' (Kipling), 170–1
 colonial knowledge regarding, 104–5
 compared to Byronic hero, 108–9
 compared to tigers, 109–10
 Die Räuber (Schiller), 105–7
 leader mourned by wife, 111–12
 origins, 104, 123n4, 125n44
 Rajput, 116–17, 123n4
 as rebels, 97, 106, 109, 123n4, 155–6
 women and children attacked by, 109–10, 111, 120, 135
 see also dacoits; pindaris; thugs
Bayley, F. W. N., *The New Tale of a Tub*, 79
Bayly, C. A., 62–3, 150n12
Bengal Annual, 13, 17, 18, 28
 circulation, 22n34
 contributor gender ratio, 23n53
 metropolitan audience of, 25–7, 51n12
 'Oriental' character of, 28–9
 price, 22n37
 see also Richardson, David Lester
Bengal Herald, 13
Bengal Hurkaru, 11, 13, 21n6, 22n39, 23n58
Bengal Weekly Messenger, 13
Bhabha, Homi, 1, 29
Brown, Samuel Sneade, 30–1
 Byron as model for, 32
 'England', 32
 England compared to India by, 36
 Hemans as model for, 32–3, 52n26
 home remembered by, 31–3, 34
 Home Letters, Written from India, 31–4, 36, 38, 41
 mother's death anticipated by, 38
 on picturesque, 34

Buckingham, James Silk
  editor of *Calcutta Journal*, 11, 96
  on tigers, 78–9
Buettner, Elizabeth, 24–5, 42
Burke, Edmund, 58–61, 69, 88n22
Burt, Thomas Seymour
  Narrative of a Late Steam Voyage, 65
  Poems, 65–6
Bux, Ram *see* Ram Bux
Byron, Lord
  'The Bride of Abydos', 32
  Samuel Sneade Brown and, 32
  Byronic hero, 108, 112–13, 125n42
  'The Destruction of Sennacherib', 112
  Don Juan, 11
  Henry Barkley Henderson and, 110–11
  James Hutchinson and, 112
  Thomas Medwin and, 109–10
  'Oriental Tales', 119–20
  quotation of, in *Confessions of a Thug* (Taylor), 105
  readership in British India, 107
  reference to, by Emma Roberts, 107
  Schiller, influence of, 106

Calcutta Courier, 17, 21n6, 21–2n28
Calcutta Gazette, 11
Calcutta Journal, 11, 96
Calcutta Literary Gazette, 13, 14, 17, 21n6, 21n16
  circulation, 22n34
Calcutta Magazine, 13
Calcutta Magazine and Oriental Museum, 10
Calcutta Monthly Register, 10
Calcutta Quarterly Magazine and Review, 13, 22n34, 22n37
Calcutta Review, 15, 20
Cameron, G. Poulett, 'Kishen Kower: or, the Maid of Odeypoor', 147, 153n61
Campbell, Robert Calder, 'Sonnet', 39
Caunter, John Hobart, 84
  The Cadet, 72, 84
Chakravarty, Gautam, 84, 156
Chaudhuri, Rosinka, 2, 19
childhood, 24, 32–3
  Rudyard Kipling on, 48–50
child(ren)
  in Britain, 34–5, 42–6

colonial, as intermediary figures, 120–3
  in India, 116, 119–21, 126n29
  Indians compared to, 162, 169, 173
  infanticide, 143, 147, 178
  mixed-race, 121
  transformation of by residence in India, 42–3
  victims of bandits, 110, 116
Chitor (Cheetore)
  defenders of, 159, 176–8, 179
  invasion of, by Alauddin Khalji, 131–2, 176, 181n11, 184n54
  invasion of, by Bahadur Shah, 137–8
Cohn, Bernard, 9–10
Collingham, E. M., 70–1, 77
Congress, Indian National, 167, 169–70
Curran, Stuart, 119–20

dacoits, 123n4
  compared to Byronic hero, 108–10
  'The Dacoit' (Sloper), 111–12
  'The Dakoit' (A. Prinsep), 115–21
  'The Decoit' (Henderson), 110–11
  East India Company campaign against, 104–5, 155
  rebel characters of Walter Scott, comparisons with 115–18
David, Deirdre, 40
Delanougerede, J. F., *Wuzeerally*, 19
Delhi Gazette, 14
Derozio, Henry Louis Vivian, 19, 21n20, 187
Dixon, Charles, 178, 184n63
D'Oyly, Charles, 72
  Tom Raw, the Griffin, 72–3, 80–1, 83–4, 86
Drummond, David, 21–2n28, 23n61
Dunbar, John, 'Sonnet – Famine', 64
Dutt, Michael Madhusudan, 19, 172

East India Company
  Anglicist tendency within, 84, 129
  James Buckingham expelled by, 11
  changing nature of, in late eighteenth century, 61
  criticisms of, by Edmund Burke, 58–9
  criticisms of, by William Thompson, 99–100
  exploitation of India by, 56–7, 63
  famine, response to, 62–3, 65
  and Indian Mutiny, 165–6
  and orphans, 120

East India Company (*cont.*)
  satires on, 11, 77
  security enforced by, in India, 147, 155
  social consequences of military actions of, 104, 123n1
  and James Tod, 128–9, 130
  see also Hastings, Warren
East India United Service Journal, 13
Eastern Miscellany, 13
Eden, Emily, 'Up the Country', 107
  childhood memories of England in, 42
  contemplation of eating the Rajah of Bhurtpore, 78
  on famine, 64
  on home, 47
  vision of future England in, 40
England
  Samuel Sneade Brown's longing for, 31, 34
  climate, 30, 34, 39, 40–1
  Emily Eden's vision of future, 40
  'England' (Brown), 32
  'England and Bengal' (D. L. Richardson), 34–5
  'An English Landscape' (D. L. Richardson), 35
  land of umbrellas, 39
  landscape of, 32, 34–5, 38, 44
  Mary Leslie on, 160
  Robert Cotton Money's memories of, 44–5
  nabobs accused of disrupting social order of, 56–7
  'Sonnet to England' (D. L. Richardson), 35
  'When I left England' (D. L. Richardson), 38
Englishman, 19, 21n6, 21–2n28
exile(s)
  British émigrés considered as, 4
  British experience of as transformative, 38–9
  'Consolations of Exile' (D. L. Richardson), 43
  'The Emigrant's Song' (P. Scott), 50–1
  'Exile' (Tytler), 37
  'The Exile's Return' (P. Scott), 39
  literary tropes of, 24, 26–8, 31, 34, 36–7, 48
  R. A. Macnaghten on, 53n52
  'An Oriental Tale' (Parker), 29

outdated customs among, 70–1
  relationship with home, 24–7
  'The Return from Exile' (D. L. Richardson), 35, 42
  Edward Said on, 4, 38
  'Stanzas Written in a Pavilion of the Rambaugh' (Roberts), 36–7
  writers as, 26–8

famine
  British observers affected by sight of, 63, 69–70
  Thomas Burt on, 65–6
  East India Company accused of indifference to, 59, 60
  East India Company policies exacerbate, 62–3
  Emily Eden on, 40, 64
  'Famine in Rajputana' (Trevor), 66
  Maria Graham on, 64
  The Grand Master (Quiz), 68
  W. H. Sleeman on, 64–5
  'Sonnet – Famine' (Dunbar), 64
food
  cannibalism, 61, 75–7, 78
  contamination of, 69–70, 73–7, 86
  excessive consumption of, 67–8, 71–2, 87
  humans considered as, 63, 69, 78, 79–82, 84
  India considered as, 57, 59–61
  Indian, 70–1, 72, 73
  turtle soup, 75–6, 78
  suitability of, for British children, 42–3
Foote, Samuel, 56
The Nabob, 90n72
Freitag, Jason, 129, 172, 183n50
Freud, Sigmund, 'Humour', 86–7

Ganore, Queen of
  'The Queen of Ganore' (Leslie), 158
  'The Rajpootni' (Mowatt), 140–1
gender roles, 5, 6, 67, 120–1, 134–5, 154
  in British society, 138, 164–5
  femininity, 68, 72, 136, 188–9
  masculinity, 113, 119, 132–3, 161, 163–4, 167
  patriarchy, 34–5, 106, 113, 178, 186
  in Rajput society, 132, 136, 138–9, 141, 145, 148–9, 179
  and readership, 27
  Emma Roberts on, 152n47, 185–7

'Tomb of the Suttee' (Keene), 187–8
  see also separate spheres
Ghosh, Kasiprasad, 19, 23n56, 97
Gibson, Mary Ellis, 2, 18, 19, 36, 156
Government Gazette (Madras), 14, 19–20
Graham, Maria, on famine in India, 64
griffin(s), 75, 81–2; see also *Tom Raw, the Griffin* (D'Oyly)

Harcourt, Alfred, 156
  Jenetha's Venture, 162–5
Hastings, Warren
  accused of corruption, 55, 59–60
  impeachment of, 10, 55, 57, 58–61, 62
  representation of, as vulture, 60
  self-portrait in verse, 61
  subject of caricatures, 61, 88n
Heber, Bishop Reginald, 75, 86
Hemans, Felicia, 'The Spells of Home', 32–3
Henderson, Henry Barkley, 108, 110
  'The Decoit', 110–11
  Satires in India, 72
Hicky's Bengal Gazette: or, Calcutta General Advertiser, 10
Highlanders (of Scotland), 25, 113–14, 119
  compared to Indians, 25, 117, 118, 160, 181n16
historiography, 130, 134, 143, 149, 152n52, 171
home, 4
  associations of, with childhood, 42–6
  associations of, with death, 37–8, 41–2
  constructions of, in Anglo-Indian writing, 30–47, 48
  'Domum, Domum, Dulce Domum' (D. Money), 45–6
  English, 30, 31–2, 34–5, 39, 44–5, 47, 48–9
  exile writers' versions of, 24–6
  exiles' ambivalent relationship with, 37–41, 48–51
  fantasy versions of, 32, 36–7
  homesickness, 27, 50
  in India, 49–51
  Irish, 35
  'Lines – Home' (Tregear), 46–7
  'On Going Home' (D. L. Richardson), 38
  picturesque visions of, 33–7

'The Return from India' (Parker), 41–2
Scottish, 35
'Sonnet' (Campbell), 39
'A Sort of Lay Jocund' (Macnaghten), 39
'The Spells of Home' (Hemans), 31–2
'Stanzas written on the River' (Parker), 30
'Thoughts of Home in India' (Parker), 44–5
unattainability of, 46–8
'The Wanderer' (Tregear), 40
'The Wanderer's Return' (Stacy), 38–9
hunting
  The Cadet (Caunter), 84
  cycle of, 83–4
  The Grand Master (Quiz), 67
  The Lady of the Lake (Scott), 119
  Tom Raw, the Griffin (D'Oyly), 83–4
Hutchinson, James, 'The Pindarree', 112
H.W.J.
  'Italy, a War Song', 96
  'The Greeks', 96

Ilbert Bill, 162, 170, 183n43
Inchbald, Elizabeth, *The Mogul Tale*, 55
India
  climate of, 15, 17, 29, 40, 42–3, 48, 72, 167
  landscape of, 36, 41, 49, 95, 105, 118–19
India Gazette, 11, 21n6
Indian Mutiny, 2, 165, 172, 174
  'Dixon Sahib' (Trevor), 178
  'Havelock's March' (Massey), 160, 182n29
  impact of, on British in India, 166–7
  Jenetha's Venture (Harcourt), 163–4
  Seeta (Taylor), 155
  'Sorrows and Aspirations' (Leslie), 156, 157–9
Indian Observer, 11
Ireland, 35, 47
  Irishness in *Kim* (Kipling), 122–3, 126n59

Jodhpur see Marwar

Kaleidoscope, 13, 19
Karnavati, regent of Mewar, 137

Keats, John, 156–7, 181n7
Keene, Henry George, 'Tomb of the Suttee', 187–8
Khan, Amir *see* Amir Khan
Kipling, Rudyard, 2, 20
  on Bengali men, 170–1, 183n44
  as child in Southsea, 48–9
  on India compared to England, 48
  representations of childhood, 49–50
  on *sati*, 188
  WORKS
  'The Ballad of Boh da Thone', 170–1
  'Beyond the Pale', 84
  'The Enlightenments of Pagett, MP', 169
  Kim, 50, 122–3, 126n59
  Letters of Marque, 188–9
  'The Moon of Other Days', 48
  'Mother Maturin', 122
  'Pagett, MP', 166
  Something of Myself, 49–50
  'To Be Filed for Reference', 122
Kishen Kower, princess of Udaipur, 5, 142
  Amir Khan on, 143, 152n53
  'Kishan Koomaree, Princess of Oodeepoor' (H. T. Prinsep), 147–9
  'Kishen Kower' (Landon), 145–6
  'Kishen Kower' (C. Richardson), 145
  'Kishen Kower: or, the Maid of Odeypoor' (Cameron), 147, 153n61
  'Kishen Kowur' (Mowatt), 146
  John Malcolm on, 143–4, 152n55
  Henry Thoby Prinsep on, 143
  Emma Roberts on, 147
  James Tod on, 143–4

LaCapra, Dominick, 85–6
Landon, Laetitia
  influenced by Emma Roberts, 138, 141, 151n40
  'Kishen Kower', 145–6
  'The Raki', 138
  works discussed in Calcutta press, 17
landscape
  British 'union landscape', 119
  pastoral, 33–3, 34, 35, 38, 41, 44, 48
  picturesque, 4, 28, 30, 33–4, 35, 52n34, 79–80, 105
  see also England; India; Scotland
Lear, Edward, 'The Cummerbund: An Indian Poem', 82–3

Leask, Nigel, 84, 110, 124n24
Leslie, Mary
  anticipation of a Christian India, 160
  conflation of England and Britain, 160
  on Indian Mutiny, 156, 158–9
  'Legends', 156–7
  'Pertap Singh', 159–60
  'Prelude', 157
  'The Queen of Ganore', 158
  Scots ancestry, 160
  'Sorrows and Aspirations', 156, 159
Life and Adventures of Shigram-Po (anon.), 75–7
Lupton, Deborah, 70
Lyall, Alfred
  Indian Mutiny and, 172
  'The Old Pindaree', 172–3
  'Rajpoot Rebels', 174–5
  'A Rajput Chief of the Old School', 175–6
  'The Rajput States of India', 174

Macaulay, Thomas, on Bengali men, 167
Macnaghten, Robert Adair, 22n28, 53n52
  'A Sort of Lay Jocund', 39, 71
Madras Comic Almanac, 14
Madras Literary Gazette, 14, 15
Madras Male Asylum Herald, 14
Maitland, Julia
  on Anglo-Indian habits of over-eating, 71
  on England as home, 47
Majendie, William, *Calcutta: A Poem*, 74–5
Malcolm, John, 124n, 143, 152n48
  A Memoir of Central India, 143
Maratha(s)
  Anglo-Maratha wars, 98, 104, 115–16, 173, 174
  Rajput-Maratha conflicts, 131, 175, 177–8
Marwar (Rajput state), 138, 179, 184n63
Massey, Gerald, 'Havelock's March', 160, 182n
Medwin, Thomas, 112
  'A Bengal Yarn', 84–5
  'The Pindarees', 109–10, 135
Meerut Universal Magazine, 14
memory
  Rudyard Kipling and, 49–50

nostalgia and, 30–1, 32–3, 42, 44–5, 46–7, 48
John Shore on, 63
souvenirs, 25
Mewar (Rajput state), 131, 181n13, 184n54
Rhymes of Rajputana (Trevor), 176–8
James Tod on, 131–2, 179
Udai Singh and, 150n18, 179
Mill, James, 134, 181n16
Mofussilite, 14
Money, David, 'Domum, Domum, Dulce Domum', 45–6
Money, Robert Cotton
Journal of a Tour in Persia, 44
'Thoughts of Home in India', 44–5
Moore-Gilbert, Bart, 2, 9, 182n31
Mowatt, Anna Maria
'Kishen Kowur', 146
'The Rajpootni', 140–1
Muir, J., 'The Heroism of Koonbha', 133, 151n25
Mutiny *see* Indian Mutiny

nabobs
accused of corruption, 5
consumers of curry and rice, 70
greed of, 57, 69
Indianised bodies of, 77, 90n72
predatory, 56–7
nationalism, 5
Bengal, 19, 168–9
European, 95
Indian, 96, 180
national tale, 121–2, 126n56
Rajput, 98–100, 174, 176

Oodeypore *see* Mewar
Orient Pearl, 13, 17
Oriental Herald, 96–7
Oriental Magazine and Calcutta Review, 12
Oriental Magazine; or, Calcutta Amusement, 10
Oriental Miscellany, 11
Oriental Observer (*Oriental Literary Observer*), 13, 14, 17, 22n34

Padmini, princess of Mewar, 132, 136, 150n19, 163, 176, 188
Parker, Henry Meredith, 28–30, 97
'Indian War Song', 97–8
'An Oriental Tale', 28–9

'The Return from India', 41–2
'Songs of Spring', 51n18
'Sonnets on Shakespeare', 52n23
'Stanzas Written on the River', 30
periodical press
of British India, 9–20
contributors, 15, 18–19
economics of, 16, 17–18, 22n37
Indian compared to British markets for, 16–17
readership, 15, 16
subject matter, 17, 21n6, 25, 36, 104, 143
see also individual titles
pindari(s), 98, 124n27
'Indian War Song' (Parker), 97–8
'The Old Pindaree' (Lyall), 172–3
'The Pindarees' (Medwin), 109–10
'The Pindarree' (Hutchinson), 112
see also Amir Khan
Pirthi Sing, death of, 139
Pittock, Murray, 112, 119, 125n50, 160
Postans, Marianne, 141
on Kishen Kower, 153n57
'The Rajpoot Bride', 138–9
predator(s), 63, 80–1, 84, 117
British considered as 55, 66–7, 70, 76
Warren Hastings considered as, 60, 61
insects, 74–5, 80–1, 90n84
tigers, 37, 55, 61, 78–9, 84, 86, 119
see also bandits; dacoits; hunting; thugs
Prinsep, Augustus, 126n
The Baboo, 121
'The Dakoit', 115–21
Prinsep, Henry Thoby
as co-author of *The Baboo* (A. Prinsep), 126n55
'Kishan Koomaree, Princess of Oodeepoor', 147–9
as translator of *Memoirs* (Amir Khan), 143

Quarterly Oriental Magazine, Review and Register, 12
Quiz (pseud.), *The Grand Master*, 66–9

Rajast'han, Annals and Antiquities of see Annals and Antiquities of *Rajast'han*
Rajputana, 66, 127; *see also* Marwar; Mewar

Rajput(s)
  bandits, 117, 123n4
  compared to Greeks, 130
  feudalism, 95, 129, 147, 171
  heroic sacrifices of, 131–2, 134, 176
  history, 128–30, 131–2, 147
  nationalism, 97, 98–100
  social organisation, 127
  see also Annals and Antiquities of Rajast'han; Chitor; Kishen Kower; Mewar
Rajputs, literary representations of
  'The Ancient Rajpoot' (Tregear), 133
  'At Chitor' (Trevor), 176–7
  'At Oodeypore' (Trevor), 177
  'Famine in Rajputana' (Trevor), 66
  'The Heroism of Koonbha' (Muir), 133, 151n25
  'Kishan Koomaree, Princess of Oodeepoor' (H. T. Prinsep), 147–9
  'Kishen Kower' (C. Richardson), 145
  'Kishen Kower' (Landon), 145–6
  'Kishen Kower: or, the Maid of Odeypoor' (Cameron), 147, 153n61
  'Kishen Kowur' (Mowatt), 146
  'Pertap Singh' (Leslie), 160–1
  'The Queen of Ganore' (Leslie), 158
  'The Rajpoot Bride' (Postans), 138–9
  'The Rajpoot Chieftain' (Tregear), 133–4
  'Rajpoot Rebels' (Lyall), 174–5
  'The Rajpoot Wife' (Arnold), 179–80
  'The Rajpoot's Lament' (Thompson), 98–9
  'The Rajpootin' (Tregear), 136
  'The Rajpootni' (Mowatt), 140–1
  'A Rajput Chief of the Old School' (Lyall), 175–6
  'A Rajpût Nurse' (Arnold), 179
  'The Rakhi' (Roberts), 136–8
  'The Raki' (Landon), 138
  Rhymes of Rajputana (Trevor), 176–8
  'The Suttee of Gorah's Wife' (Trevor), 176
  'The Third Sack and After' (Trevor), 177–8
  see also Annals and Antiquities of Rajast'han
Ram Bux (pseud.), 183n38
  'The B. A.', 168
  Boojum Ballads, 167
  'The Bounding Babu', 168–9
  'Mr Thomas Atkins on the Congress', 169–70
  'Young India', 169
Rice, Mrs, *The Nabob: A Moral Tale*, 56
Richardson, Catherine, 'Kishen Kower', 145
Richardson, David Lester
  on childhood, 42, 43
  compares England and India, 40
  as editor, 12, 13, 15, 17, 18, 19, 21–2n28
  on England as home, 26, 31, 34–5
  on *sati*, 135
  see also Bengal Annual
  WORKS
  'Consolations of Exile', 43
  'England and Bengal', 34–5, 52n32
  'Home Visions', 31
  'Introductory Sonnet', 27–8
  'Introductory Stanzas' (1830), 25–6
  'Introductory Stanzas' (1831), 27
  'On Going Home', 38
  'The Return from Exile', 35, 42
  'Sonnet to England', 35, 42
  'Summer and Winter', 28
  'The Suttee', 135
  'When I left England', 38
Roberts, Emma, 83, 141, 187
  and *Annals and Antiquities of Rajast'han* (Tod), 136–7, 151n42
  on the British in India, 23n49, 43, 52n32, 81
  on Byron, 107
  career as writer on India, 28, 146–7
  on children in India, 43
  as editor, 13, 14, 17, 105
  on female agency, 137–8, 141, 152n47, 186–7
  on Bishop Heber, 75, 86
  on Indian women, 79–80, 147, 148
  on Kishen Kower, 147, 148
  poetry of exile, 36–7, 46
  on *sati*, 185–7
  on thugs, 105
  see also Landon, Laetitia
  WORKS
  'The Ganges', 37
  'The Ghaut', 79–80
  'Indian Graves', 46
  'The North-Wester', 52n34
  Oriental Scenes, 28

'The Rajah's Obsequies', 186–7
'The Rakhi', 136–8
Scenes and Characteristics of Hindostan, 23n49, 43, 52n32, 75, 81, 107, 135, 147, 152n47
'Stanzas Written in a Pavilion of the Rambaugh', 36–7
'The Suttee', 185–6
Rowlandson, Thomas, illustrations of, in *The Grand Master*, 68

S (pseud.), 'The Famine Relief Officer', 70
Said, Edward, 1, 2, 4, 38
sati, 2, 135, 147, 151n34
   British interventions against, 135, 178
   Rudyard Kipling on, 188
   Kishen Kower's death considered a form of, 147, 149
   parodied in 'An Oriental Tale' (Parker), 29
   'The Rajah's Obsequies' (Roberts), 186–7
   'The Rajpoot Wife' (Arnold), 180
   Emma Roberts on, 187
   'The Suttee' (D. L. Richardson), 135
   'The Suttee' (Roberts), 185–6
   'Tomb of the Suttee' (Keene), 187–8
sati rescue, 135
   'A Bengal Yarn' (Medwin), 84
   by Job Charnock, 135
   'Julian and Gizele' (Medwin), 135
Schiller, Friedrich, 104
   Die Räuber, 105–7, 124n8
Scotland
   India compared to, 95–6
   The Lady of the Lake (W. Scott), 113, 118–19
   landscape of, 118–19
   Mary Leslie, Scots ancestry of, 160
   'Lines: On hearing the Bagpipes of the Cameronians at Chinsura' (Vetch), 35, 52n36
   Scots rebels, 113–14, 160
   Waverley (W. Scott), 113–14, 119
   see also Highlanders
Scott, Patrick
   'The Emigrant's Song', 50–1
   'The Exile's Return', 39
Scott, Walter, 11, 95–6, 107
   cited by Emily Eden, 107
   cited by George Trevor, 184n62
   The Lady of the Lake, 113, 115, 118–19

   landscape in works of, 118, 119
   narrative technique of, 117, 184n61
   rebel / outlaw figures in works of, 113–14, 117
   Waverley, 113–14, 117–18, 119
separate spheres (gender roles), 132, 139, 141, 150n21
Shakespeare, William, 52n23, 64, 105, 152n56
Shelley, Percy Bysshe, 'Ozymandias', 101–2, 176
Sheridan, Richard Brinsley, 60, 61
Shigram-Po *see Life and Adventures of Shigram-Po*
Shore, John, on famine, 63
Singh, Udai *see* Udai Singh
Sinha, Mrinalini, 167
Sleeman, William Henry
   on bandits, 104–5, 155
   famine relief work of, 64–5
   on *sati*, 151n34
Sloper, Samuel, 'The Dacoit', 108, 111–12
Spivak, Gayatri Charkravorty, 1–2, 136, 137
Stacy, W., 'The Wanderer's Return', 38–9

Taylor, Philip Meadows, 2, 182
   Confessions of a Thug, 105, 154, 181n3
   Seeta, 122, 154–5, 156, 161–2
Thackeray, William Makepeace, *Vanity Fair*, 70
Thompson, William Francis
   India, 99–100
   'The Rajpoot's Lament', 98–9
thugs
   Confessions of a Thug (Taylor), 105, 154, 181n3
   criminal nature of, 104–5, 123n4, 155, 180–1n2
   Seeta (Taylor), 154–5
   W. H. Sleeman on, 104–5, 155
Tipu Sultan of Mysore, 57, 78
Tod, James
   career, 127–9, 131
   as colonial historiographer, 129–30, 132
   on Kishen Kower, 143
   representations of, in late Victorian literary texts, 172, 177
   see also Annals and Antiquities of Rajast'han

Tom Raw, the Griffin (D'Oyly), 72–3, 80–1, 83–4, 86
Touchstone, Timothy (pseud.), 56
  Tea and Sugar, 77, 90n72
trauma, 85–6, 90n, 91n99, 158
Tregear, Vincent, 151n24
  'The Ancient Rajpoot', 133
  'Lines – Home', 46
  'The Rajpoot Chieftain', 133–4
  'The Rajpootin', 136
  'The Wanderer', 40
Trevelyan, George Otto, on the Great Exhibition, 25
Trevor, George Herbert
  'At Chitor', 176–7
  'At Oodeypore', 177
  'Dixon Sahib', 178
  famine relief works, 66
  'Famine in Rajputana', 66
  'The Mayo College', 178
  'The Suttee of Gorah's Wife', 176
  'The Third Sack and After', 177–8
  on James Tod, 177
  Rhymes of Rajputana, 176–8, 184n62
Trifler, 12
Trumpener, Katie, 121, 126n56
Tytler, J., 'Exile', 37

Udai Singh, ruler of Mewar, 179, 150n18
Udaipur *see* Mewar
United Service Gazette and Literary Chronicle, 14

Vetch, G. A.
  'Lines on a Sweet Briar in India', 42
  'Lines: On hearing the Bagpipes of the Cameronians at Chinsura', 35
  on Scotland, 52n36

Ward, William, on *sati*, 135
Webb, William Trego, 'Ode to a Mosquito', 81
Weekly Examiner: and, Literary Register, 14
Wellesley, Richard, on the conquest of Indian territories, 57
Wendeborn, Friedrich, on nabobs, 57
Wheeler, Margaret (Mary Wheeler), 158–9, 181n9
White, Daniel, 2, 29

Yeldham, Walter *see* Aliph Cheem
Young, Colonel, 83
  'The Mosquito's Song', 81, 87

EU Authorised Representative:
Easy Access System Europe Mustamäe tee 50, 10621 Tallinn, Estonia
gpsr.requests@easproject.com

Printed and bound by CPI Group (UK) Ltd, Croydon, CR0 4YY